JOHN McLEOD CAMPBELL
ON
CHRISTIAN ATONEMENT
SO RICH A SOIL

JOHN McLEOD CAMPBELL
ON
CHRISTIAN ATONEMENT

SO RICH A SOIL

GEORGE M. TUTTLE

Principal Emeritus, St. Stephen's College
Edmonton, Canada

1986

THE HANDSEL PRESS
EDINBURGH

Published by
The Handsel Press Ltd.
33 Montgomery Street, Edinburgh

© 1986 George M. Tuttle

British Library Cataloguing in Publication Data

Tuttle, George M.
   John McLeod Campbell on Christian atonement:
   so rich a soil.
   1. Campbell, John McLeod   2. Atonement—
   History of doctrines—19th century
   I. Title
   232'.3'0924   BX9225.C29

   ISBN 0 905312 51 1

Typeset by Jo Kennedy, Edinburgh
Printed in Great Britain by
Clark Constable, Edinburgh and London

CONTENTS

FOREWORD

A few years ago, while teaching for an academic year in the Vancouver School of Theology, I came across Dr. Tuttle's doctoral dissertation in the library of the University of British Columbia, on 'The Place of John McLeod Campbell in British Thought Covering the Atonement,' and was so impressed by it that I encouraged him to have it published. McLeod Campbell was a remarkable Scottish theologian – thought by many to be Scotland's greatest – whose theology was hammered out on the anvil of his pastoral experience. Here was an invaluable study, not only of McLeod Campbell's theology of atonement, but also of his influence on subsequent thought, not least on nineteenth-century Anglican theology. Now Dr. Tuttle, from his own rich experience as a pastor and teacher in the training of men and women for the Christian ministry, has written this splendid study showing how McLeod Campbell's theology is such fertile soil and so relevant for us today.

As a young minister in Row in Dunbartonshire, Campbell was aware of a strong 'legalistic strain' in the religion of Scotland, coupled with an introspective lack of joy and assurance which he believed derived from the high Calvinism of his day, with its doctrine of a 'limited atonement,' that Christ did not die for all but only for an elect number. Generations of Scots had been taught to 'examine themselves' for 'evidences' of election. But this had produced an inward looking, too often guilt-ridden, attitude which contrasted so sharply with the joyful triumphant faith and assurance of the New Testament church. So he tells us he made it his early concern to give to his people 'a ground for rejoicing in God' by directing their minds away from themselves to the love of God the Father as revealed in the whole life of Christ, and supremely on the Cross.

He soon came to see that our answer to the question of the extent of the atonement depends on our view of the nature of the atonement. The doctrine of a limited atonement, in the federal Calvinist tradition, especially as taught by John Owen, the English Puritan, and Jonathan Edwards in North America, flowed from two convictions about the nature of God. The first was that justice is the essential attribute of God, but the love of God is arbitrary, seen in his will to elect some individuals and send Christ to die for them. John Owen had taught that love is not God's nature, but his will. This, Campbell saw, was not true to the New Testament and the Christian doctrine of the Trinity, that God as Father, Son and Holy Spirit, is Love in his innermost Being, and has created us and redeemed us in love and for love – for 'sonship.' With the ancient fathers, in their negation of Sabellianism, he saw that what God is towards the world in love, in creation and redemption, he is in his eternal nature, as the Triune God.

The second was that in the federal (covenant) scheme, law is thus prior to grace. God is related to all humankind by 'the covenant of works (law)' and only to some by 'the covenant of grace' in redemption. Hence atonement was construed in terms of the view that God would only be gracious if law was satisfied and sin punished, that is, by Christ fulfilling for the elect the conditions of the covenant of works (law). McLeod Campbell saw that this inverted the Biblical order, that grace is prior to law, that 'the filial is prior to the judicial.' Both creation and redemption flow from grace, and law is 'God's heart coming out in the form of law.' Law is the gift of grace, reveals our need of grace and leads to grace. The Incarnation and the Atonement, which must be held together, are the Father's act of sending his Son to fulfil for humankind the filial and judicial purposes of creation. Atonement is God's act of grace in which he takes to himself for us his own divine judgments 'in order that we might receive the adoption of sons.' The filial purposes of creation and incarnation are secured by atonement. Hence atonement must be interpreted in terms of both the Trinity and the Incarnation, 'retrospectively' removing condemnation on past sin and 'prospectively' leading to sonship.

In our own day, theologians like Barth, Rahner, Moltmann, Jüngel and von Balthasar have all seen how Western theology has too often operated with concepts of God which owe more to Aristotle and the Stoic Lawgiver, than the New Testament, and has consequently drifted away from seeing the centrality of the Christian doctrine of the Trinity. McLeod Campbell discerned this long ago, and saw its implication, both for the pastoral ministry and for our understanding of the doctrine of God, that the sufferings of Christ the Son on the Cross reveal the suffering Love of the Father. 'He who has seen me, has seen the Father.'

Dr. Tuttle's book is profoundly relevant for the contemporary situation both theologically and pastorally in its concern to show that the Gospel is the Good News of God coming to restore to us our lost humanity, 'to bring many sons to glory' – and therefore good news for every creature.

James Torrance

ACKNOWLEDGEMENTS

It was a Canadian scholar of Scottish background, Dr. George Johnston, who first confirmed my intention to pursue a study of John McLeod Campbell. Opportunity was afforded by Union College of British Columbia (now Vancouver School of Theology) for research at Emmanuel College, Toronto, Canada, yielding a doctoral dissertation under the careful and caring supervision of Professor W.O. Fennell. Dr. Norman Porteous, formerly Principal of New College, Edinburgh lent encouragement for publication of the material in a considerably revised and updated book form. Throughout this process, Professor James Torrance of the Faculty of Divinity in the University of Aberdeen has been a constantly helpful critic of my thinking, a counsellor in writing and a painstaking reader of the manuscript, without necessarily endorsing all judgements of fact or opinion.

The staff of many libraries have been most helpful in research, while Mrs. Lucille Donnelly of Sidney, B.C. proved more than an expert typist through suggestions for improvement of phrase.

I am immensely thankful to all these and to others; yet a special expression of gratitude is due to my wife Helen R. Tuttle (born in Kirkcaldy, Fife, Scotland) for constant practical help and for her thoughtful insights included in these pages.

George M. Tuttle
January, 1985

A STORY

There was once a village set by a quiet river in an open valley. People drew water from the stream for household needs, and for their kitchen gardens. The fields beyond were sown each spring for the summer season to yield a crop. Then one year unusually heavy rainfall in the surrounding hills raised the river to overflowing. Water ran in the streets, threatened homes and places of business.

The community acted quickly enough. Neighbours joined to throw up dykes around their buildings, though they were helpless in the face of flooded fields. They could only await the drain-off and a return to normalcy.

The events of those days are largely lost to public memory now, though a few records of interest found their way into the archives. As providence would have it, however, the subsiding waters left a layer of silt over those fields; and from that time until this whoever has had a mind to cultivate them has been nourished by the fruits of so rich a soil.

I

THE MANNER OF THE MAN

On May 24, 1831, a young minister of the Church of Scotland was on trial for preaching a view at variance with official doctrines of the church as laid down in the Westminster Confession. The case had moved for many months through several levels of church courts until, after an all-night debate, the General Assembly brought the trial to a dreary end by voting to depose from its ministry John McLeod Campbell of the parish of Row.*

The case was closed, yet the issues it had raised remained actively on the conscience and in the mind of the church for decades. The judgement was never reversed; yet the events surrounding the trial gave impetus to a movement whereby the Confession, though never altered, could be interpreted with a new freedom. Meanwhile, the minister who had been rejected entered providentially into a new freedom as a theologian destined to enrich the minds and stir the feelings of countless Christian people.

My first notice of John McLeod Campbell came through brief summaries of his views in general works on the Christian doctrine of atonement. A special curiosity was aroused, however, through occasional references to him by church historians who testified to his importance for this or that turn of events in the life of the Scottish church without enlarging fully on those events.[1] That curiosity was lifted to the level of a consuming interest by the number and variety of testimonials to Campbell's stature as a theologian which my eyes grew accustomed to spot throughout the literature. Even a full century after his death, a ranking theologian who would later become a Moderator of the Church of Scotland could extol Campbell as a prophet in his own day and as a contemporary of ours.[2] Another in that same year offered it as his judgement that John McLeod Campbell was 'one of the greatest (if not the greatest) of our Scottish theologians.'[3]

What was there about this man forced out of the normal practice of ministerial vocation, who could by alternative means achieve even more than the original goal? What sorts of thoughts suited for their times, and dated in their manner of expression, may nevertheless come across as seasonable for succeeding generations?[4]

John McLeod Campbell was born a minister's son in 1800 near Kilninver on the west coast of Scotland. His early home life was

---

* Pronounced Roo, the spelling later reverted to its ancient form of Rhu.

evidently happy and secure. True, the death of his mother when he was only six years old was hardly a normal experience; but that the father and son were thus brought into a relation of mutual affection and dependence which grew with the years, is demonstrated by their standing together through many a crisis, and may be traced through a lifetime of correspondence. At Campbell's ordination the father could testify that his son had never caused him a moment's pain since the day of his birth.[5] And at the moment of his son's deposition from the ministry he addressed the Assembly, saying: 'I will never be ashamed to be the father of so holy and blameless a son.'[6] Most of the company present were giving embarrassed assent in their hearts, for many had already acknowledged the moral and spiritual quality of the man they felt obliged to charge with heresy. Incidentally, many of our sources comment on the probable connection between this father-son relationship and Campbell's warm exposition of the divine Fatherhood which became so central in his theology.[7] At all events, the boy grew up in an atmosphere of deep religious persuasion, quiet culture and humane attitudes. He flowered as a gentle, honest and generous person. These qualities were accompanied by virtues which could easily be misdirected – a strong sense of conviction, fidelity to truth and tenacity of purpose. These, as we may well understand, could display themselves to disadvantage under the pressure of a trial for heresy. To some he seemed even to court trouble deliberately. Certainly it was with no little difficulty that the generous side of his nature was maintained at all. Years later Campbell himself told how during that trial the very content of the love of God which he sought to uphold as the ground for his doctrines proved a reminder that this love must be the tone of his response to the charges laid against him. The struggle was not an easy one; yet all sources agree that over the years Campbell became a man of rare virtue. Of his mature manner of thought Principal Shairp of United College, St. Andrews, remarked, 'Penetrating inwardness there was, and watchful conscientiousness of thought, but at the same time eminent sanity of judgement. Above all, you felt that all his thoughts and feelings breathed an atmosphere of perfect charity.'[8] As for other aspects of his character, Campbell's distinguished kinsman, Dr. Norman McLeod, in a sermon shortly after Campbell's death, spoke of him as the best man he had even known in Christ-like qualities.[9] Surely this is extreme language of the sort one often hears in a funeral eulogy; yet over and over again, both before and after his death, such phrases were used by people of high and low estate to describe John McLeod Campbell: 'transparent simplicity,' 'goodness,' 'saintly,' 'heavenly nature.' This is the sort of person he was taken to be.

During his pre-theological education at the University of Glasgow Campbell tackled a wide range of subjects with enthusiasm and success. Perhaps most important for the work he was destined to do were his studies in philosophy, especially the so-called Scottish school of 'common sense' philosophy initiated by Thomas Reid. Campbell had already enjoyed a propensity for accepting the world around him as it seemed by nature to present itself. He would not therefore have been amenable to idealist philosophies which distance themselves from natural objects by formulating truth in terms of ultimate and all-embracing ideas. Nor would he be happy with that other contemporary alternative, Hume's scepticism, which tended to lock one inside the mind by affirming that what appears to be the case is really a function of the mind. Reid had opted for a basic assumption that there is a correlation between what objects and events are perceived to be with what by nature they really are. Indeed they offer to the mind their own evidence for what they are, and hence provide a basis on which we may understand and respond to them. In a sense they are their own interpreters for those who are willing to observe and listen. All experience is thus deemed to be founded on objective facts of the world around one.

However much some might criticize this view as resting on an unwarranted and naive assumption, it proved in practice to encourage a mentality in Scotland favouring scientific pursuits. Campbell himself felt the tug of science. It drew him during graduate studies to take some classes in chemistry and mineralogy; and later he would bring a similarly empirical attitude to bear on what he believed to be the primary and pivotal object, God. It was this style of thinking which led Campbell to observe a natural flow of connection from incarnation, to atonement, to sanctification in Christian experience.

Campbell's twin interests in science and religion lasted a life-time. He pondered the new questions raised by Darwinian theories, and felt the challenge to traditional religion in Comte's positivism. It was apparent too that his responses to these problems could command attention. When Dean Mansel delivered the Bampton lectures of 1858, thinking to commend the Christian faith by an exposition of philisophical agnosticism and reliance on Christian externalism, Campbell found himself concluding that this attempt to trace and mark the limits of religious thought was a failure.[10] He believed that speculative philosophy could not be dismissed so easily without damage to an important element in the human approach to reality. Then when the controversial *Essays and Reviews* came out two years later, occasioning widespread discussion and arousing fears on the part of some that the very foundations to Christian faith were being undermined, Campbell was naturally concerned but was at the same time somewhat surprised that Christians could feel themselves to be in so vulnerable a position. His own response was characteristic. The love of truth prevented him from joining in any hasty outcry against the results of inquiry. He persisted with the question 'Are they true or are they false.'[11] The prompting of friends soon brought his views to publication in *Thoughts on Revelation* (1862). In this book he dealt with the issues of the natural and supernatural, identified the ground for Christian faith and endeavoured to state a doctrine of inspiration.

It might well be asked how Campbell responded to the so-called Romantic Movement with which his life-span so closely co-incided. The cold rationalism of the eighteenth century had starved the human emotions. But the contemplation of nature through human nature was awakening people again to the feelings and moral sensitiveness of the inner life. Campbell breathed the new atmosphere with enthusiasm. He loved the poetry of Wordsworth and the romantic lore of Scott. References to them punctuate his writings with ease, yet for him the truest stirrings of inwardness were always to be measured by the objective facts of experience, especially the facts of revelation recognized in the person of Jesus Christ.

As for the feeling side of the faith, Campbell was very much influenced by the writings of, and about, three men whom he later referred to as his 'Row Companions' – Henry Martin, David Brainerd and Henry Dorney. He acknowledged that for a considerable period he owed more to them than to any others: said he, they 'shared with my Bible the whole of my reading.'[12] These sources helped to strengthen his own inward witness to kinship with God by the spirit and to contemplate the biblical experience of 'union with Christ' as a ground for stating Christian doctrine. To know this helps one to understand both the message in Campbell's preaching and the way he goes about his theological task.[13]

Mention of life in the Spirit reminds one that Campbell characteristically approached theology from the deepest levels of faith and devotion. It was natural, therefore, for him also to probe the theology of worship in at least some of its manifestations. This indeed happened, triggered by an interest in Roman Catholic tendencies in certain sections of the Church of England, a reading of works generated by the Oxford Movement and lengthy conversations with Henry Manning (later Cardinal). These ventures prompted his first book, a work on the Eucharist entitled *Christ the Bread of Life* (1851). It was not at first readily received, perhaps partly because of its difficult style; but as his other books appeared it gained in favour enough to merit a second edition in 1869 which was reviewed in the *Spectator* with high praise.[14] The continued relevance of the book is witnessed to through multiple references by Dr. T.F. Torrance in essays on questions of liturgies and the Eucharist published in 1975.[15]

Above all, Campbell from his earliest years had been steeped in the scriptures; and his interpreters have counted him first and foremost a biblical theologian. It becomes a matter of importance therefore to know how he regarded the Bible. What was its authority for him? How did he think it should be read, interpreted and used in theological argument?

Today, historical criticism of the Bible is taken for granted as a worthy and fruitful approach to the scriptures. John McLeod Campbell's work belongs, however, to a pre-critical period. He had hammered out the main tenets of his theology and had said all he was ever to say on the central doctrine of the atonement before the battle began over the application of historical criticism to sacred writings. John T. McNeill remarks that Campbell was perhaps the last theologian of real originality who comes under this category.[16] Yet Campbell did live to see that struggle begin, and partly because of this was led to turn back the pages of memory to explain his attitude to the Bible in former years.

When Campbell began his ministry in 1825 he had settled quite simply and believingly on the affirmation in the Shorter Catechism that the scriptures are the only rule for teaching 'what man is to believe concerning God, and what duty God requires of man.'[17] He had no hesitation about receiving the scriptures as the means of God's revelation to us, and was assured that they would confirm and clarify any other utterances of the mind of God 'whether in nature, in providence or in conscience.'[18]

Campbell early found the seat of authority for faith elsewhere than in an ecclesiastically approved creed, or even in the external features of biblical language. God's Word is authoritative because it carries its own evidence with it. And where are those evidences best recognized? – in the mind and heart, in the conscience of the believer where God is recognized for who he is and his commands are known to be true as issuing from him. This recognition of the truth about God is more than an intellectual matter; it is moral, personal, and inwardly acknowledged. The Bible is thus the vehicle of God's Word, but it is only recognized as God's Word through the response it arouses in conscience. Neither an external examination of the scriptures nor an institutional imprimatur upon its words can be the final ground for acknowledging the truth of revelation in the Bible. Not even miracles are enough to persuade the believer. 'In the gift of conscience' says Campbell, 'my God has put the needed – the only needed – scales into my hands.'[19] These words were written at the close of his life, but they are amply illustrated in his early sermons, for he founded his appeal for acceptance of the gospel on this principle from the beginning of his ministry.[20] Though he did not employ the language in the earlier stage, Campbell was ultimately to identify that response in conscience to the Bible message as Reason and Revelation bearing witness to each other. He seems not to have known a time when he did not adhere to a conviction that Reason and Revelation have a common origin in God and present themselves to faith as two harmonious witnesses to the one truth. By Reason here he means of course more than the powers of intellect and the perception of logical relations. It signifies a response of the whole person. By Revelation he is thinking in particular of God's Word as expressed in Holy Scriptures.

Campbell's reliance on the inward response to God's Word amounts to a denial that Biblical documents in themselves have any special authority. Since the truth must commend itself to every person's conscience in the sight of God, the determining factor in Biblical interpretation is an attitude of mind and heart divinely prepared to hear that truth. Moreover, this 'conscience' is capable of cultivation under the

Revelation of God in Christ to the point where it is clear that the only true glorification of God by us is through life as sons and daughters to a parental God. For Campbell, in Christ alone we know God to be the Father of our spirits, and in this knowledge we have a clear-cut instrument for the continuing interpretation of scripture. The words will be read and understood as glorifying a personal and loving God.

What did this mean in practice? Campbell had not arrived at the point where he could see that there might be real inconsistencies in its wholeness. Apparent inconsistencies disappear when each passage is seen in the fullest light. So Campbell did not twist phrases to demonstrate the harmony of each part of scripture with all the rest; nor did he insist on literal acceptance of the words as they stand so as to turn a blind eye to inconsistencies. He was saved from this not by exposure to the results of Biblical criticism as known to us now, but by the application of his own principles. Infallibility and consistency could only be discerned internally as Bible passages bear witness to the purpose of God that people should glorify God in their relating to God. God is not inconsistent, though we may have to wait long to hear rightly. As Campbell applied this view of the authority of the Bible he found himself sometimes having to reserve judgement for years if necessary for the truth to convince the soul that God was being glorified in a manner suited to his will that men and women should come as children to a loving parent – in accordance, in other words, with the revelation of God as Love. An interesting sample of this sort of waiting is described by Campbell as late as 1861 with reference to the uncertainties he had encountered at Row on the doctrine of election. Certain passages had given him great trouble. He was even tempted to think the Apostles in error; but by suspending decision he had come to see, at several points, that what had appeared a stumbling block really was something quite different. Of this experience Campbell recorded:

> This process is indeed still incomplete, for the hardest knot of all is still to unloose, the ninth of Romans. But I do not doubt that if the Apostle's words ever come to convey to my mind just what he intended, they will be then conveying what I shall be able to receive, and shall see to be in harmony with those of his words which I now feel that I understand.[21]

Having found a point of departure satisfying to conscience under God, Campbell faithfully followed its implications. Of course his exegesis was not always correct from the standpoint of historical criticism as accepted today. His exegetical method, however, possessed a devotional quality which saved him from the narrow Protestant Orthodoxy of his time, and would save us from the literalism of ours. With him there was no literalism amounting to bibliolatry. He eschewed the proof-text method of argument employed by persons of a dogmatic and doctrinaire turn of mind. His over-riding concern was to discover a meaning which commended itself in the light of God as the 'Father of our spirits,' to use a favourite phrase. This is the quality in Campbell's use of scripture which commands consideration and respect even when one cannot entirely accede to his interpretation of a particular point.

To one type of limitation in his handling of the Bible Campbell owned up with characteristic candour. His own theological leanings and his practical orientation rendered him prone to favour for attention those scriptural passages which connected themselves with his primary interest in the notion of humanity as meant to glorify and rejoice in God. Those favoured parts included, for example, the Fourth Gospel and the Letter to the Hebrews.[22] Actually, Campbell's preaching covered a reasonably wide variety of Bible texts; and in his major work, *The Nature of the Atonement and Its Relation to Remission of Sins and Eternal Life,* he moved as freely through the Bible as the subject required. If there was a tendency often to repeat certain themes, this was through no faulty motive on his part.

Campbell knew that he had come to his particular view of scripture almost imperceptibly. He says that if anyone had surprised him too soon with questions about the authority of the Bible, he might have fallen back on an appeal to some external evidence. As it was, he found himself led along this other pathway – inward and spiritual, yet somehow very practical. Having this manner of approach, and having so much self-awareness concerning his own predilections, he proved to be in a better position than most to meet the onslaught of controversy over Biblical criticism when it did develop. He regarded the new thinking to be among the 'permitted regions of thought' and held that 'there must be a mind in which they can be trodden with safety,' and against those who carelessly imagined that now at last the truth of the Bible was to be properly sifted he entered a caveat that the claim of the Bible to be what we accept it as being must be independent of historical criticism.[23]

PART ONE
A UNIVERSAL ATONEMENT

II

THEOLOGICAL RESPONSE TO
A PASTORAL PROBLEM

John McLeod Campbell was inducted to the ministry in the parish of Row in 1825. Entering upon his work with the enthusiasm of youth and with a real sense of vocation he set out quickly to meet the people. On the very first day he began to be aware of a deep religious need among them. His final visit that day was with an elderly couple in a little cottage. As he came away they walked with him to the top of a hill overlooking the waters of the Garelochhead. The old man bade farewell with the words: 'Give us plain doctrine, Mr. Campbell, for we are a sleeping people,' and his wife added a word from the scriptures which in retrospect appears to have had a prophetic ring: 'Be thou faithfull unto death, and I will give thee a crown of life.' (Rev. 2:10) Campbell never forgot this experience. In round after round of the pastorate, after listening to the questions people were asking, he came to have an awful sense of what he called 'the want of living religion.' For these people in their need he really cared, and he knew that he had work to do beyond anything imagined.

It turned out that these people were confronting age-old conundrums arising from the mystery of the experience of election under God: questions about how to live in relation to the promises and demands of God, to grace and to law. These can be detected in the vocational struggles of Abram, Jeremiah and St. Paul; also in the pilgrimage of Israel and in the New Testament Church. They get raised as questions about the conditions of pardon, how one is assured of divine favour, who is included, and so forth. They have emerged with particular sharpness in the face of a need for renewed sense of purpose and direction, as, for example, in the Reformation of Luther and Calvin. Long before Campbell's time in Scotland, two phrases had been employed to identify a certain polarity in dealing with these matters: the 'gospel strain' and the 'legal strain.' A fair reading of John Calvin, for example, would place him in line with the gospel strain in theology. Calvin had singled out God's call to Abram as a model for the divine relation to humankind (Gen. 12:1-3). It rested on God's initiative in the covenant and on God's faithfulness for its fulfilment. Abram was not given to know all that would be entailed by freely responding to God's call, but he was given a prior promise of enablement to meet every requirement and of an ultimate blessing for all humanity. Abram participated in the covenant by trust in God for who God is and what God says. The subsequent promised renewal of the covenant in the vision of Jeremiah (31:31-35) bore the same stamp; so also in the new covenant through Christ. In this view grace always precedes and enables works, and every Christian doctrine is informed by this priority. Calvin realized the subtle ease whereby the order can be reversed, against which no mere set of rules can guarantee. Indeed, some of his own successors allowed for such reversal in their development of so-called Federal Calvinism.

Instead of adopting Calvin's single model of a covenant of Grace (whether the old or the new) these later Calvinists fastened upon the notion of two covenants. The first was made by God the creator with Adam as the federal head of the race. It was based upon a presumed human ability to recognize and obey God's laws in the world, and in all things to 'glorify' the Creator. God promised life and blessedness as a consequence of such obedience. This was a 'Covenant of Works.' In Adam's failure, however, all humanity was deemed to have forfeited these benefits. They 'became dead in sin, and wholly defiled in all the faculties . . . utterly indisposed, disabled, and made opposite to all good and wholly inclined to all evil.'[1] In such a state men and women cannot possibly meet the demands of God's law and are therefore deserving of eternal punishment. The only conceivable way out would be if God, who is supremely sovereign, should provide that way. This was believed to have happened through a second move, a 'Covenant of Grace,' whereby God mercifully granted a means to eternal life. Yet theologians, taking account of scriptural references to a final judgement and the apparent double outcome – some to eternal life and some to perdition – felt bound to the notion that this double outcome was rooted in the purposes of the sovereign God from the beginning. It appeared therefore logical to conclude that the new covenant in Christ was made only for those destined ultimately for salvation – the elect. This called for a doctrine of limited atonement.

Campbell was to discover that Federal Calvinists, having begun with a Covenant of Works based on the requirements of law under a sovereign God of justice (the legal strain), were unable to shake off a 'works' mentality even in their honest effort to declare the good news of God's love. In their Covenant of Grace that mentality simply shifted to focus on the human responsibility to offer reparation and faith as a means for meriting the gift of Christ, thus placing conditions against the promise of the gospel offer. In addition, the morality and service themes essential to the first covenant were carried over to the second as additional grounds ('evidences') whereby the believer might be tempted to measure the probability of his or her inclusion among the elect.

No doubt it would be possible to show that the gospel strain often did come through in the preaching of many a strict Calvinist. How could it be otherwise when the scriptures were read and expounded by persons who had some feeling for the power of Christ's love? Yet the constellation of ideas characteristic of the 'federal scheme' had been enshrined in the Westminster Confession as official standards for the Church of Scotland.

For nearly two hundred years it had informed the catechisms whereby succeeding generations had been trained up. So Federal Calvinism carried inherent problems. They were bound to show from time to time.

Campbell came to see that these several problems focussed in the doctrine of election by a limited atonement, while his own reading of the gospel message led him to proclaim a universal atonement. It would be rash of course to imagine that he had no predecessors in this. Elements of the problem had been present from the earliest centuries of the Christian era, and took a recognized form at the time of the Pelagian controversy in the early fifth century. In modern times the issue arose most strongly in the Arminian controversies and in the effort to settle the question at the Synod of Dort in 1618 in which some British Reformed theologians took part. It is safe to say that even by that time every possible logical refinement had been worked out between the extremes of universalism and particularism whether of divine intent or actual outcome in redemption. Moreover, the Arminian question was a constant one thereafter in all the non-Roman churches of Britain.

The Westminster divines thought to stifle Arminianism through their Confession of 1646, and its adoption in Scotland carried that same notion as one of its purposes. Yet the issues would not die. Long before Campbell's time one or other of them occasionally reached the church courts. Witness the condemnation by the General Assembly (1720) of the so-called Marrowmen who promoted the unconditionality of the gospel, though they had not questioned it as effective for the elect only though offered to all. Yet the specific question of a universal atonement was cause for the deposition of Thomas Mair from the ministry in 1757; and by the end of the century the case of William McGill had gone to the bar of the Presbytery of Ayr before being dropped. Campbell's preaching was bound to call such names to mind. Yet he was destined to come to the fore as the central figure in the turn-around from the federal scheme to a renewal of reformation theology.[2] This proved so for a variety of reasons, including the timing and drama of his trial for heresy as a man of undoubted character and devotion, and the broader range of questions to which he later brought some system. Yet a major reason for the final effectiveness of his work lies in the fact that, while he did possess abilities for thorough academics, he was first drawn into preaching and pastoral conversation at the most elemental and passionate levels. He dealt with the questions as they happened to arise rather than by plan. Answers suggested themselves through an agonizing struggle, and often by quiet surprise.

Campbell 'dug in' at two points. first, he sought to study the actual spiritual condition of his people. He resolved to avoid confining discussions of religious matters to the times and places ordinarily set apart for the purpose. It would be a matter for any occasion. His underlying motives were practical, as described in a later reflection on his early ministry:

No forming by much reading an acquaintance with what had been thought and taught in the past, neither any amount of free exercise of my own mind in weighing theological questions, could in the least have been a preparation for my subsequent work such as my pastoral experience at Row has been . . . As compared with what is engaged in as the study of Divinity, it was in some sense the Baconian *direct contact* with nature in the substitution of induction for *speculation*. It has I feel, been a gain to me and not a loss that my pastoral work thus stood first in order, and that my thinking has been stimulated by the exigencies of that work, and not by any love of speculation or craving for originality.[3]

Professor Dickie sums up the matter in contemporary phrase: 'Campbell tried to work out his theology from the actual human situation. He was the right type of existentialist.'[4] This approach is eminently represented in Karl Barth's early sense of demand for solid pulpit work in wartime and Reinhold Niebuhr's pastoral dealings with Detroit auto workers, both men no doubt thus finding pivotal bearings for their later academic theological reflection.

The other point of departure for Campbell was the study of the scriptures. In fact, the study of the human scene drove him to meditation upon scripture as a source of diagnosis. If there was a gnawing religious problem among his people, then surely an examination of Biblical Christianity would enable him to see what that problem was.

This double reliance on pastoral experience and on the scriptures is amply demonstrated in a thousand pages of the Row sermons. Taking into consideration the language habits of the day, these sermons read well and sustain interest. Unlike Campbell's private correspondence, they contain few references to current events; yet by constantly bringing Bible passages to bear upon imagined human situations and upon the interior life of the hearer they breathe an atmosphere of practical Christian faith and life.[5]

It becomes a task of some importance to trace out Campbell's dealings with his parishioners' theological problems which led within about five years to proceedings in the church courts.

Even through their Calvinist inheritance people could be told that faith is not a human achievement. It is the gift of God by the Spirit of God. Nor was it to be exulted in by those who had it, thus making of Christ a work. Yet they suffered over a persistent question: 'How do I know that I have this true faith, the kind of faith which assures eternal salvation? How can I know that I am one of the elect?' One could turn to the Westminster Confession and find it said of the certainty of salvation: 'this certainty is not a bare conjectural and probable persuasion . . . but an infallible assurance of faith.'[6] But one could also find that 'this infallible assurance doth not so belong to the essence of faith, but that a true believer may wait long and conflict with many difficulties, before he be partaker of it.'[7] In other words, even among the elect, only a few will know early in life; most will not know until well on in life and may even have to wait to the point of death. The earnest person is therefore left in a state of uncertainty, and even of anxiety, as to his or her salvation.

We are told by Campbell that in the face of this problem current teaching had satisfied itself with the notion that if a relationship with Christ was producing love to God and neighbour, that is, showing forth the Christian graces, then a person might be considered to have a real and saving faith. Observe that even those of Arminian turn of mind, for whom peace with God always has a personal history to which one can point, included themselves in this category; for they were forever searching within themselves for the evidence of conversion experience. Whether by Calvinists or Arminians, the so-called 'evidences' of repentance, believing and Christian character were extolled in preaching and hopefully searched for in private meditation.

Campbell's pastoral observations led him to see that Calvinists were succumbing to the very danger which Calvinism officially sought to avoid, for the anxious questioner was focusing attention upon the self's awareness of goodness and achievement. This was in fact to regard some act of one's own as the key to salvation and as ground for assurance of faith. It meant also a suspension of trust in Christ, a denial of God's grace, and cutting off of the flow of love and good works which proceeds from the true faith. A person might thus be found in a worse state than before, the mind turned anxiously upon self. This was the religion of a people turned in upon itself – a sort of 'me generation,' to use a phrase coined more recently.

Campbell observed other aspects of the same religious problem. He felt, for example, that repentance too often proved to be merely regret at the experience of suffering the unhappy consequences of sin under God. He recoiled from what appeared to him to be a hollow and hypocritical profession of repentance. He also felt that people were choosing what they believed to be eternal interest in preference to temporal ones not because of the intrinsic value of the former but through self-concern as to their salvation. Even their praises to God seemed to be 'verbal tributes to God as just, holy and good . . . not because their hearts are full of His excellence and enamoured of his beauty, but because they think it will please Him and recommend themselves to Him.'[8] In so far as people could persuade themselves that these features of repentance and praise were real fruits of the Spirit in the New Testament sense, they could rest satisfied, and they could receive the approbation of others whose sights were set for such 'evidences' as guarantees of the reality of faith and thus of election. Campbell had been seeking to recommend such manifestations only as the fruits of a *true* faith which he urged upon them with great earnestness.

At first people failed to respond to Campbell's sermons in the manner he had hoped. They often praised his preaching, but continued in their old style. It became even more evident that theirs was a hollow faith. This led him to plead for greater honesty in looking at themselves. Quite a few did some soul-searching and did acknowledge the spurious character of the 'evidences' to which they had been trying to point. They were driven back to acknowledge that they did not know Christ for what he truly is; but they pleaded now on the ground that at least they *desired* the faith of Christ. Campbell detected even here the self-regarding character of their coming to God. The underlying problem, of course, was that they were in fact treating faith in Christ as a 'work.' The call to trust him was only an added demand of the law. The preacher suspected that even his preaching led them to regard faith as a 'third commandment' which prodded them to further self-examination and to greater self-despair.

Campbell was tempted to comfort people by telling them that, after all, their situation was really not so bad when compared with other people who likewise were found wanting. Yet he allowed himself the pastoral pain of admitting to them how serious he considered their spiritual state to be. He also tried to show that this discovery of their true situation was not news to God; nor was it anything which the Gospel failed to take into account, or which could rightly hinder them in hearing what the Gospel really had to say. Was not their problem one of failure to see Revelation for what it is, namely, God's parental love ready to receive sinners though they be sinners, to pardon and provide. Campbell had been immersed in a fresh study of the New Testament and, as will be shown later, in a contemplation of Martin Luther. More and more he was impressed by the fact that his parishioners were not seeing what had already been given to them in Christ.

> I speak under the conviction that there is much misapprehension as to what is our right state before God . . . we feel as if we were first to be in the right state – in the condition in which God would desire to see us, and *after this* should be emboldened to have confidence towards God, and to rejoice in God – that we must first be righteous, and then be warranted to have peace before the Lord – that we must first be made what we ought to be, and then look to God with joy and confidence, as children to a father.[9]

What has to be done has already been done freely and unconditionally. The forgiveness sought has already been declared. God in Christ has in fact come to us. It is not through something done by us that we have title to come to God with confidence. Campbell comments: 'I used to say, "If you knew the mind of God towards you as the Gospel reveals it . . . knew as really your own the unsearchable riches which you have in Christ, you must needs rejoice in God through our Lord Jesus Christ".'[10] He tried to show that even the common doctrine that we are first to repent and believe, if this be regarded as setting the conditions on which we earn an interest in Christ, is really 'the old system of good works under a new name.'[11] Repentance is not something which in any sense removes the barrier between God and ourselves. It is acknowledging that God has removed that barrier and 'the going back when the barrier was removed.'[12]

Likewise, humility and contrition are not prerequisites to God's acceptance of us; they are rather to be seen as growing from trusting in his acceptance.

Campbell was setting forth the Gospel as a declaration that humankind may rest assured in the love of God to them in Christ, pardoning sin and giving eternal life. The preacher's message was an invitation to believe what God says, to let God be God, to know that in the prior act of pardon we have only to rejoice.

Some Christians in every generation have responded to the Christian message in the manner of Campbell's congregation. The gospel comes across to them as a burden rather than a lift. The indicatives of the 'good news' are not really heard as such, but only as the imperatives of yet another moral demand. This can take individual form in moral standards to live up to, or the form of societal goals for which to strive. The hearer is reminded of failure to be what he or she is meant to be both in private and in public affairs. To be sure, these concerns belong to us as human beings and are not lost to Christian view. The Christian life is founded not on what we are and do, but with who God is and what God has done. God's gifts are seen to precede demands, to put things right in our favour, to promise grace even in the midst of failure. In that awareness one finds the motivation to be and to do, and the reason for rejoicing. Without it one is left stoically to press on, reminded constantly of impossible odds.

Perhaps the most characteristic words in the Row sermons are the words 'rejoice,' 'joy,' 'delight.' The condition of rejoicing in God is an inclusive one. To repent of one's ways is to delight in God's ways. To be humble is to have joy in dependence upon God. To be righteous is precisely to delight in God.

This experience is not reserved for the future only. The invitation to delight in God is addressed to us in every moment of time and in every circumstance. It is not something to work and wait for, or something which comes into play at the hour of death or even only in the critical moments of life. It belongs to life's routine. Says Campbell: '*Now* there is *in* the keeping of God's commandments, not *for* or *after*, but *in* the keeping of them, an exceeding great reward. "Because I delight in the law of the Lord", the Psalmist says, "I walk at liberty".'[13] The new spiritual situation in which all humanity stands is not simply the negative removal of a barrier to their coming to God. It is also the positive offering of power so to come. You not only have pardon for past sin, but enablement to delight in God, to sympathize with God's condemnation of evil, to love what God loves, and to live as children in God's family. God's work in Christ is two-fold: both to reveal the loving God in whom we are given the right to rejoice, and to make available the Holy Spirit to enable us to live in the light of that revelation. As Campbell put it Christ is 'not merely one in the *thought* of whom I can come to God, but in whose strength I can come . . .'[14] Thus it became Campbell's business as a pastor and preacher to encourage people not to consider their own achievements or their own feelings towards God, but rather to see what God has done for them and what God's continuing feelings are toward them – and in these things to be glad. Because of the prior pardon of God he taught that 'their first step in religion would require to be *resting assured of his love in Christ to them as individuals*, and of their individually having eternal life given to them in Christ.'[15] This was Campbell's doctrine of Assurance of Faith which he was preaching when rumours began to circulate that this preacher was carrying the doctrine of assurance too far. Of more immediate importance, however, is the fact that ensuing discussions pressed him in a natural pastoral sequence towards finding the foundation for assurance of faith in the universal extent of the atonement. Only if the Gospel declared Christ to be God's gift to every human being, can anyone be sure of title to rejoice.

In a later recollection of the situation Campbell remarked that he had never thought otherwise of the atonement than that it had universal import. It seemed to have been the plain meaning of scripture.[16] He notes too that many of his Calvinistic friends were groping after a way to express the true relationship of faith to newness of life. Some had come to believe that in a certain sense Christ was the gift of God to all: a sort of 'divine deed of gift,' like providing a medical doctor in a society to whom anyone feeling the need could turn for aid. But to Campbell's mind this was a half-measure which pivoted about the sense of human need and human response, rather than about the divine intention and provision. So Campbell was moved to press what appeared to him to be the 'natural and obvious' meanings of scripture as showing the universal extent of atonement. Preaching on I Timothy 2:6, for example, he felt the need for constant repetition and emphasis: '*He gave* himself a ransom *for all*.'[17] Today it seems unbelievable that such emphasis should be thought necessary; yet it really was a moot point in Campbell's time requiring more than casual notice. Long uncritical acceptance of the notion that Christ had died for the elect only could not easily be rooted out. It amazed him to find that familiar words such as 'God so loved the world' (John 3:16) and 'Come unto me all ye that labour' (Matt. 11:28) could be interpreted as giving the atonement only a limited reference. True, there are passages in which the context makes it clear that a certain few people are addressed, but these ought not to be taken to mean that the same words may not be addressed to others. In handling Isaiah 55:1, for example, Campbell considers it worth considerable time to clear up the question whether the intention of the invitation is particular or universal: 'Ho everyone that thirsteth . . .' Nor did he pass over some of the more difficult passages such as the prayer of Jesus 'not for the world, but for those you have given me' (John 17:9). He declared it to mean not that Christ's love is limited to some but that only that he appropriately asks a blessing upon those who have acknowledged him.[18] Admittedly he also says Amen to God's judgement against those who refuse to trust God.

Campbell sometimes appears to be 'reaching' for answers. Occasionally the argument trails off into a general appeal to the congregation not to let anyone persuade them to the contrary by 'vain words' and 'ignorant reasonings.'[19] The fact is that at this time he had not worked out a complete system of theology. The sermons reveal a strange mixture of orthodox Calvinistic terminology along with the central fact of the love of God revealed in Jesus Christ means that the gospel invitation is by its nature given to all. This was the valid point he felt impelled to preach upon incessantly. He knew there was need for reconstruction in theology, but his own efforts in this direction were confined to occasional thrusts. The immediate problem for Campbell, however, was not further to work out his theology but to avoid certain dangers of misinterpretation and faulty application of the doctrines he was already preaching. Captured as he was by the themes of pardon, assurance and universal atonement, he was not insensitive to the temptations which so readily attend them. He knew that some would think him open to a charge of antinomianism. Such a charge did in fact come from several sources. Some of the critics Campbell felt were merely perverse people who kept rising to the defence of law and morality because to hear the vices of stealing or drunkenness preached against provided them with false ground for personal comfort. They liked to hear the condemnation of things which did not obviously apply to them so as by indirection to be puffed up, and avoid the proper point of repentance in themselves. These people affected outwardly their concern for the well-being of society by declaring that these doctrines of God's love and pardon would lead people to feel they may do as they please. But Campbell detected their inward fear that the truth of his doctrines would force them to recognize the poverty of their own spiritual life.

There was another group, however, with whom Campbell had a great deal more sympathy. These were serious-minded Calvinists in whose lives the underlying truth of the assurance of God's love for them was being demonstrated though they shrank from identifying it as such by reason of negative conditioning in theology. They appreciated the importance of personal appropriation of Christ, but they had a dread of the antinomianism historically associated with a false sense of assurance. Their continued concern for the fruits by which people are thought to have a true faith kept them bound to the 'system of evidences' and hindered them from fully abandoning themselves to God. In preaching to these people Campbell sought to lift up the true object of God's saving act in Christ as not their release from the demands of righteousness but as an actual fulfilment of righteousness by having in them the mind of Christ. The only freedom from condemnation which the Apostle Paul, for example, contemplated had for its purpose 'that the righteousness of the law might be fulfilled in us.' (Rom. 8:4) Campbell would have us observe the precise wording, 'fulfilled in us' not 'imputed to us' for it is not at all intended that we should do without the righteousness of the moral law. The purpose is rather that we should be enabled to rejoice in the rightness of God who receives us as we are and sets us free to be what we are meant to be in Christ.

As a faithful pastor, Campbell also set out to show that to have an assured faith in the love of God promotes practical personal righteousness, both of the self and in relation to others in society. To critics who suggested that such assurance would lead to pride he countered by challenging them honestly to ask themselves how, when truly associating personal pardon with the suffering love of God in Christ, they could possibly be proud of themselves. Observation of humility displayed by forgiven persons proves the case. And to anyone who imagined that a person assured of pardon would become careless of sin Campbell commended the reading of Hebrews 10:19-22 as witnessing precisely the opposite. What force does the phrase 'full assurance of faith' have in this passage? Campbell replies that far from causing indifference, the passage represents it as a means of access to the enjoyment of communion with God.[20]

So there *are* to be fruits of the Spirit which arise from delighting in what God is. We are to expect 'evidences' of faith. We may rightly look for them as the test of faith in others, though being careful when discovering them in ourselves lest they tempt us to think of them as the ground of our acceptance with God. The fruits of faith are not new grounds for faith. They are rather 'additional proofs of the great truth we believe at first.'[21] Thus did Campbell seek to dispel any suggestion that his views would absolve people from moral reponsibility.

There was another closely related danger. Some people might take Campbell's doctrine of universal atonement and pardon to mean universalism as to salvation. The natural question was to ask: 'If God so loved all people as to give his son to die for them, is it conceivable that he would ultimately allow any to perish?' Campbell's reaction was characteristic. It appeared to him a plain meaning of the Bible that some do in fact choose the path of destruction; so that was to be accepted as such. Then he probed the point to discover the error of drawing a logical conclusion from a false conception of the relation between love and righteousness.

In Campbell's view the New Testament is unequivocal as to the fact of judgement when the sheep and goats are to be divided, when there will be a final reckoning as to the handling of talents in this world. What then is the human situation? He took his cue from the Parable of the Fig Tree (Luke 13:6-9) to describe it as a present condition of forgiveness and a future prospect of judgement. The present condition of the human race is that God has already forgiven us all. We are free to repent and believe, to trust Christ for his salvation. This is the day of grace. But it is not automatically a permanent condition of things. It is preliminary to a day in which God will judge men and women according to their deeds in the body.

Observe, however, that this fact need not introduce insecurity into the

Christian life, for judgement itself is not based on any moralistic interpretation of the law. It is based on the response to God's gift in Christ. Were men and women too proud to receive this gift? Were they too stubborn to turn towards the light? Do they continue to frustrate the Divine Love? If so then there is nothing except to be abandoned – to be left in outer darkness. Campbell kept warning his hearers: 'There is a condemnation which arises out of a dispensation of grace . . . there never was a gift given of God in respect of which God did not hold the creature receiving it accountable.'[22] If we neglect so great a salvation how shall we escape the day of wrath?

In denying universalism as to salvation Campbell also pointed to the character of God as Love. He declared it a delusion to think that because God loves someone, that person must thereby necessarily accept that love and live. If people ultimately perish it is not because God does not love them or has failed to reveal love to them, but because they would not believe that God means what God says in the offer of pardon. Everyone is invited to accept forgiveness and to trust God for eternal life. Whoever refuses is judged by that refusal. There is therefore a judgement which love cannot, and will not, keep back; or more positively stated, there is a judgement which love must exercise. Time after time these sentiments were repeated from the pulpit at Row. Campbell preached warningly, but always on the background of a primary conviction as to the love of God for every person and an open invitation into God's fellowship.

There were also devoted persons of a strictly Calvinistic turn of mind who showed alarm when Campbell's declaration that Christ died for *all* seemed to imply that the sovereign God wills that none shall perish. They asked: 'If God wills that none shall be lost, are you not concluding that ultimately all shall enter into life?' They feared that Campbell's doctrines implied a denial of final judgement and a confounding of distinctions between good and evil. Was he not emphasizing divine mercy at the expense of God's moral government?

Campbell acknowledged himself a kindred spirit with these 'narrower Calvinists,' because he respected their high sense of seriousness in religion. But he was amazed that the things he was already saying about the day of reckoning had failed to satisfy their apprehensions. Campbell knew that people schooled to think of God in terms of his sovereignty would have difficulties if they applied strict logic to the saying that God 'will have all men to be saved.' (I Timothy 2:4). He pleaded with them to hear no more and no less than what the words in their context declared about the mind of God towards us. Our best response to these words should not stem from speculative hopes or fears but from faith and obedience. We are not to think: 'Well then, all will enter into salvation and we need have no anxiety over ourselves.' Nor are we to fear lest the moral life be confounded by a supposed universalism of salvation. Rather we are to pray: 'Oh that this will of God be not frustrated. Let me be a channel of it.'

Campbell simply did not want to leave the believer in that state of uncertainty which so often characterized strict Calvinists. There is a kind of certainty open to the believer, even though it be not the certainty of salvation. He makes a distinction at this point between a prophecy and a promise. God does not prophesy as a certainty the salvation of this or that person; but does promise the certainty of salvation to any and all who trust him for it. The gospel proclaims that salvation is free to all; it does not assume as part of the good news that all shall in fact accept and possess life.[23]

Campbell's faithful attention to the Row parish, including the opportunity again and again to meet with people's questions for the sake of clarity, was beginning to show results. When he was offered a choice to serve elsewhere he remarked that evidence of a solid revival among his people was good reason for his remaining at Row.

Meanwhile, Campbell had found among his nearby ministerial colleagues some men of like mind; and a few further afield with whom he could correspond. He had also attracted the warm friendship of the lawyer Thomas Erskine who had already published on themes similar to his own. So Campbell had much to be encouraged about. At the same time this very broadening of contacts, plus frequent attendance at his church by people on holidays from Glasgow, served to bring him forward as a major figure in re-opening some highly sensitive theological issues. Rumours were spreading. Misunderstanding was mounting. Campbell would soon find himself caught up in controversy, charged with heresy and deposed from the ministry.

III

ECCLESIASTICAL RESPONSE TO
A THEOLOGICAL PROBLEM

To appreciate the Church's official response to John McLeod Campbell's preaching on the universal extent of the atonement one must consider the circumstances of the time. The predominant element in those circumstances was the Church of Scotland's position in the national life and her desire to safeguard that position. From the time of John Knox, Scotland's story could be read in the records of the Kirk. The Reformers had bequeathed a doctrine and a polity which were applied with greater thoroughness than they themselves could have imagined. After the Union of Parliaments in 1707 the Kirk remained the chief expression of the national spirit, and by the beginning of the eighteenth century it had achieved well-nigh despotic power over Scottish life. Ecclesiastical opposition was negligible. The native Episcopalian group was small and unpopular by virtue of old Jacobite sympathies. Papists had to lie low; and the non-conforming sects of English origin made relatively little headway on Scottish soil. The Church of Scotland did suffer a few secessions from her midst in the eighteenth century, but these did not immediately affect her power. During Campbell's youth the Kirk seemed as firmly founded as ever in the national life.

In spite of this outward show of strength the discerning observer could see that not all was well with the national Church, even though none could have predicted the tragic disruption which would occur in 1843. The Church of Scotland was suffering from theological bankruptcy and party strife. For generations two factions had been struggling against one another, under banners as Moderates and Evangelicals.

Moderation was a product of the age of reason and a growing confidence in the secular development of the nation. New intellectual currents were flowing which challenged traditional doctrines.[1] Under philosophers such as Francis Hutcheson the Moderates learned to think of God as desiring the well-being of all his creatures under divine law, and of humanity less depraved than portrayed by traditional Calvinism; more self-reliant, and possessing sound guides in reason and conscience. In harmony with their new interest in humanity the Moderates emphasized the great value of learning and literature; and their preaching veered away from details of doctrine towards the so-called 'practical' moral themes. They despised crude haranguing and suspected emotionalism ('enthusiasm') in religion as cheap and unworthy; yet they did represent a freer approach to strict Calvinism as early as 1719 to prompt William Dunlop's admission that in some quarters the reformed confessions were 'not only undervalued as mean and useless, but exclaimed against as unjust, arbitrary and inconsistent in their frame and tendency with the liberty of mankind.'[2] Some Moderates would have been willing to give up subscription to the Westminster Confession as obligatory; but most, while sitting loose to many of the standards, still clung to the Confession as a symbol protecting the church's establishment.

Evangelicals, on the other hand, reacted negatively to the new mood. They held tenaciously to Calvinistic tradition, being full of zeal in defending its finality. They believed that the most proper pulpit subject was some elaboration of the dogmatic system. 'To depart from that system, or even criticize it, might entail everlasting death. Its judgements upon those who did not accept its standards were fiercely censorious; and its characteristic documents are usually abusive.'[3] Evangelicals were narrow and harsh, but theirs was a religion of courage and intensity not altogether out of place in an age which took too lightly the fundamentals of the Christian faith.

The Moderates enjoyed a clear ascendancy in the mid-eighteenth century, but by its end they were experiencing serious set-backs. The flow of new thought had not stayed with the optimism of Hutcheson but moved through successive stages to the scepticism of Hume. There was little left to feed the soul. Also enlightened persons sustained the shock of seeing the French Revolution moving towards some awful excesses. Many Scots who had thrilled to the themes of 'liberty, equality and fraternity' found their ideals disturbed and their faith in cultured humanity crumbling. Then came the Age of Romance which uncovered and expressed an element in human nature long suppressed, and the Age of Reason was eclipsed. The Moderates lost vitality. They had no word for the new age. It was under these conditions that the Evangelicals, convinced of the truth of their doctrines, seized the opportunity to become the ruling party in the Kirk.

The Evangelicals who came to the fore in the early nineteenth century, however, were of a somewhat different complexion from their counterparts of previous generations. Long contacts with Moderates had led them to appreciate some of the 'finer' things of life. They were reading works such as the Waverley novels, if not too publicly; and they were putting a premium on eloquence and learning in the pulpit. At the same time, among those who remained Moderates by party affiliations there was a new willingness to lean again on the tried truths of Calvinism. Many a pastor of either persuasion could faithfully perform the tasks of ministry without the parishioners being aware of party affiliation. Indeed, a leader among the Moderates could be quoted in 1833 as saying: 'that in the course of the last forty years there had been a gradual approximation, on the part of the clergy of what are called the two sides of the Church, to a closer resemblance of one another in all the great features of their public teaching.'[4]

It seems that not only had something of each side been absorbed by the other, but the driving force of each had been spent. Traditional antagonisms remained to flare up around lesser issues – sometimes merely trivial and personal matters. There should have been peace; yet skirmishes continued long after the reasons for warfare had ceased. So the energies of the Church were being sapped to no good purpose and the stage was being set for the great Disruption on quite different grounds, practical and political.

Meanwhile both sides had long neglected theology. Evangelicals, by definition as it were, stood for no changes in theology. The Standards of the Church had been set at Westminster in 1646 and there were to be no alterations. Even exposition of the Confession had to be done with fear and trembling, lest the interpreter be suspected of heresy. And the Moderates, for all their love of learning, had failed to cultivate theological thought as such. Geddes MacGregor uses strong words to describe the situation: 'Throughout a century in which Scotland had produced scarcely a singly noteworthy page of theology, the Kirk's Calvinism had hardened almost to the point of sterility.'[5] For neither party was the Westminster Confession pivotal to the church in any living way. Indeed, it has been reliably claimed that it would be quite impossible from sermons of the mid-nineteenth century to reconstruct even the outlines of the Confession. Yet it remained in the background to be brought out in the face of any apparent threat to the establishment.

Campbell's relationship to the party question turned out to have important consequences. His father had been numbered among the Moderates, though with no taste for useless controversy. The son refused any party label. He could see too much of good and ill on each side. He felt that neither group represented the truth as it ought to be put to a generation woefully in need of the gospel. He therefore retained unhampered freedom for obedience to the truth as he saw it. He even maintained a hope for better times. He longed for a spiritual awakening among those who, as he put it, were 'slumbering upon the downy pillow of moderation, or storming in the popular clamour of high-flying church contention.'[6] Those better times were too slow in coming. Neither party was ready to change. Meanwhile, Campbell's choice of an independent course tended to arouse suspicion in both camps and bring them together in opposition to his doctrine.

Towards the end of the year 1827 the ministers of Glasgow became alarmed at the rumours about Campbell's preaching on assurance of faith as grounded in a universal atonement. They invited him to come for a discussion on the subject. He accepted and was at the time well received. But the event proved thereafter only to stir more disquiet. Campbell was greatly disappointed. Of Edinburgh he sorrowfully reported that he was much spoken against there also. When one prominent preacher heard about a new appointment to the Greenock pastoral charge near to

Campbell he had exclaimed, 'Good, he'll be a capital fellow for knocking the Row heresy on the head.'[7] By the spring of 1828 Campbell was admitting a growing sense of crisis in the religious controversy of the day and that he himself would be found in the centre. He wrote to his father, '. . . it has become the epidemic disease of the present age that men should find peace in the combination of an orthodox creed with much religious bustle; but heart religion has been at a low ebb . . .' To intimate friends he confided that he could see 'winnowing times coming,' and expressed the hope that he himself might be found properly ready.[8]

Campbell could hardly have known that the time would be so short and that when the storm broke he would be at its very centre. Before the year was out a few of his parishioners sent a petition to the Presbytery of Dumbarton complaining that their minister's teaching was antinomian in character. The petition proved abortive due to technicalities in the document. A second petition a year later signed by three or four individuals also failed. One of its signers proved not to be in good standing as a member of the church; and the only signer to appear before Presbytery agreed to withdraw the petition for a time. At last, however, early in 1830 a memorial signed by twelve heads of families was brought to the Presbytery with more success. It claimed that following upon the previous petitions a number of other 'unprofitable questions' had been raised and more 'pernicious doctrines' had been introduced. It begged Presbytery to 'take measures for effectually checking that constantly increasing, most painful and pernicious state discord into which the Parish has fallen; and for securing our youth from unavoidably falling into what we conceive to be hurtful errors.'[9] At the same time a counter petition was presented, signed by eighty householders and heads of families. It declared that their minister had faithfully proclaimed the gospel and urged that Presbytery do nothing to weaken his hands. Unfortunately, the Presbytery declined to receive this favourable word on a technicality, perhaps thus showing the mood which would prevail throughout. At any rate the case was now officially before the church courts. For fourteen months it moved through almost every possible step provided for processing a suit in the Church: petition, counter-petition, interview, Presbytery visitation, transforming charges to a statement of libel, hearing arguments from legal counsel for prosecution and defence and appeals to higher courts until a decision was reached. The core of the lengthy libel was as follows:

> Mr. John McLeod Campbell . . . you are indicted and accused
> . . that albeit the doctrine of universal atonement and pardon
> through the death of Christ, as also the doctrine that assurance
> is of the essence of faith, and necessary to salvation, are con-
> trary to the Holy Scriptures and to the Confession of Faith . . .
> yet true it is and of verity that you . . . hold and have re-
> peatedly promulgated and expressed the foresaid doctrines . . .[10]

Observe that the order in which the doctrines had been worked out in

Campbell's pastoral experience had by this time been reversed. His people had first confronted him with the problem of assurance of faith. They wanted to be sure of their salvation. This led him to invite them to trust in the pardoning love of God and therefore rejoice. But how could anyone be certain that the pardoning love of God was for him or her? How could one know of inclusion for sure? These questions had pressed Campbell to go a step further. He had declared the gospel to mean that Christ died for all and not just for a certain elect few. The atonement of Christ is universal in extent and is therefore the ground on which the doctrines of pardon and assurance may rest. Thus when the charges were laid against Campbell this third doctrine, the universal extent of the atonement, was properly brought forward to first place as the key to the whole discussion of his views.

During the debates in the Presbytery, the Synod, and in special committees about five hundred pages of evidence had piled up. Meanwhile also church people generally were being aroused by sermons and open letters designed to refute Campbell's views. Most of these seem to have been motivated by unreasonable fears concerning Campbell's alleged universalist and antinomian tendencies, the very things he had taken such pains to warn his people against.[11] Barclay of Irvine, in a bitter attack short-titled *Strictures*, dubbed his own efforts 'small shot,' but reminded Campbell that 'small shot may do effective execution' and, as if to guarantee the worst, predicted that the 'big guns' would soon follow. So church leaders were losing all sense of proportion. Complications of thought and feeling were making considered judgement almost impossible. Thus by the time it reached the General Assembly of the Church of Scotland the end result had become a foregone conclusion. In the closing moments of that meeting still another petition arrived from Row, signed by ninety-five per cent of the parish and proving beyond all doubt their confidence in their minister. It told how his zeal had stirred in them 'such a searching of the Scriptures, such feeling regarding divine and eternal things, as had not formerly occupied so much of their attention.' This petition arrived too late for discussion purposes, but could not in any case have meant much in the dying moments of an all-night debate from which more than half the Assembly members had already taken their leave. The remaining group voted 119 to 6 for Campbell's deposition.[12]

Before dealing more fully with the course of the argument at Campbell's trial for heresy, it is important to take account of some general dynamics at work. On the one hundredth anniversary of Campbell's induction as the minister at Row, when a memorial to his name was being unveiled, the speaker for the occasion said of that heresy trial:

> None can read the sorrowful record of that case without being painfully aware that there was nothing in it which could possibly justify so catastrophic a climax. It was a succession of confusion of thought, bungling of phrases, misinterpretation of ideas, and

persistent mutual misunderstanding.[13]

This is certainly the feeling one gets in reading the record of proceedings. Yet, while we cannot justify either the manner or the conclusion of the trial, we can do two other things. First, we can understand something of why it happened as it did. Second, we can discern at this distance certain great and good results which stemmed providentially from the deposition of John McLeod Campbell.

While the preacher at Row knew that at some points he was at variance with the Standards of the Church, and that opposition was being stirred up, nobody could have foreseen how tangled and frustrating the business would become before it was over. Our advantage is that of retrospect.

Here was a young man, whose pastoral experience had brought him to a fresh possession of a notion as old as the gospel itself – the love of God for the whole world. In some of its implications at least, this idea cut straight across the doctrinal tradition of a powerful Church. People are not easily told that things they have considered fundamental in matters of faith are false. Even less are older people happy when so challenged by a youth only beginning his vocation. It is not surprising that the records show samples of sarcasm drawn from seniors:

> Some of us might have been his father; and, without any great arrogance, I may say, that we had as much divinity as he has before he was born; and we may be allowed to have made some addition to it during the thirty years he has been in the world.[14]

Then take account of the party cross currents already described. G.D. Henderson remarks that with the eclipse of the Moderates there was a reaction favouring orthodoxy which reached its height at the very time of Campbell's trial.[15] And J.H. Leckie makes the further observation that Campbell's unwillingness to join either the Moderates or the Evangelicals left him without the normal personal loyalties which accrue from party affiliation.[16] The Evangelicals to be sure acknowledged Campbell's fervour as commendable, but they suspected him as the son of a Moderate and certainly held him accused of holding incorrect doctrines. As for the Moderates, if Campbell had been willing in any way to revive their cause, some of them might have come to his defence. But they remained dominated by other motives.

H.F. Henderson commented on an element in Scottish character in a work on the religious controversies of Scotland:

> Scotsmen have never relished their spiritual food too highly seasoned. They have a strong distaste for the element of en-thusiasm and religious assurance. They have enjoyed a religion that they could argue and fight over, but they have not readily taken to one that has abounded in rapture and ecstasy.[17]

When therefore Campbell pressed for personal awakening, personal assurance and what he called 'heart religion,' he was already rendering himself suspect. His phrases 'feelings of the Father' and 'delight in God' would be embarrassing to the dour Scot. Accidents of geography and name connected him by rumour quite falsely with an ecstatic movement in his part of the country led by two Campbell sisters (no relation to him). He was known to be a friend of the eccentric Edward Irving whose case was on the agenda for the same Assembly meeting. While he did not agree with Irving, he was suspected by association.[18]

Beneath any general difficulties in handling the feeling side of the faith lay a radical fear of any disturbance of peace and order in relation to the establishment. Studies of the voting patterns in the General Assembly of the Church of Scotland between 1826 and 1841 reveal a tacit agreement that divisions over matters of doctrine and morals, appearing somewhat unseemly for the national church, should be dealt with at the Presbytery level.[19] If such issues did come forward to the Assembly they could take the form of legal and disciplinary matters rather than of doctrinal cleavage. The worst fear was that 'fanaticism,' 'enthusiasm' and 'pentecostal outbursts' of any sort might surface at the Assembly to threaten the wellbeing of the church and the authority of the Standards. Thus did the Evangelical party member James Barr reveal the true concern when he wrote (more in the language of Moderates) to warn that in Campbell's teachings the Kirk faced the prospect of exchanging 'a rational and enlightened piety for the caresses of a wild, ignorant and frantic enthusiasm.'[20] Like Annas and Caiaphas fearing a disturbance in the time of Jesus the leaders of both Evangelical and Moderate wings sought to avoid a popular movement which might threaten the Establishment.[21] Whatever party doctrinal differences may have continued to exist these were set aside in favour of strict adherence to the Westminster Standards. Party feeling would find expression only in such minor ways as jockeying for procedural control and eminence in the debate itself.

No fair assessment of the situation can be made without acknowledging Campbell's own contribution to the atmosphere of contention. He had a sense of self-confidence and conviction which under the pressure of the circumstances impressed some as unreasonably dogmatic.[22] A virtue may sometimes thus appear a vice. They interpreted his responses as the latter; and they were irked.

Campbell persisted also in using terms in an admittedly unusual fashion. He knew this created a problem, and so reconsidered his wording more than once; but felt that rephrasing might only bury the issue.[23] He was battling for a principle and he believed that honest people would try to catch the meaning of his words; but they would not. So this became a recurring theme of his trial – the fact that they continued to employ his phrases in a manner different from his meaning.

It became a struggle over semantics. Perhaps the best illustration of this was his use of the word 'pardon.' By the divine pardon he did not mean a general absolute amnesty. That would indeed be playing into the hands of antinomianism and universalism. Nor did he mean the kind of pardon a person prays for in reference to a given wrong, because this implies that the suppliant has already returned to the fellowship and knows God's constant mind towards him. And he did not mean a conditional pardon whereby *if* one repents then God will forgive – that is pardon of the Arminian variety. He did mean the unconditional pardon which proceeds from the good will God bears towards men and women revealed in his action in Christ bestowing upon them the title to return to him. Every person is in this sense now in a position of pardon. Campbell certainly had a point to make, but one cannot easily exclude old meanings and put new ones in their place. Even his close friend, Robert Story, who later staunchly supported Campbell at the trial, felt the force of this problem. He pleaded that Campbell's meanings be seen for what they were; yet he openly admitted the unfortunate use of the term 'as fitted to mislead, as not framed to give right conceptions of the truth.' But he asked that 'truth not suffer although clothed in unseemly garments.'[24] Afterwards, Story told how day after day he had entreated Campbell to disavow his claim to the novel use of a word and simply be free to declare to everyone that nothing prevents a return to God except one's own unbelief in God's love.[25]

The situation was made even more difficult by the fact that the very terms Campbell chose for his purpose, universal atonement, pardon and assurance, had already gathered a stigma through the Marrow controversy of the previous century. Campbell could show both that the language had been misconstrued at the time,[26] and that in any case the Assembly's condemnation of the *Marrow* in 1720 could not be invoked as a binding rule against him, since it had not first been remitted to the Presbyteries. The fact remains, however, that Campbell had chosen phrases guaranteed to give trouble. He had not intended it so; yet, once chosen, he held to them as a way of pressing his accusers to face the issues head on. He acknowledged this in a private letter many years later.[27] Indeed, it is possible that if he had withdrawn his words the case might have been dropped and lost in the past. As it was, his explanations did not have the power he hoped they would have to alter the hostile attitude towards his views. The changes which in subsequent years did begin to show in the church were the result of moral forces stemming from the fact that a saintly minister had suffered deposition – it took that and more than that to alter the mind of the Church.

One more factor in the dynamics of the situation should be mentioned. Each side was founding its case on different grounds of authority, though neither side realized this at first. Much debate was necessary before the gulf between them was finally revealed to be Campbell's predilection for the scriptures and theirs for the Confession. At the beginning each party claimed to base its case on both the scriptures and the Confession. By the climax of the trial for heresy Campbell's opponents were standing firmly on the Confession as such, interpreting the scriptures on its terms. To counter this Campbell was resting his case on the Bible and was even beginning to question the Confession's compatibility with the Bible. These points will be illustrated as we consider the course of argument in that trial.

IV

THE TRIAL
ATONEMENT – LIMITED OR UNIVERSAL?

It seems incredible now that there was ever a time when it was necessary to make a case for the universal extent of the atonement. Yet Campbell, as a matter of historical fact, lived in just such a time. What might seem to us as shadow-boxing proved for him to be a real and fundamental debate. He was questioning a central tenet of a proud theology, and he was deposed on that ground. It therefore becomes important to follow the main course of the argument.

Campbell opened his defence at the Presbytery by summarizing his position that God through Christ gave himself for all humankind 'without exception and without distinction. And this the scriptures teach.'[1] In his initial effort to demonstrate this Campbell employed the method of typology familiar to his hearers but not so to us: looking for New Testament understandings through 'types' in the Old Testament. Our assessment of his position now would likely rest on how these arguments were adequately matched by the less figurative methods he used with reference to other passages. He endeavoured to show that the scriptures do not portray the work of Christ in any excluding fashion as for some only. Admittedly there are passages which have often been so interpreted. John 10:27 might appear to suggest that Christ had a favoured group of sheep in his fold. John 15:16 may seem to mean that certain persons have been chosen out above others. Ephesians 5:25 likens Christ's relationship to the Church as that of a man choosing a wife. These do indeed suggest some sort of exclusiveness, yet it was Campbell's view that when examined more closely it becomes clear that these passages only contain the assertion of a part of a wider truth, and we make a mistake in 'understanding the statement of the love manifested to some, as amounting to a denial of the love manifested to the rest.'[2]

Turning to passages which appear to have a more positive and inclusive character, we are invited to consider what might be the plain meaning of several portions of scripture. Look at John 3:16 'God so loved the *world* that he gave his only begotten Son, that whosoever believeth in him might not perish but have everlasting life.' Surely, *world* here does mean all men. Said Campbell, 'nothing but a distinct statement that the *world* does not mean the *world* can limit this statement as to the object of the work of Christ.'[3] Similarly he pointed to I John 2:2 'He is the propitiation for the sins of the *whole world*.' Or turn to Romans 5:18 '. . . as by the offence of one judgment came upon all men to condemnation;

even so by the righteousness of one the free gift came upon all men unto justification and life.' 'No words' says Campbell, 'could be more fitted to mislead us than these are, if the *all* upon whom the judgment hath come to condemnation, be not the same *all* upon whom the free gift hath come to justification.'[4] So also for the glad tidings 'which shall be to all people' in Luke 2:10.

Campbell approaches I Corinthians 15:1-3, in a slightly different manner: 'moreover, brethren, I declare unto you the *gospel* which I *preached* unto you. For I delivered unto you *first of all*, that which also I received, how that Christ died for our sins according to the Scriptures . . .' Paul is here regarded as referring to his first message to the Corinthians. He had spoken to them *before* they had heard of Christ; yet he included them as numbered among those for whom Christ dies. 'The fact that Christ died for them was not inferred from the fact that they were believers, but was itself the fact which at his first appearance among them he had asked them to believe.'[5]

If we turn from passages which proclaim the gospel to all people and consider the requirement of repentance which is properly associated with the gospel, we find that this demand also implies the universal extent of the atonement. In the fifth chapter of II Corinthians Paul wants to be sure his readers have not received the gospel in vain. He calls upon them to be reconciled to God, because of God's act of Love in making Christ 'to be sin for us, who knew no sin, that we might be made the righteousness of God in Him.' (V.21). Campbell marks it as clear that the point and power of the exhortation would be lost 'if any of them could turn and ask what proof there was they *they* were the objects of the deed of love upon which he founded it, and that he was not in the condition to tell them with certainty that they were.'[6]

The command to be concerned for others, to love others and to pray for them, likewise suggests the universal reference of God's work. In I Timothy 2:1-6, we are bidden to pray for all persons, including those in authority as rulers 'for this is good and acceptable in the sight of God our Saviour who will have all men to be saved, and to come to the knowledge of the truth; for there is one God and one Mediator between God and men, the man Christ Jesus; who gave Himself a ransom for all to be testified in due time.' Were there no willingness on God's part to save all, it would be scarcely meaningful to be asked to pray for all. This same passage, of course, in the hands of the strictly logical thinker, who begins on the premise that God is Almighty, and that what God wills *per se* cannot be frustrated, opens the way for universal salvation. Campbell's opponents were quick to accuse him of just such a conclusion.

The passages Campbell chose for their 'plain meaning' as to universality are usually well handled; and the thinking he applies to passages which appear to him to *imply* universality exhibits a marked feeling for the context in each case. When you examine them in the light of twentieth century commentaries, you find Campbell's thinking

generally confirmed. But there are exceptions in passages where he
seems to be teased into drawing more from the statement than the facts
will allow. For instance, his readiness to see universal reference in Isaiah
53:6, is hardly warranted: 'all we like sheep have gone astray, and the
Lord laid upon Him the iniquities of us *all*.' The *all* here does not
originally mean all humanity but a particular people who are being taught
how God deals with them. This is not to say that Christians may not
properly find here a happy phrase to witness to what God in fact has done
universally in Christ, but it should be looked at from that perspective if we
are to draw a meaning of the universality of the atonement from it.
However, a fair reading of the majority of Campbell's interpretations
leads the reader to be amazed that they failed to impress the minds of his
hearers. He himself could hardly conceal surprise. When the case went
by way of appeal from the Presbytery to the Synod it was pointless to
repeat scripture commentary which by that time was before everyone in
print; so Campbell settled for a brief summary, and for some general
comment as to his meaning:

> It is not a question as to the meaning of this or that passage of
> the word, but the great question of what God would have us
> believe concerning himself. And if the Doctrine is true then
> must it be found not in one passage only, but must pervade the
> whole revelation which God has given of Himself.[7]

Moreover, he claimed that thought must pivot around Jesus Christ and
what he was to people and what he did for them as revealing the nature
and purposes of God. Surely we must believe that in fulfilling the Law of
righteousness as a man living for others, Jesus Christ must be reflecting
God's love to all. In Campbell's view the secret of God's character is
revealed in the work of redemption and as he put it: 'Christ came not to
change his Father, but to declare his Father's Name.' When we see the
love of God in Christ, we are not seeing *some* love in God which is
coaxed forth from God in consequence of the work of Christ, but we are
seeing a work which arises from the very heart of our Creator who is also
our Redeemer. In fact, in the Redeemer we see who the Creator really is.[8]
Here was a theological statement Campbell would one day develop in his
work on the nature of the atonement. Other statements at this juncture
show him to be verging upon questions whose importance he would not
identify until the final stages of the trial, namely, how to relate God's
apparent election of *some* only to God's clear love for *all*. We come to
that in due course (p.50). Meanwhile, what about the Assembly's
response to Campbell thus far?

What Campbell's accusers had to say in direct response to his
arguments from scripture do not make good reading. This was, as G.D.
Henderson affirmed, not because they were utterly without reason but
because they failed sufficiently to lay hold of the subject in hand.[9] They
were disposed, as I have indicated, to turn away from scripture to found
their accusation on the Confession of Faith. This was evident very early

in the proceedings when a certain Mr. George, agent for the libellers, declared that in establishing the relevancy of the libel he felt himself 'not called upon at all, according to my conception, to enter upon the wide field of Scripture controversy.'[10] Then pointing up the fact that ordination vows are solidly linked with acceptance of the Confession, he concluded: 'I am persuaded that the Presbytery will consider any detailed reference to the Scriptures altogether unnecessary.'[11] This mood was underlined by a minister at that same session of Presbytery: 'We are far from appealing to the word of God on this ground; it is by the Confession of Faith that we must stand; by it we hold our livings.'[12] Campbell was thus confronted with a constant struggle to secure what he felt to be a fair facing of what the scriptures declare. The records of the trial reveal mainly generalizations and evasions. A good sample is seen in the way in which a representative member of Presbytery put their case to the next higher court, the Synod: 'Any individual who can take the Scriptures in his hands, and maintain such a doctrine as Mr. Campbell has done, has a mind so formed that I cannot easily comprehend how it arrives at such a conclusion.'[13] Yet in his own address he completely ignored Campbell's exposition. He merely listed the passages which had been cited by the Assembly Act of 1720 and considered that perfectly sufficient to secure judgment against Campbell.

Another eminent clergyman undertook to do something more, though he too skirted Campbell's argument, substituted another passage which he dealt with out of context, and then made an appeal to turn from Scripture to the Confession. Of the passage which speaks of Christ giving himself a ransom for many, he declared:

> Our Saviour does not intimate that the benefit of the atonement was to be universal – it was to extend to *many* . . . at all events supposing there might be some ambiguity as to what is the sense in which they are to be understood, our Church has not left us at liberty – she has decided the question; and to us who have subscribed her standards, her authority is law.[14]

At the same meeting still a third key person spoke of the Church as nationally established. In effect, ministers have a contract with the Church and State as worded in the Westminster Confession. They exercise their office only on agreed terms, and must therefore be judged on those terms.[15]

So Campbell turned to a consideration of the Confession. He had expected to do so for the wording of the libel so obliged him. As to the universality of the atonement, he began by claiming that the most that could be said to substantiate a charge against him was that the Westminster Confession of Faith is silent on the subject. He would show that the silence could be explained by the history of the Confession in a manner which leaves the way rightly open to an acceptance of the doctrine of universal extent of the atonement.

Campbell reminded the courts at each level that Protestantism had come into existence as testifying against error in the Church of Rome. Had the protestors felt error to have existed around the question for whom Christ died, surely it would have been singled out for the attention which so great a theme would warrant: 'I cannot believe that if the Reformers disagreed with her in this, they would protest against her masses, penances and a thousand other things, and not lift one voice against the doctrine of universal atonement.'[16] Campbell read from the Roman Catechism of the Council of Trent a statement which on the face of it is difficult to interpret in any other way than as an explicit doctrine of the universal extent of the atonement. This is further emphasized by its marginal title expressly stating that Christ made satisfaction for the sins of the 'whole world.'[17] Since with all this the Reformers had no apparent quarrel, Campbell claimed that in favouring a doctrine of universal atonement he was standing well within the true Reformed tradition. Further in support of this claim he quoted from the Confession of Faith used in the English congregation at Geneva, which according to Campbell's source had been 'received and approved by the Church of Scotland in the beginning of the Reformation,' though later superseded by the Confession of 1560:

> Thus of his free mercie, without compulsion, he offered himself up as the onlie sacrifice to purge the sinnes of all the world, so that all other sacrifices for sinne are blasphemous, and derogate from the sufficiencie hereof. (Dunlop's Confessions) Vol. ii, p. 5.[18]

Alongside this he put quotations of similar wording from the Confession of both Saxony and Augsburg, and a further reference to the Confession received by Scotland from Geneva: 'for we teach and beleeve that this Iesus Christ, our Lord, is the onely and eternal Saviour of *mankinde, yea and of the whole world.*'[19]

Campbell presented these in somewhat rapid-fire style, it being obvious to him that they clearly favoured his view, and that the burden of proof must therefore rest with the opposition. With the Westminster Confession, however, one does find a change. Here is a statement only of what has been done for the elect and not for others. Campbell gratefully points out that the Church was 'witheld, through the superintending mercy of God, from stating that Christ did not die for all,'[20] but he must regretfully acknowledge its failure to say that Christ did die for all. He believed, however, that his contemporaries were reading too much into this point of silence; so he felt it necessary to take account of the historical situation which produced the Confession.

Prior to the time of the Westminster Assembly there had been a widespread disposition to have England, Scotland, and Ireland parallel their political ties by religious conformity expressed through a common Confession and a single form of Church polity. The question of a common statement of doctrine presented itself as a reasonable possibility, for differences of belief did not appear to be very great. But obstacles of a polity character did loom large and ultimately proved insurmountable.

Campbell reminded his audience that the act of Parliament appointing the Assembly of Divines at Westminster stated specifically that they were named with deliberative powers 'for the setting of the Government and Liturgy of the Church of England.' But in regard to matters of Doctrine their task was only 'the vindicating and clearing of the doctrine of the said Church from false aspersions and interpretations.'[21] The Assembly had the articles of the Church of England as the basis of their discussion. The second of these articles allows for a very possible interpretation favouring the universal extent of the atonement. Christ is one 'who truly suffered, was crucified, dead and buried, to reconcile the Father to us, and to be a sacrifice not only for the original guilt, but also for the actual sins of men.' And if there be any doubt left, says Campbell, Article 31 is even more precise. 'The offering of Christ once made, is that perfect redemption, propitiation, and satisfaction of All the sins of the whole world, both original and Actual . . .'[22] Moreover the Anglican Catechism used at that time in preparation for Confirmation sets forth the Apostles' Creed and then appends certain questions:

Ques. 'What doest thou chiefly learn in these articles of thy belief?'

Ans. 'First, I learn to believe in God the Father who made me and all the world. Secondly, in God the Son, who hath redeemed me and *all mankind*. Thirdly, in God the Holy Ghost, who sanctifieth me and all the Elect People of God.'[23]

In regard to the extent of the atonement, the Church of England was manifestly in harmony with the Reformed tradition as cited above.

The Articles also contained a statement on Predestination and Election (#17) which speaks of those whom God has 'chosen in Christ out of mankind' and the benefits deriving to them as what can be witnessed to, but makes no mention of others, as would occur in a clear statement of double predestination.[24]

Now what kind of statement came from the Westminster Assembly's discussion in its Article III, 6? While they refrained from saying what God's purpose might be towards the non-elect, they did make a negative reference: 'Neither are any other redeemed by Christ . . . but the elect only.'[25] Campbell presses his point that the word 'redemption' in the Anglican Article 31 clearly has the force of an oblation for the sin of all people. In Westminster's use, however, the word 'redeemed' introduced an ambiguity. Strict Calvinists tended to equate it with the whole work of atonement done in Christ, his death for the remission of sins. The redemption of the elect constitutes the full extent of the atonement. Thus the atonement is regarded as limited. But the word 'redeemed' may still be confined in its reference more particularly to the actual deliverance of the elect as such. In this case nothing is being said of the non-elect in their relationship with Christ, and there is consequently no ground for a denial of universal atonement. Campbell adhered to this interpretation and upon it he based his argument from silence.[26]

Campbell even sought to explain the mind of the Westminster Assembly in their wording of this section of the Confession. There had been forces at work, he claimed, which quite naturally led Westminster to give greater prominence to the doctrine of election than otherwise they would have done. It has often been claimed that the Anglican Articles were open to Arminian interpretation; witness the words of caution against this possibility included in the statement on predestination and election of Article XVII. No doubt it was felt that a greater emphasis upon election might help to circumvent misgivings. Further, certain members of the Assembly who had already been teaching a limited view of atonement pressed for a restrictive statement at this point. But there were others who freely assumed a doctrine of universal atonement and a few more who did so with only slightly greater caution. These people clearly would not be satisfied with any statement which implied that the benefits of Christ's death were limited to the elect only. They were prepared to say, for example, that 'Christ did pay a price for all, with absolute intention for the elect, with conditional intention for the reprobate, in case they do believe.'[27] True, they did allow that there was no direct assertion of universal atonement, but they would hardly have signed the finished document had they felt that this compromise involved them in a denial of the doctrine as such. Finally, says Campbell, if we are to assume that the Westminster Assembly took its terms of reference seriously, then we must 'expect no *new* Doctrine in the Westminster Confession of Faith, other than that contained in the previous Articles and Catechisms of the Church of England.'[28] Some guardedness or some elaboration here and there might be expected, but nothing which could be thought as new or in direct contradiction of the old. Finally, Campbell reminded the court that the Westminster Confession had been received in Scotland 'as in nothing contrary to the received doctrine of this Kirk.' That is to say it was held to be in harmony with the Scots Confession of 1560 and the Palatine Catechism which were then in use. Campbell quoted the following words from the earlier Confession as favouring a universal atonement:

> But yet we avow that he remained the only well-beloved and blessed Sonne of his Father, even in the middest of his anguish and torment, quhilk he suffered in bodie and saule to mak the full satisfaction for the sinnes of the people.[29]

Admittedly, it can hardly be claimed that the phrase 'of the people' used here necessarily refers to all people. It could have reference to the elect people of God. But Campbell is more to the point when he refers to the Palatine Catechism (better known as the Heidelberg Catechism) which was used by the Reformed Churches of Germany and the Netherlands as well as in Scotland:

> Ques. 37 'What believest thou when thou sayest, He suffered?'
> Ans. 'That in the whole time of His life which he continued

here upon earth, but especially in the end thereof, He sustained, both in body and soul, the wrath of God against the *sinne of all mankind*.'[30]

Campbell had thus ranged widely through the confessional literature in search of support for his stand on the universal extent of the atonement.

How did the various trial bodies meet his handling of the Confession? As already observed when he had argued from the scriptures they had progressively pressed for reliance on the Standards of the Church. Now when he did turn to Confessional statements there was a parallel tendency to disengage themselves from any Confession in the Church's heritage except that of Westminster as it stood. They crisply refused to look at other sources. Said one: 'We must not go back to any confession before the Westminster, for to it we must bow.' Even the Bible apparently was to come under the authority of the Confession, for the same gentleman continued: 'By my subscription, I am bound to receive the Bible in the sense of the Westminster Confession.'[31]

Possibly Campbell was injudicious in some of the authorities to which he appealed. His reference to the Church of Rome would increase their animosity. And certainly he could gain no favour in Scotland by founding so much of his argument on the derivative character of the Westminster Confession 'as it came to us from England.'[32] It was a sensitive point. Some took the opportunity to say disparagingly that the Church of Scotland distinguished herself precisely on this point, that Anglicanism allows for universal redemption while the Kirk knows the truth of particular redemption. Campbell was told that he might very well go to England to preach his doctrines. As for his other sources, whether Lutheran or Calvinist, they said:

> You may just as well tell us of vitrified forts, or anything else in natural history, as tell us about Geneva Confessions, or Wirtemberg Confessions, or any other Confession than the Westminster Confession, to which all of us have subscribed in the most solemn manner.[33]

The Westminster Confession was an important part of the Revolution Settlement. It was the trade-mark of the Church of Scotland. Even a hint of questioning the Confession smacked not only of heresy but of disloyalty. It is no surprise that Campbell met with feelings of outright hostility before the case was through.

Campbell was right (if not tactically wise) to recall the materials of the Confessional tradition. Taken as a whole they favour a positive doctrine of the universal extent of the atonement. As to the Westminster Confession in particular, however, his argument from silence appears to bear less weight. Among those who drew up the Confession, those who favoured a limited view of the atonement seem to have had a controlling influence which prevented the mood of earlier Confessions from finding a fully positive expression. Campbell's contemporaries therefore had good reason to suspect that if he were to view the matter with complete clarity he would find himself out of sympathy with the Confession of West-minster. And it was to this Confession only that they felt called upon to adhere.

This brings attention to the question held in abeyance: the relation of the divine love (which purports to yield a doctrine of universal atonement) to the Calvinistic doctrine of election. Campbell was not at the time questioning the current conception of God's electing only some to salvation. The reader is left with a still unanswered question: How is Campbell to reconcile the fact that God loves us all, and that Christ died for all, with the notion that God effectually saves only some?

Campbell propounded as scriptural the fact that some receive the grace of God into believing hearts while others refuse God's gift. There is a double outcome. He was quite prepared to say that those who receive the Word do so by virtue of 'that work of the Father, whereby they have been made willing to receive the Son to reign in their hearts.'[34] In other words, while God loves *all* and Christ died for *all*, there is an action of the Father through the Son by the Spirit whereby God elects only *some* to salvation. Campbell points out that election has reference to ultimate salvation and not to prior atonement. He rings the changes on the fact that God elects 'unto obedience' (I Peter 1:2), and effects a calling 'out of darkness into his marvellous light' (I Peter 2:9) and he affirms that 'that light of the sun of righteousness – that glory of God in the face of Jesus Christ (i.e. atoning love), was altogether independent of their being brought to know it – it was the manifested grace to all men – *IN their being brought to KNOW it, was their election shewn.*'[35] The question asserts itself as to how the love of God shown forth in the atoning work of Christ can really have universal meaning and value if God effectively elects only some people – this would appear, in effect at least, logically to mean the exclusion of others.

The same problem arises in Campbell's dealing with Confessional statements and comes to focus in his treatment of the Westminster Confession. In his eagerness to show himself in harmony with the Confession, again he leaves Christ's atonement for all and the election of some to salvation as two distinct doctrines. They are placed side by side, the bearing of each on the other not being shown.

One of Campbell's chief opponents indicated the point of no return for the court when he identified the doctrine of election as 'really the leading doctrine of our Confession' and holding first place in it. 'Everything,' he continues, 'seems, by the Confession, to be included in God's eternal decree – all that takes place on earth is included in that decree.'[36] This of course includes the thought that people can do nothing of themselves; God is Almighty. He elects some to redemption and by his Spirit enables them to respond to his call. To the strictly Calvinistic mind it was not logically possible for others to be included. They are simply the non-elect, though, paradoxically, held to be without excuse. On this basis, whoever claims that the death of Christ is also for the non-elect is open to two charges. First, that this portrays a sacrifice insufficient to its declared purpose of redemption, hence being derogatory to Christ as making an aspect of his work to be of no effect. Second, that in any case the doctrine of a universal atonement serves no good end, since the sacrifice of Christ is conceived as only removing the barrier to a return to God without actually enabling that return, and there is thus no benefit to humanity. By the time the case reached the Assembly the logicians had cornered Campbell on this dilemma.[37] It was clearer to the court than it was to Campbell that, if he meant what he said, he could not be regarded as adhering to the Confession at this point. His persistence exasperated them. So much so that some began openly to cast aspersions on his much publicized Christian character. 'I cannot give him credit,' said one, 'for that respectability of character which has been reported of him.'[38]

Various writers have observed that Campbell was already getting past the dilemma without realizing it, that he was growingly 'conscious of a message which he could not as yet formulate.'[39] There were signs of a struggle to express this message during the trial, prophetic signs of what would yet come:

> I direct your attention to the real source of the difficulty in receiving the truth of God which I now set forth. *It is the not realizing God's character* as apart from God's power. It is one thing to be the Almighty – it is another to be love . . . God has come forth in Christ, as a servant, to show his character, as apart from his power. There is no glory in power, simply as power. Power belongeth to God alone; but if we would praise the power, it is because of the character according to which that power acts.[40]

Thus to Campbell the pivotal point of theology must be the Divine Love as revealed in Jesus Christ. If to the contrary we start with the premise as most important that God is Almighty, then in regard to salvation we have two alternatives. We can argue from the double outcome of salvation and destruction that these are alike the will of God in an arbitrary fashion. That is, they are alike pleasing to him, which really means that they can reveal no character. If on the other hand we place the Love of God at the centre but still persist in asking how a God who loves all could possibly allow any to perish, we still display an underlying primary premise that God is Almighty – we have not really grasped the character of God as Love.

The core of the problem, Campbell claims, is that we will not recognize a will in God which the wicked oppose, disappoint and frustrate; that God may be grieved and that things may take place against God's loving will. There is in other words always an open possibility in the relation of God to us in time. If this is so, then as Campbell himself did not at that time fully appreciate, there was need to reappraise the Calvinistic doctrine of predestination so as to take this possibility into account. And to do that would require a new conception of the *nature* of the atoning work of Christ. Campbell's opponents saw better than he did himself the threat he posed to their theological system. He had the nub of the matter in his heart, but had not yet applied it to the central citadel of the Westminster Confession. They for their part held that citadel to the end.

Eugene Bewkes describes the situation in a memorable way: 'There was no seeing eye to eye. The church forces never really understood the defendant at all. The prosecution and defence were like two stars each moving in its own orbit, each far removed from the other. Campbell moved in a wider ellipse. He saw their limits but was out of their range.'

It is only fair to admit that occasionally the opposition came close to acknowledging the validity of Campbell's position, especially when challenged to consider the underlying assumptions of their own preaching. Dr. Dewar of the Tron Church, for example, made two very significant speeches to the Synod in which he admitted that the atonement is the proof of the love of God to mankind and that the death of Christ is the foundation on which the proclamation of mercy may be made to all sinners without discrimination. But in each case he drew back from following the implications of these facts which Campbell sought to recommend as true.[41]

In summary it may be said that Campbell had become possessed of a central truth of the faith which had been vividly impressed upon him in his pastoral work. But he had not quite realized that this would run counter to the Confession to which he had signed his agreement at ordination. His opponents, on the other hand, held tenaciously to that Confession, realizing the threat inherent in Campbell's message but failing to see that their own preaching often proceeded on assumptions which were in agreement with Campbell. On the logical front he was the loser; this they knew. On the existential front he was to be a winner; this they could not foresee.

One final fact must be taken into account. It has often been noted that Campbell's deposition had this great value, that it freed him to embark on his really great work on the nature of the atonement. But we should not miss the fact that the trial itself was a liberating experience. He was being delivered from the fetters of Confessional authority in a manner he had never anticipated and to an extent he might never have achieved on his own. The process is a traceable one.

As a newly ordained minister Campbell had not doubted his adherence to the Westminster Confession. It was when he first felt the pressures of preaching and the pastorate that his concern for universal atonement was cultivated, and in turn he began to see that people could cling to long-cherished doctrines without full awareness of their meaning. He saw too that they may so hold a doctrine as to make less effective the word of God. He deplored this from the pulpit: 'I now charge with so doing, all who teach that Christ only loved some, and only died for some.'[42] He was already leaning more on the Bible than on the

Confession, and he believed that no doctrine should be preached when not explicitly and demonstrably present in scripture. He was ready to remind people that there were many doctrines expressed in scripture which did not find their way into the Confessions.[43] At the same time he believed that the universal extent of the atonement proclaimed in the Bible had found its way into the Confessions whether explicitly or implicitly. As the opposition pressed for the decision of the trial to rest chiefly upon the Westminster Confession, Campbell made it clear that he was willing to defend himself on this ground but that he could by no means give over to the Church's Standards the priority which belongs to scripture. He felt indeed that even to prove the Standards to be in his favour would not add any authority to doctrines already demonstrated from scripture.[44] His claim to support from the Confessional tradition was not therefore of primary importance. Then, when it appeared that the evidence was slim for his argument from the silence of the Westminster Confession, Campbell found himself questioning the wisdom of its framers. The members of the Assembly had been 'guilty of a great sin' by refusing to set forth the *whole* truth on this subject. He spoke thus to the Synod.[45] By the time the trial had reached the Assembly Campbell had moved to the place where he would put his case entirely upon scripture:

> I hold, that the Confession of Faith cannot be made *directly* the ground of a charge of heresy . . . I hold, that it has no authority but a derived authority, and that this the Church has again and again recognized . . .[46]

And in a final burst he declared:

> It is a far more solemn thing, and accompanied with a far higher sense of responsibility, to apply the word of God to prove the character of a doctrine, than to apply a Confession of Faith; and therefore do I contend for the application of the word of God, and for it exclusively.[47]

Was Campbell beginning to suspect that possibly his views did not after all square completely with the Confession? Was the dilemma with which he had been challenged leading him to glimpse the disparity with scripture which sounded through the silence of the Confession? Was there a fundamental conflict between the Confession's statement on the work of Christ and a full-orbed doctrine of the love of God? We cannot say precisely when Campbell himself became conscious of any change in his allegiance to the Confession, but we do have an interesting report in this connection from his close friend A.J. Scott, whose open dissent from some parts of the Confession had led this same Assembly to withdraw his licence to preach.[48] Scott tells of his conversation with Campbell when it was all over:

> After that dreary night in the Assembly, the dawn breaking upon us as we returned at length, alike condemned, to our lodging in the new town of Edinburgh, I turned round and looked on my companion's face under the pale light, and asked

him, 'Could you sign the Confession now?' His answer was
'No. The Assembly was right, Our doctrine and the Confession
are incompatible.'[49]
This by no means implies that Campbell was discarding the whole
Confession. It means only that on one great issue he had been forced to
realize the inadequacy of the Confession. This had cost him his position
in the Church. At the same time, however, he was being liberated from
the obligation always to justify his thought in terms of traditional
doctrinal statements, important and useful as he knew them to be. From
then on, in comparative isolation and in newly confirmed spiritual
freedom, Campbell was impelled to follow the next logical steps of
working through questions as to nature of the atonement on which he
would publish fifteen years later. Meanwhile, he was privileged to
observe how his earlier insistence on the universal extent of the
atonement might ultimately alter the church's attitudes towards it
Westminster standards.

V

AFTERMATH:
CAMPBELL'S CONTRIBUTION TO A CHANGING
THEOLOGICAL CLIMATE IN THE CHURCH

In the closing moments of that all-night session of the Assembly which deposed Campbell from the ministry, and immediately after the sentence was pronounced, the Chief Clerk of the court stood in his place to utter words of solemn triumph and warning. Somehow in his weariness the phrases slipped out with precisely the opposite of his intended meaning. 'These doctrines of Mr. Campbell,' he declared, 'will remain and flourish after the Church of Scotland has perished and been forgotten.' In the hush that followed, Campbell's friend Thomas Erskine, who had been observing the proceedings from the gallery, could be heard to whisper: 'This spake he not of himself, but being High Priest – he prophesied.'[1] The reference of course was to Caiaphas who had favoured the death of Jesus by way of an expedient to protect the nation from disaster (John 11:47-53).

The Chief Clerk had uttered at least a partial truth. 'These doctrines of Mr. Campbell' joined those of his predecessors in a dramatic and telling way. They began to gain favour not only in the church which had cast him out but among thoughtful people throughout the land. Still other names were added to the list. For example, eight years after Campbell's deposition a young minister of the United Secession Church by the name of James Morison experienced a spiritual awakening which included a new awareness of the universality of Christ's atonement. As a result he wrote a book on the subject, and was summoned before the Church courts and deposed. Morison then went out to found a new sect known as the Evangelical Union – otherwise dubbed the 'Morisonians.' Ultimately he headed their theological school.[2]

In this period too representatives of the Independent churches were publishing in Britain and America in promoting a 'modified' form of Calvinism which allowed for the notion of universal atonement.[3] It was to their writings that the Canadian, Robert Peden, appealed in 1850 when he was suspended from the ministry by the Toronto Synod for preaching universal atonement.[4] As for Methodism, though it never gained a strong foothold in Scotland, it did add fuel to the fires. These so-called 'Evangelical Arminians' stressed the universality of the atonement: 'We are North Britons, contending for a principle generally denied in our country to be sound.'[5]

By 1847 Campbell was remarking on 'a great breaking up of Calvinism' in his own country. It remained for historians to estimate his own considerable role in that process.

One might have expected that all this ferment favouring broader views in theology would lead to changes in the Confession itself. But this was not to be. As a symbol of religion in Scotland the Confession has always been more than an intellectual statement of faith. Scotsmen were not likely to alter the Confession if it proved possible to live with it on a less stringent basis. Subsequent Scottish theology has shown what could be done by way of broader interpretation in theological research and preaching while the Confession was retained as it stood. There was also, however, a measure of official recognition for the practical changes which had taken place. This came in a series of Declaratory Acts liberalizing the formulae of subscription to the Confession. A candidate for ordination had always been expected to declare belief in the whole doctrine of the Confession. In 1889 the Assembly of the Church of Scotland agreed to omit the word 'whole.' In 1903 the situation was further relieved by a declaration required to be read publicly prior to the oath of subscription at ordination. It indicated the sense in which the Confession was to be taken as authoritative. The Confession was regarded as an infallible rule of faith and worship only in so far as it accords with the Holy Scripture interpreted by the Holy Spirit. It can be argued that this had always been the implicit principle of the Confession. Yet in Campbell's case the leaders of the Kirk had been unwilling to conduct his trial in those terms in 1831. The declaration of 1903 was designed to give some leeway to individual conscience. This change in attitude may be detected in a comment by Professor W.A. Curtis during his inaugural lecture in this same year at Aberdeen University. He asserted that the General Assembly of the Church of Scotland recognized that the Westminster Confession in its details could 'no longer be claimed to represent the spontaneous beliefs of the great majority of our teachers and preachers.'[6] By 1910 even the wording in the subscription oath of the Established Church had been amended with the consent of Parliament to read: 'I hereby subscribe to the Confession of Faith, declaring that I accept it as the Confession of the Church, and that I believe the fundamental doctrines of Christian faith contained therein. To our generation all these changes may seem of slight importance; but their importance should not be missed. They reflect a very considerable alteration in prevailing theological attitudes. Henceforth the clergy could have greater freedom in their handling of any given part of the Confession.

Meanwhile other branches of Presbyterianism had also taken steps to recognize the practical situation without altering the Confession itself. Both the United Presbyterians in 1879 and the Free Church in 1892 passed Declaratory Acts defining at certain points the sense in which the Confession was to be understood. They denied that the doctrines of sin and grace mean that human responsibility has been destroyed and that people as such have no power whatever to act virtuously. They denied that some infants are eternally lost, that there is fore-ordination to destruction or that divine grace is not extended to persons beyond the reach of the appointed means of grace. In both churches these moves were made in response to overtures from those who sought to relieve their scruples concerning the Confession. The church courts recognized the existence of the problem but wanted also to conserve the Confession inviolate. When appointing their committee, for example, the Free Church Assembly declared: 'The Church can contemplate the adoption of no change which shall not be consistent with a cordial and steadfast adherence to the great doctrines of the Confession.'[8]

In English Presbyterian churches similar discussions had been taking place. These came to a brief halt in 1888, but in 1890 a committee chaired by Principal Oswald Dykes was commissioned to draw up interpretations of the faith. They presented Twenty-four Articles which revealed a liberalizing tendency, similar to that in Scotland. Instead of the word 'elect', for instance, they used phrases like 'Christ's people' or 'everyone who repents and believes.' In the article on election nothing is said about reprobation. The terms of adoption of this report, however, were sufficiently ambiguous to render their authority for the Church debatable. Some say these Articles had no authority beyond a statement for information and consideration. Others give them well-nigh Confessional status. Curtis concludes that whatever the precise terms of adoption, they were intended not only to give some relief to conscience vis a vis the Westminster Confession, 'they were also intended to be accepted as a virtual substitute for it, and with great cordiality.'[9] It would appear then that all these acts did reflect great changes in theological attitude and did provide protection for those who ventured a freer interpretation of the Confession.

Turning to persons who by common consent have a sort of unofficial authority in matters of the Confession, we find the less rigid attitude expressed. Macpherson, whom H.F. Henderson describes as 'the latest orthodox defender of the Confession,'[10] appears at least cautiously to follow the argument from silence which Campbell used at his trial and which allowed for a belief in the universality of atonement without denying particular salvation.[11] Mitchell's introductory chapter to the minutes of the Westminster Assembly may be cited similarly.[12]

Mark this, however, that these moves bespeak only a liberalization in the use thus far made of the Westminster Confession. Though the Church acknowledges the right to alter, and even to create substitute standards, the Confession itself remains the principle subordinate statement under the scriptures. Ministers of the reunited Church of Scotland (1929) are required to subscribe themselves as professing agreement with 'the fundamental doctrines of the Christian faith contained therein.' Yet many found this an uncertain and hampering position to be in, and therefore still pressed for further review. Thus in the 1980s the whole subject came back on the agenda in the Church of Scotland.

While there is no doubt that Campbell clearly anticipated much that was to take place, it is impossible to speak with precision of his share in the changes which came about. It is easy to attach a person's name to the trends of a given time; but this does not provide satisfactory proof. Other names can be associated with the same events. The fact is, however, that keen observers of Campbell's own day, as well as students of church history since that time, have tended to single him out for special attention. Other names are often linked with his – Erskine, Maurice, Irving or Morison – but usually Campbell's name comes to the fore.

When delivering the Baird Lectures at Glasgow University towards the close of the nineteenth century, Professor R.H. Story made some comments about Campbell's place in the changing theological climate. In describing the shift in balance of power from the Moderates to the Evangelicals, Story explained how neither group had been conspicuously successful in probing the deeply spiritual and moral meanings of Christian doctrine. Then he proceeded to speak of Thomas Erskine and of McLeod Campbell as the pioneers of a movement which did finally stir the mind of the Church and ultimately broke the bonds of the Westminster Confession. Of Campbell in particular he remarked:

> The Church has long repented of its act of narrow-minded injustice, and has recognized the truth of the teaching which, sixty years ago it branded as unsound . . . .The liberty of prophesying, of which Campbell was the pioneer, is now the Church's secure possession.'[13]

Possibly Story's remarks reflect personal leanings, for his father had been an intimate friend and supporter of Campbell in the Row days. At the same time, he had observed the intervening years at first hand, and as an able Church historian he was equipped to interpret what happened.

An estimate of a much later date is contained in the Hastie Lectures given also at Glasgow University in 1930 by A.J. Campbell. Of McLeod Campbell he said:

> No sooner was he cast out of the Church of Scotland than his influence began to make marked headway within the Church. For the next fifty years the most impressive school of thought within the Church of Scotland bore his stamp. Spreading as a leaven, his work took effect even among those who regarded the Church of Scotland as an evil thing, and prided themselves on being the most unyielding of dogmatists (i.e. the other Presbyterian bodies) . . . Under the stress of circumstances they learned to speak of the Confession much as McLeod Campbell had spoken.[14]

The lectures tell how after the Disruption of 1843 the Free Church and the United Presbyterians, as well as the more conservative elements in the Established Church found their chief targets for criticism in John

Caird, John Tulloch and Norman McLeod and others who 'kept alive the teaching of McLeod Campbell.' These men, it is said,

> . . . declared a gospel that was universal, spoke of the Father-hood of God more than of His sovereignty, and led the way back from the traditionalists and their cast-iron dogmas to the study of the Person, Life and Teaching of Christ. By the end of the century the old rigidity had disappeared so completely from Scottish life that few could have believed that it ever existed.[15]

The sources abound in testimonials of this kind. Dr. J.H. Leckie writes that the Campbell case was 'the opening episode in a war for greater freedom of teaching which went on for more than fifty years,'[16] while A.B.D. Alexander declares in *The Shaping Forces of Religious Thought*: 'Campbell has done more than any other to emancipate his countrymen from the harsher elements of Calvinism.'[17] Judgements of this kind from persons who have a right to make them cannot be ignored.

There is another aspect of the situation rarely referred to in the literature, namely, an apparent defection of members from the Church of Scotland to the Episcopal Church arising from difficulties with the Westminster Confession. The Bishop of Argyll and the Isles, Alexander Ewing, was in a position of first hand knowledge on this matter. When in 1872 Dean Stanley lectured at the Philosophical Institute of Edinburgh on Scottish ecclesiastical history (later published as *The Church of Scotland*) Ewing wrote him a letter of appreciation in which he inserted a critical comment:

> I would mention, if you would excuse, that you have omitted an act which, if injurious but discreditable to the Establishment, is yet the hinge on which most of its recent history turns – the deposition of Dr. Campbell. To that is mainly owing the influx into the Episcopal Church of a valuable portion of the Estab-lishment, and their desertion so weakened the latter, that at the disruption the Calvinist party carried the day. Now, however, Dr. Campbell is the boast of the Establishment. At a dinner given him on the occasion of his being made a D.D. by the University of Glasgow, three years ago, I asked the chairman, Norman McLeod, if they would now turn him out? He replied, 'We owe much to Luther, but the theology of our days owes a far greater debt to Dr. Campbell. It was our glory to have brought him up,' and – I whispered – 'to turn him out?'[18]

Even allowing for the close friendship between Ewing and Campbell, and for the blood relation between Campbell and McLeod, this item of conversation is a highly significant indication of how the Scottish Churches generally came under the influence of the deposed minister, John McLeod Campbell.

I have said that Campbell was not alone in his doctrines. Nor was there lack of others to pick up his concerns after his death, often independently and from quite different perspectives. Witness on the one hand D.L. Moody's powerful and popular preaching of a 'free gospel,' and on the other, a new climate of thought among academics.[19] Yet these factors in no way detract from Campbell's rather special role.

There is still a further question. Why does Campbell's name thus keep coming forward? The answer appears to lie in a combination of factors.

It should be remembered that Campbell's case was kept more than usually in the public eye through a volunteer publisher in the person of R.B. Lusk of Greenock. Lusk sympathized with Campbell sufficiently to make it possible for many of his utterances to have open presentation in print. It was he who had arranged the shorthand recording of Campbell's sermons. He provided similarly for the full proceedings of the trial. A heresy trial is normally accompanied by much gossip and misrepresentation, and Campbell suffered his share of these. But Lusk's factual reporting did much to keep at least the more thoughtful people informed, and ultimately to enlarge the sphere of Campbell's influence. People could read for themselves what Campbell had really been saying. They could see that he was neither Socinian nor Arminian and that the charges of antinomianism had been utterly unfounded. The Lusk materials greatly helped his cause both at the time and for later generations.

There seems to have been a measure of providential timing whereby Campbell's appearance on the scene coincided with movements of the Spirit which turned in a fresh way to scriptures for guidance. Some devotees went to all sorts of extremes of religious enthusiasm and biblical interpretation; but Campbell came to the scriptures with a more measured stride. He found in them an objective source which he could put alongside the church's traditional statements of doctrine to the point where he challenged the church at the heart of its institutional life in the church courts with the priority of the scriptures over the Westminster Confession, the latter to be recognized as truly subordinate. It was Campbell more than any other who publicly identified the point at which the church itself had fallen into the error of making an idol of its cherished Confession of faith. Shades of all this linger into our own day, so that knowledgeable persons do not speak of it without some reference to John McLeod Campbell.

Personal and moral factors also shared in making Campbell's influence upon the Church greater than would otherwise have been the case. To all concerned the Christian character of this man was completely evident. He maintained a gracious attitude towards his accusers. He had no bitter words for his judges. Yet the proceedings throughout his trial presented the spectacle of a truly good man being victimized by party strife, and prejudicial argument favouring the status quo. His more sensitive opponents could hardly fail to have believed that a great wrong had been done. There is evidence of much heart-searching both among those who attacked him and among friends who failed to come forward in support of Campbell.

Even the great Dr. Thomas Chalmers seems to have been found wanting. It is sometimes stated that to the end of his days Chalmers took comfort in the fact that he had not voted for the deposition of McLeod Campbell.[20] It should also be said, however, that neither did Chalmers exert himself at the time. He chose to be absent on other business, explaining to his son-in-law William Hanna: '. . . it would have required a whole month to have mastered the recent authorship on these topics and to have prepared myself to my own satisfaction.' 'Nor did he ever question,' says Hanna, 'either the necessity or the justice of the Assembly's decision though he did allow that the underlying differences had probably not been so great as they appeared.'[21] Chalmers was the only churchman with sufficient stature to have gained a fairer hearing for the accused. He already knew that others would speak against Campbell with far less preparation than he himself possessed. Yet he simply allowed events to take their course.

When, after many years, Campbell was finally vindicated there were doubtless others who also 'took comfort' that they had not opposed Campbell. Only two or three, however, could say that they had actually supported him. John T. McNeill summed up the truth of the matter when he said that the trial and deposition of Campbell had given the Church 'a bad conscience.'[22] Somehow people felt the necessity to justify themselves for what had taken place, and the Church as a whole came to regret its action. After the Disruption of 1843 even conservative Free Churchmen preferred to disclaim responsibility for this unhappy event of their history.

Add to this the fact that for the rest of his life Campbell supplemented his courageous witness at Row by most valuable writing. Above all *The Nature of the Atonement* (1856), as the natural theme beyond the question of its extent, exercised an influence far beyond the limits of church courts and official standards. We have yet to deal with that phase in detail. Suffice it now to say that Campbell the pastor and preacher was overtaken by Campbell the author. This was precisely the right order in favour first of self-awareness and then of change.

The theological climate was indeed changing in Campbell's own lifetime. As the years rolled by he realized more and more that a new time had come and that he had played an important part in it. For reasons of health in 1860 he retired from Glasgow to Rosneath within sight of Row across the Gareloch. Until his death in 1872 he lived in a house provided by a friend to which he gave a Gaelic name, Achnashie – 'field of peace.' The place became his family centre; the time an opportunity for reflection and further writing. Honours came as well. In 1868 Glasgow University conferred upon him an honorary doctorate, with public appreciation noted in the *Glasgow Herald*.[23] There were close-in testimonial occasions too, as when a group of persons highly placed in church and university life met in philosopher Edward Caird's home to make a special presentation: 'We desire,' they said, 'to express our conviction that your labours and example have been the means of deepening religious thought and life in our country; that your influence has been a source of strength and life to the churches . . .'[24] It was this same Dr. Caird at the turn of the century who remarked concerning the Row heresy trial and its aftermath: 'In this case it may fairly be said that the heretic has in the long run converted the Church.'[25]

PART TWO
THE NATURE OF THE ATONEMENT

VI

A COMPARATIVELY INDEPENDENT MIND

John McLeod Campbell loved the Church of Scotland and dreaded the very thought of leaving her ministry. Yet after his deposition he expressed no word of bitterness or recrimination. In a farewell sermon to the people of his parish (preached in a field because he was debarred from the sanctuary) he made no direct reference to the awful experience of that trial. On another occasion he commended his successor to them and urged that they receive him in good faith. This was not done for dramatic effect. It was a simple-hearted acceptance of the experience of rejection which he had many times preached about at Row as the possible lot of a Christian.[1] Principal John Tulloch witnessed to the fact that Campbell never ceased to have a warm heart towards the Church which cast him out.[2]

Nor did Campbell have any appetite either for shifting to another church body, or for founding a sect of his own. All such suggestions he turned aside, including one from Henry Drummond.[3] For a time he travelled as an itinerant preacher. Then in 1833 some interested friends secured him a chapel in Blackfriars Street, Glasgow. Here he served for about twenty-five years, except for a few intervals due to poor health. He preached three times a Sunday and often on week-days, counting himself also a pastor to the poorer people of the city. He had neither ministerial standing nor any denominational connection. Since his father had been able to supply a small income for him, he laboured without salary.

Initially these were lonely years from the standpoint of one cut off from the church he loved, and from the many benefits available for a promising young man. In a letter to his sister he described himself as like a sailor shipwrecked on a lonely island from which he had no escape.[4] He acknowledged himself to be 'a nobody in Glasgow.' Yet the perspectives of history allow us to sense how providential was Campbell's isolation. Having been deprived of the normal fulfilments open to one in the church at large, he found himself nevertheless in a marvellous setting for the maturation of mind and heart. This included the challenge of responding to ordinary people in the congregation and in the neighbourhood, correspondence and dialogue with a circle of friends who lived at the growing edges of theological awareness, and the satisfactions of family life. It afforded him also time for study, reflection and writing which would re-introduce him somewhat to the wider church.

The few to whom Campbell remained a faithful minister could not know, as we know now, that his courageous stand in the trial of 1831 had already added impetus for change in the national church; nor could they ever have guessed that one book in particular germinating in their pastor's mind would one day have a theological impact far beyond the Church of Scotland.

It is true of course that in no pursuit does a person exist as an island unto the self. So a theologian's views will rightly bear the marks of heritage, home, the ruling ideas of the times and all the round of private reading and experience. It is important to search out the circumstances of a person's life which may have influenced the development of his or her thought. My biographical references to John McLeod Campbell have been minimal, and thus far selected mainly to show how his early thought was shaped in part by the practical problems of the ministry. However, in approaching a study of his mature views on the atonement it becomes appropriate to consider the extent to which he was influenced by other writers, whether contemporary or antecedent. This may be doubly important in Campbell's case because of some neglect and even misconception as to his sources. I have mentioned the so-called 'Row companions' (p.14), books of both theological and devotional value in Campbell's early formation, and above all, the Bible as his primary resource. What about others?

Thomas Erskine of Linlathen (1788-1870) is the person most often acknowledged to have influenced John McLeod Campbell. Erskine was a lawyer by training whose private means afforded him an opportunity to pursue religious contemplation and theological writing. Through conversations with a wide circle of friends, and by a series of books, Erskine stimulated a vital mood in theology which affected British theology far more than is generally realized. His books were small in size but weighty in matter. He began in 1820 with *Remarks on the Internal Evidence for the Truth of Revealed Religion* which identified him as an apostle of the 'Christian consciousness'. Then followed books on the meaning of faith, the unconditional character of God's gift in the gospel, a study on atonement, and one on the doctrine of election. After 1837 Erskine ceased to publish; yet for another thirty years he influenced the thought of his generation through an interchange of visits with leading men of the time. Still one more book appeared posthumously in 1871.[6]

Thorough evaluations of Thomas Erskine's work have only lately been made (not overlooking the valuable effort on *Erskine of Linlathen* in 1899). My purpose is only to estimate his bearing upon Campbell.

Erskine and Campbell were the warmest of friends. They visited each other's homes frequently, sometimes travelled together, and exchanged letters on all sorts of topics. The Campbells even named a son Thomas Erskine.

In literary endeavour, three of Erskine's works were in circulation before the publication of Campbell's sermons. Two more appeared still twenty years in advance of Campbell's book on the atonement. It is therefore not surprising that the careful reader of Campbell's sermons and of his defence at the trial for heresy finds many striking similarities to Erskine's writings. Some of these have been documented elsewhere.[7] It can be shown also that certain ideas in Campbell's *Thoughts on Revelation* run parallel to Erskine's 'Internal Evidence.' Of elements in common between their respective views on atonement some notice will be taken below. There is plenty to suggest that Campbell must have relied heavily upon Erskine as first in the field. This conclusion is strengthened by the fact that many of Campbell's contemporaries assumed his inspiration to have been Erskine. For instance, when in 1830 a leading Edinburgh preacher published sermons in opposition to the doctrine of universal pardon, the attack was directed mainly at Erskine, with the young Campbell regarded as one of Erskine's associates.[8] Various subsequent observers settled for the notion of Campbell's dependence upon Erskine. It is said, for example, of Erskine that '*The Nature of the Atonement* would probably have never seen the light if it had not been for Erskine's earlier writings on the subject.'[9]

In spite, however, of all that has been said favouring a material dependence of Campbell upon Erskine, opinions to the contrary, or at least of a qualifying character, have also been voiced. Robert Mackintosh offers a footnote comment on Campbell's 'supposed dependence upon Erskine? They were comrades; not master and pupil.'[10] Likewise, Professor Bewkes insists that earlier assumptions be revised, claiming that we should not think of Erskine as the head of a school of thought of which Campbell was one of several representatives.[11]

Take account also of external evidence. Early in 1826 Campbell wrote from Row to his father about his satisfaction at reading 'Erskine's *Internal Evidences.*' It is obvious from the reference that the author's name is known at least by reputation to both men. Evidence is lacking here and elsewhere to establish whether Campbell had yet come upon the only other work of Erskine's available at that time: *An Essay on Faith*. In this particular letter, however, Campbell recalls a previous conversation with his father on a subject he was now reading about in Erskine; and quite unaffectedly he comments on Erskine's way of putting it in 'language which you remember was mine.'[12] There were thus indications of like-mindedness between the two men even before Campbell came into contact with Erskine's written word.

What of their first personal meeting? In his senior years Campbell could not recall the precise time, whether in 1827 or 1828.[13] Nor was William Hanna any more certain on the point when he edited Erskine's letters for publication. The occasion seems to have centred around Erskine's chancing to hear Campbell preach in Edinburgh in the spring of 1828. Erskine is said to have remarked to a friend who accompanied him: 'I have heard today from that pulpit what I believe to be the true gospel.' Dr. Hanna comments on Erskine's surprise and delight that 'at least one minister of the Church of Scotland' had been expressing thoughts in 'almost the very form' in which he himself had been framing them.[14]

Whether conversations between the two men took place that day is not clear. It is enough to say that within a few months Erskine took up temporary residence near Row to hear more of this message and to gain the friendship of the young preacher. A.J. Scott was there also, and the three men were amazed to discover their unity of mind on so many matters. Years later Campbell wrote to Robert Story about that memorable time:

> That historical independence which we mark when two minds, working apart and without any interchange of thought, arrive at the same conclusions, is always an interesting and striking fact when it occurs; and it did occur as to Scott and myself; and also as to Mr. Erskine and me.[15]

In a similar vein he told his daughter how he had come into contact with Erskine and Scott 'having before – each, and each separately – come to the same light of the divine love in which I was rejoicing.'[16] Obviously Campbell thought of himself as characteristically thinking in common with Erskine and Scott rather than in dependence upon either of them.

D.J. Vaughan, a good friend of Campbell's in England, sought to sort out the Erskine-Campbell-Scott relationship shortly after Campbell's death. Among other things he noted Hanna's comment that each of the three had 'moved in separate orbits; each having a path of his own, which with absolute independence he pursued,' though not without manifesting, as we have seen, a oneness of mind, 'each a living spring and fountain-head of intellectual and spiritual refreshment, which has flowed from them by many channels to the world around.[17] He also pointed out that Erskine, having been the first to publish, did much to prepare the way for Campbell's fuller and more finished handling of their common themes.

If the 'master-pupil' terminology used later by R.S. Franks is an overstatement in one direction, Vaughan's phrase 'entire independence' moves too far in another. Campbell must be seen as having first achieved the general outlines of his thought quite independently of Erskine. Then followed more than half a life-time of close contact which could hardly fail to influence both men. But Campbell was not during this period developing ideas which belonged distinctively to Erskine. He was carrying his own ideas a stage further. Thus they celebrated a deep-running consonance of thought and feeling. They could not be independent of one another in any exact sense.

As for literary acknowledgement, the very nature of their relation made that unnecessary. There is not a single notice of Erskine in Campbell's *The Nature of the Atonement*. Yet about this, his greatest achievement, Campbell confided to Erskine: 'In writing it you were mentally present with me . . . as one on whose sympathy I could calculate.'[18] Here is a clear indication of the manner of Campbell's reliance upon Erskine. He found in his older friend corroborative support in all that mattered to him in both preaching and publication. If he had never read Erskine's works or entered into that friendship, Campbell would still no doubt have preached as he did at Row and written later on the atonement in much the same vein as he did in 1856. Yet Erskine's inspiration and support gave Campbell more confidence and helped to clarify his thought and lend a flavour to all his work.

Frederick Denison Maurice (1805-1872), the great representative of the so-called Broad Church Movement in England, is another name to be taken into account when considering possible influences upon John McLeod Campbell. They were contemporaries, and very good friends, though they saw one another only between lengthy intervals.[19]

In April of 1838 Campbell speaks of meeting 'a Mr. Maurice of the Church of England' who had been previously known to him only as 'the writer of *Letters to a Member of the Society of Friends* advocating the claims of the Church of England.'[20] The first edition of this publication was 1837, six years after Campbell's deposition, which established the fact that Maurice had no influence on Campbell's thought at Row or in the heresy trial. As for possible influences later we cannot be certain. After their first meeting the two men followed each other's careers with considerable interest. Campbell's letters show him often critical of Maurice's conclusions, though respectful of his aims and motives. He sometimes found himself drawn round to an opinion of Maurice's after second thoughts. With regard to Maurice he learned the value of waiting to see.[21] Certainly he read Maurice's works; and he had the highest regard for Maurice's place in Anglicanism as 'the foremost man of their Church . . . the only man who is attempting to deal with the mental difficulties of his generation in a free and fair spirit. [22]

Maurice, along with Campbell, had been befriended by Erskine; yet more readily than Campbell he can be thought to depend on Erskine. One of his publications (*The Prophets and Kings of Israel*) was dedicated to Thomas Erskine. Of this action Maurice wrote to Erskine: 'I wished to tell others how much I believe they, as well as I, owe to your books; how they seem to mark a crisis in the theological movements of the time.'[23] For our purpose it is important to add, however, that Maurice's acknowledgement of Erskine on another occasion specifically included Campbell as one of the springs of his thought. In an autobiographical letter he recalls his steps as a young man toward fresh insights into the gospel, '. . . helped much in finding an answer to the question by Mr. Erskine's books . . . and by the sermons of Mr. Campbell.'[24] This was written of the period just prior to 1835, which means that before Campbell read anything of Maurice's, or met him personally, Maurice had already recognized him as one of his teachers. More than twenty years later, upon the publication of Campbell's *The Nature of the Atonement*, Maurice wrote to him in appreciation. Venturing also to add a few qualifying comments, Maurice was careful to point out: 'In all spiritual truth I feel that you are so much the teacher, and I the learner, that I am afraid of putting myself in the wrong position.'[25] These words could be credited to modesty on Maurice's part. Yet brought into association with all the evidence they appear to put the emphasis in the right place. In seeking to know whether Campbell may have depended upon Maurice, we find the facts tending to favour just the reverse.

With regard to the content of *The Nature of the Atonement* two important points remain: one a verifiable fact, the other an open question. As to the first, it might easily be assumed that Maurice's *Doctrine of Sacrifice* published in 1854 would be fresh in Campbell's mind as he wrote his own book on the atonement for publication in 1856. However, the fact is that he deliberately refrained from reading it until afterwards. Campbell felt it necessary to explain this action to his publishers as an advantage to all concerned.[26] The question remaining open is whether Maurice's other previous writings had any direct bearing upon Campbell as he worked on *The Nature of the Atonement*. Maurice's *Theological Essays* of 1853 represent an obvious possibility. It contains a chapter summarizing his views on the atonement at that time in which emphasis rests upon the love of God the Father. He also opposes the current interpretation of Christ's work as one of penal substitution, preferring to think of Christ as the representative head of the race rather than as a substitute for humanity.[27] These same themes appear in Campbell's volume; but it must be said too that they belonged to Campbell's message more than twenty years before at Row. Campbell stood in no special debt to Maurice along these lines. However, it could be that Campbell's knowledge of the *Theological Essays* was one of the factors prompting him to pursue his writing without further reading Maurice on the subject in order precisely to continue on a course genuinely his own.

Without doubt Campbell was encouraged and helped by what he found in Maurice as a person and as a writer. With Maurice, as with Erskine, he discovered a great degree of like-mindedness in facing the theological issues of the day. Yet, while he shared in the early influences over Maurice, and was on that score held by the latter in highest honour, it must be maintained that Campbell wrote in all but complete independence of Maurice.

Friedrich Schleiermacher (1768-1834), the German theologian, brought a strong influence to bear upon Campbell's contemporaries in Britain. Did Campbell depend on him? A number of responsible writers have answered in the negative. Principal Tulloch recognizes that Schleiermacher was a pioneer in working out a theology of the Christian consciousness. He also claims, however, that Thomas Erskine was working concurrently along the same lines in Scotland without guidance from Schleiermacher; and he associates Campbell with Erskine at this point. Otto Pfleiderer's word on this question should have special value since his study of theology in Great Britain during the nineteenth century is appended to his larger work on German theology. He accepts Tulloch's opinion. Pfleiderer offers his judgement after describing Erskine's general role in theology and Campbell's contribution to the doctrine of the atonement in particular:

This is manifestly the same reconstruction of the Christian doctrine of salvation which was effected by Kant and Schleiermacher in Germany, whereby it is converted from forensic externality into ethical inwardness and a truth of direct religious experience. Erskine and Campbell appear, however, to have reached their convictions in entire independence of German theology by their own absorbing study of the Bible.[28]

The fact that Pfleiderer tends to equate the experience-centred theology of Schleiermacher with the revelation-orientation of Erskine and Campbell (in error, I believe) might cloud one's sense of his overall authority on the main point at issue; yet there were others who also agreed that Campbell worked independently of Schleiermacher. Witness Vernon Storr, who made an even closer study of the period.[29] The word of these authorities is not called in question. Yet their failure to present adequate internal evidence for their judgement prompts us to search out supporting facts, and on one point to offer a qualifying comment.

Schleiermacher had been a professor of theology at Berlin for fifteen years before Campbell began his ministry. His most important theological treatise, however, (Der christlicher Glaube), was not published until 1821-22. Campbell was leaving university by the time the first British scholars were reading this work in the original German, though of course Schleiermacher's name was by this time a familiar one. Campbell himself had no facility with the German language. Whatever he may have known about Schleiermacher he derived from secondary sources in English. Interpretive articles were appearing in British periodicals. As for English translations of Schleiermacher's writings, these were exceedingly slow in coming. Nothing of vital importance for atonement theory was translated until well past the time of Campbell's writing The Nature of the Atonement. In fact it was more than a century before an English edition of Der christlicher Glaube appeared.[30] If translations had been achieved more speedily Schleiermacher's ideas would have spread faster and with even more telling effect than they did. In this connection Richard Brandt's thesis on Schleiermacher is revealing. He includes a study of Schleiermacher's influence on Protestant theological thought. It is no surprise that Campbell's name does not appear, but it is surprising that no other British theologian is named whose work can be dated prior to Campbell's book on the atonement.[31]

It is by no means suggested here that Campbell knew nothing about Schleiermacher's thought. His knowledge was probably that of an average British reader of secondary sources. Moreover, it is known that when he was writing The Nature of the Atonement during 1855 he had before him Schleiermacher's position on the subject at least in outline. It is found in one of the few books Campbell refers to in his text and included in his bibliography, namely, William Thomson's Bampton Lectures of 1853, The Atoning Work of Christ. Thomson had included a brief summary of Schleiermacher's view together with some illuminating notes on the subject in which Campbell's one-time teacher, Sir William Hamilton, is quoted at length upon Schleiermacher's characteristic ideas.[32] Hamilton speaks not only of Schleiermacher's emphasis on the mystical union of Christ with his members, but also of the advantages of a representative as against a substitutionary view of the atonement. Once again (as in Maurice's case above) here are themes which appear in Campbell's *The Nature of the Atonement*, but are found also in his sermons preached many years earlier. There is no way of knowing with certainty whether in that earlier period he was conscious of affinities with Schleiermacher. There is nothing to show that he was aware of any. Campbell's first expressed interest in Schleiermacher occurs in the *Memorials* in relation to a period toward the end of his life. He had been reading the translated portion of Schleiermacher's biography with considerable care and interest. A letter to his son at the time (1868) shows that this was his first serious savouring of Schleiermacher's thought. Much of it was to him, as he said, 'a new phase of the German mind.'[33]

Having regard then for the known facts, it appears proper to conclude that Campbell cannot be said to have relied upon Schleiermacher.

Albrecht Ritschl (1822-1889) is another German whose theology found a welcome in Britain during the nineteenth century. He was a younger contemporary of Campbell's, but he does not figure in the latter's writings. A survey of Ritschl's most important publishing dates indicates that he could not in any case have affected Campbell's thinking on the atonement prior to 1856. There were still other writers of about the same time, belonging to the so-called Erlanger School, whose writings show some interesting parallels to Campbell's. Gottfried Thomasius, for example, held a doctrine of Christ as representative man which allowed for the possibility that Christ entered into the human consciousness of guilt. His thought bears similarities to the concept of vicarious penitence with which Campbell is usually credited.[34] But Thomasius published along these lines very shortly after Campbell. The possibilities of any direct connection between the two men must be discounted.

Martin Luther, the great reformer, was a major figure to whom Campbell turned for help. For the record, however, two things must be made clear: First, Campbell did not profess to be an authority on Luther. Apparently he did not even range the field of Luther's works. At least when offering direct reference to the Reformer's writings he confined himself mainly to one volume: *A Commentary on St. Paul's Epistle to the Galatians.*[35] Second, Campbell's insights into the meaning and importance of justification by faith alone did not originate in a direct study of Luther. We have Campbell's own statement to the effect that reading Luther confirmed and supplemented thinking in which he had already been engaged, yet he would always remember 'the bright shining of the light of the Gospel which there was to me in his commentary on the Epistle to the Galatians.'[36] At what point he turned to Luther's

Commentary on Galatians is not specified; but whoever reads Campbell's sermons, examining the cautions and comforts offered to his people, will be sure that early in his ministry he counted on Luther's aid. He does not cite Luther by name, yet the sermons yield many phrases which turn the mind to Luther: references to God's 'strange work,'[37] the claim that 'it is most righteous that those who will not know God as God, in his love, should be made to know God as God, in his wrath,'[38] and emphasis on the importance of the personal pronoun in reference to God's forgiveness 'for me.'[39] Indeed, in a sermon on Hebrews 3:2 there are passages which could well describe Luther's religious experience.[40]

Twenty-five years later, when preparing to write *The Nature of the Atonement*, Campbell returned to a closer study of Luther's *Commentary on Galatians*. He acknowledged the extravagant and sometimes fanatical tone of Luther's language on the work of Christ, and felt that Luther had failed to set forth a clear intellectual apprehension of the nature of the atonement.[41] Nevertheless, he was convinced that the basic elements of Luther's theology, as reflected in his doctrine of justification by faith, provided the right substructure on which to found an adequate view of the atonement. Campbell therefore included a chapter on Luther more than one third of which consists of direct quotation. This is a most unusual procedure for Campbell. Even then, he claims to have 'reluctantly curtailed' his references.[42] Remember also that Campbell appended further notes on Luther to the subsequent editions of his book.[43] Moreover, the central portion of the *Reminiscences* is occupied with faith as understood by Luther.[44]

I cannot venture to judge the degree of accuracy with which Campbell interpreted Luther. It is sufficient to indicate that Campbell felt himself a kindred spirit, and that in shaping his own view of the atonement he acknowledged himself to be following up the implications of Luther's doctrine of justification by faith alone.

Luther's emphasis on the love of God as the ultimate source of the atonement in Christ, and his understanding of the believer's appropriation of Christ, entirely suited Campbell. They augmented his thinking at Row as he sought to deal with pastoral questions. They were reviewed again twenty-five years later as helpful background for a statement on the nature of the atonement. Thus far Campbell recognized Luther as his teacher. The next steps were his own.

Patristic Affinities in Campbell

In considering possible sources of Campbell's thought with particular reference to the Row period, Geddes MacGregor remarks: 'It seems plain that he was very much better read in the Fathers of the early Church than were the vast majority of his judges.'[45] This may possibly have been the case; but the statement as it stands is misleading without certain qualifications.

Consider first the fact that so far as any direct reference may be concerned, the Fathers are conspicuous by their almost complete absence from the documents. It may be expecting too much to find references to patristic literature in the Row sermons; but when Campbell was on the stand for heresy in 1831 surely he would have pinned down some of his points by citing the Fathers if he had really felt their support for him was sufficiently strong. Yet his habit was to trace the several British traditions back to the Reformation and then to skip all the way to the New Testament (and vice versa). His lack of emphasis on the doctrines of the Fathers could hardly have been in deference to the sensibilities of the courts; for Campbell had been quite willing to risk the antipathy of Calvinists by reference to Anglican and Lutheran sources.[46]

The same situation prevailed in Campbell's work on *The Nature of the Atonement*. Indeed shortly after its publication in 1856 the *Literary Churchman* brought forward a criticism that the book failed to take account of teachings in the ancient Church. This afforded an occasion for Campbell to explain himself to his publishers in a letter which is an important document on this question:

> As to the 'teaching of the Church', in the large sense of the words, I cannot doubt that such an acquaintance with the Fathers as some enjoy would have enabled me to engraft my book on the past with some advantages. But the end which I had in view was so purely by manifestation of the truth to commend myself to every man's conscience in the sight of God that, even had I had the necessary qualification in respect of reading, it would have interfered with the simplicity of my aim to have availed myself of it.[47]

Allowance must be made for Campbell's modesty about the limitations of his knowledge. Very probably he had read more widely than he admits, and would in any case have known something of the Fathers from university days. Yet the fact is that he took little direct account of patristics in any of his books. In introducing the second edition of *The Nature of the Atonement* he had occasion to make a comparison between Henry Oxenham's historical approach and his own, indicating simply: 'I have not gone further back than the Reformation.'[48] In the *Memorials*, which contain lengthy and varied discussions on theological matters, Campbell rarely mentions any of the early church Fathers.[49] The conclusion is therefore inescapable that patristic sources played no conscious part in the development of Campbell's thought.

Admittedly, Campbell will be found to have ideas which immediately remind the reader of one or other of the Fathers. There are good reasons for this. First, just as it may be said in the study of psychology that seeds of the various modern schools of psychology may be found among the ancients, so also in theology there is scarcely a theme upon which the Fathers did not touch. Some of these were barely hinted at and then left undeveloped. Thus it is almost impossible for moderns to speak on any point in theology without crossing some path marked out by the ancient church. Campbell is no exception in this respect. Second, the Fathers lived relatively close to New Testament times. They were used to beginning with the scriptures. Whoever makes a profoundly fresh start in Bible study is likely to duplicate a number of patristic conceptions long since neglected. R.S. Franks says of Thomas Erskine, for example, that the patristic type of thought which appears in his writings arises not from a knowledge of the previous history of theology but from independent Bible study.[50] So also for Campbell. His lack of direct reference to theologians of the ancient church in no sense suggests their relative unimportance. It is better to recognize how the demands of preaching and pastoral care drove him back to the very scriptural foundations which yielded among the ancients, as they did for him, an incarnational approach to the atonement.

I have concluded thus that Campbell pursued his course with a greater degree of independence than has sometimes been credited to him. This is true in relation to those nearest him, whose inspiration and support he was ready to acknowledge. It is true also in regard to most other resources available to him, whether present or past. It must be emphasized again, however, that he gave primary place to the scriptures. To them he went in long and earnest meditation. More than any other source, the Bible lent its tone to Campbell's writing.

VII

FOUNDATIONS FOR A DOCTRINE OF
THE ATONEMENT

As John McLeod Campbell moved towards his own statement of the doctrine of atonement he knew something of the breadth and variety of the efforts by Christians to understand the meaning of Christ's work, especially in its Western forms. There are some, for example, who approach the subject through a study of the history of religion in general. They are impressed by an apparently universal phenomenon: human longings for the favour of God, or of gods, presumed to be the source of life, and to whom men and women know themselves responsible. The idea of atonement arises from the consciousness of need for reconciliation between the human and the divine. By way of meeting this need, what does God expect of us, and what may we hope from God? History records practices designed to express answers to these questions. It has therefore been thought that an historical study of the origin and development of this theme would yield an understanding of the nature of atonement in general, and hence a basis for an intelligent view of Christian atonement. Campbell, however, set this method aside. He believed it was unable to account for the utterly unique elements in Christianity which commend themselves to conscience as superseding all previous ways of reconciliation.

Most Christian theologians have tended to take for their starting point some particular idea of God, speculating on what such a God requires of humanity and what God will do for or against those who fail in those requirements. For example, some have begun with the general notion of God as Love, an idea which certainly belongs to the Christian faith. God loves everyone. Any refusal or denial of that love is sin. Yet the love of God continues to confront sinners, even in the suffering love of God's Son in Christ on the cross to melt their hearts and draw them back to him. These ideas have usually been associated with the name of Abelard (1079-1142), and the so-called 'moral influence' theory of the atonement. Emphasis rests on the subjective changes effected in us by Christ's work. Campbell appreciated elements of truth in this view as too often overlooked in traditional views of atonement. Yet there were for him even more important features of atonement which this view fails to emphasize; namely, the so-called objective and Godward aspects of Christ's work.

Others (especially in the several forms of Protestant orthodoxy) have often assumed that the central truth about God is righteousness and a consequent demand for righteousness in the human scene. Failure to

76

fulfil these demands creates the problem of atonement, since the demands of righteousness must somehow be satisfied before reconciliation can take place. While in this view the love of God may still be recognized as motivating atonement, the tendency has been to consider righteousness in the divine nature as the determining factor in atonement. Disobedience to God's will rightly rouses God's wrath and brings punishment upon the offender unless some other solution can be found which equally meets the demands of justice and so placates that wrath. The determining question is how to satisfy a just God. In some doctrines the mercy of God has been kept so far in the background as to affirm that God is essentially just and only accidentally loving.

According to Campbell there are fundamental truths in all these views of the atonement, partly because they *begin* with elements of truth, and partly because these elements in turn gather to themselves other features of the Christian heritage, though the latter are coloured by the former. Campbell therefore had great respect for those who so earnestly worked out these doctrines of the atonement, and for systems of theology which, in spite of certain inadequacies, had been bulwarks of the Church's faith.

Having been reared in a church and society dominated by thoroughgoing Calvinism, from some features of which he had early turned away, Campbell felt an obligation to focus in some detail on Calvinist alternatives as to the nature of atonement. So he selected for careful study the English Puritan John Owen (1616-1688) whose Calvinist influence had penetrated to Campbell's own time and place. Motivated by a profound disapproval of Arminianism, Owen had developed a systematic approach to Christian redemption based on the divine decree and sovereign intention in Christ.[1] At its core was the concept of a just God who required that justice be satisfied, and of a Christ who gave himself as a penal substitute for the elect out of humankind by way of appeasing the divine wrath and winning their salvation. This view purported to carry every possible logical refinement of the Westminster Standards for the subject in hand. To Campbell it seemed most *clearly to represent* what he called 'the older Calvinism' to which he wanted to give a good hearing. Hence a full chapter in his book, coupling with Owen the American Jonathan Edwards (1703-1758).[2] He admired the spirituality and mental powers of both men. Especially did he recognize the unassailable logic of Owen's system by which he would have felt himself bound if only he could accept Owens' presuppositions. There was the rub.

Campbell also cautioned his readers not to imagine that Owen's strict Calvinism accurately reflected all the actual feelings existing in the churches of his day. Many a Calvinist had been struggling to formulate altered understandings of Christian atonement in response to the Arminian challenge. They tended to favour a concept of universal atonement as reflecting the divine love; and they suspected the notion of imputed guilt as a violation of justice rather than a vindication. They were finding strict Calvinism too mechanical and impersonal to take proper account of faith as the human response to God's action in Christ.

With these concerns in mind several theologians, including John Pye Smith, Thomas Jenkyn, Ralph Wardlaw and George Payne, had developed a revised Calvinism based on a re-interpretation of divine justice in accordance with a figure drawn from civil law, and associated with the name of the Dutch legal authority Hugo Grotius. It involved a distinction between the hard exactness of distributive justice to which a judge must adhere and those acts of discipline measured out by a benevolent governor whose overriding purpose is the maintenance of well-being among the people – spoken of as rectoral justice. Campbell's affinity both with their motives and with several of their conclusions led him to study these theologians and review them for his readers in some detail.[3] Yet he found himself forced to conclude that no matter how much the language of this 'modified Calvinism' was cushioned it could not escape the fact that an appeal to justice of any sort must finally be founded on justice as understood distributively. So Campbell came right back to the question of pre-suppositions – where to begin.

On balance, Campbell suspected that traditional starting points were insufficiently biblical and that discussions were carried on without heeding Luther's warning to abstain for the 'curious searching of God's majesty.' While not disdaining speculation in its rightful place, Campbell felt that theologians have approached the atonement too much in the light of their own reasoning about the attributes of God and not enough by engaging in rational analysis after a due study of the record of Revelation. Hence certain fundamental determining facts were left out.

Campbell believed that the first step in atonement discussion should be a study of the biblical account of Christ's work. One should let the passages lead into an awareness of the mind of Christ as he gave himself a sacrifice for the sins of the world. Campbell described this method as learning to see the atonement by its own light.[4] It arises naturally from his basic conviction about the priority of Revelation over religious experience: 'The grace which brings salvation is itself the light which reveals both our need of salvation, and what the salvation is which we need,'[5] so that our strange religious longings for an unknown God are brought to focus in relation to God as revealed to be in Christ.

So the scriptures provide the requisite material for theological formulation; and within the Bible the New Testament has a prior importance. Campbell believed that if one yields oneself to the mind of Christ as revealed through the New Testament then certain fundamental ideas commend themselves to conscience as the proper foundations upon which to begin constructing a statement on the nature of the atonement. Campbell was well aware that those who stood outside the Hebrew-Christian tradition would be impatient with his approach. He was beginning with givens which they would consider at first necessary to prove.[6] He attempted no formal list of presuppositions, but several may nevertheless be clearly recognized as involved in his general principle that the atonement should be seen by its own light. These may conveniently be considered under four headings.

1. *The Atonement Originates in the Love of God*

The atonement centres in the self-offering of Christ for the salvation of the world. But to understand the nature of this work of Christ it is necessary to recognize its source in God. It must therefore be seen in the light of his character as Love and of God's purpose for the human race.

The love of God has never been entirely lost to view in any statement of the atonement claiming to be Christian. This was true of the most rigorous Calvinism, as well as of the modified forms of Calvinism which Campbell had reviewed. Modified Calvinism in particular had urged that the divine mercy be regarded as the root-cause of the atonement. In developing their systems, however, the leaders of both schools allowed the requirements of justice to assume the primary importance. They felt the problem to be one of finding a suitable way to satisfy the claims of justice (whether distributive or rectoral) in order to render forgiveness possible. They tended thus to present the atonement as an expedient which must precede forgiveness – an action which enables love to express itself in the form of forgiveness. 'But,' says Campbell, 'the scriptures do not speak of such an atonement; for they do not represent the atonement of Christ as the cause, but, just the contrary – they represent the love of God as the cause, and the atonement as the effect.'[7] It was God's so loving the world as to *give* the Son that originated the atonement.

It is the very nature of God to love, continuing to love us in spite of our alienation and enmity. The love of God survives our denial and reaches across the gulf which separates us from what we are meant to be. It is God who provides the atonement. Therefore it is important to remember that forgiveness, as the form in which love is manifested, precedes the atonement, and that any statement on the atonement should always have this clearly in view. This means avoiding any conception of the atonement which suggests that God must be moved to accept the unacceptable. It is God himself who makes the move. This theme is constantly apparent in Campbell's writing. It was his message from the pulpit at Row:

> Do not imagine that Christ, the Son, came to change the Father: he came to reveal the Father – he did not come to make God kind, but to show us God's kindness – 'Herein God commendeth his (that is God's) love towards us, in that while we were yet sinners Christ died for us.'[8]

The same theme came through at his trial for heresy.[9] The divine love is the ground and source of the atonement Christ made for us.

Observe how Campbell's argument assumes that God's love is best expressed by the parent figure, the New Testament fixing attention upon the character of God as the Father of Jesus Christ, and our Father. It is against a loving Father that we have sinned; and to such we are reconciled. This is the pivotal point of Campbell's whole discussion of the atonement.[10]

While emphasizing the thought of love as the mind of God towards us, and even unhesitatingly speaking of the 'feelings' of God for us, Campbell was aware of Thomas Chalmers' warning against a 'meagre and sentimental piety.'[11] So to interpret God in a parental relation to us as children allows us all too easily to lose sight of God also as judge. Yet Campbell does not forget the inexorable judgement of God upon all unrighteousness. God does oppose sinners. The earnestness with which Protestant orthodoxy put the claims of a just God was therefore not altogether mistaken. There is a sense in which the claims of justice *do* stand in the way of reconciliation and must be accounted for in any atonement made. Every serious effort to understand the ways of God with the human race must reckon with divine justice, and somehow show its harmony with love. In Campbell's opinion, however, to reconcile love and justice requires giving primacy to one or the other; and if so, then love must be first. He believed that the revelation of God in Christ yields a view of love which envelops righteousness, and that this view commends itself to conscience as one listens to the biblical record. Erskine once wrote to him: 'When you speak to me of the love of God, I always feel sure that you mean a love which includes and implies righteousness.'[12] Not only does righteousness come under the aegis of love in Campbell's thought; it even takes on some of the qualities of love, as illustrated in the following passage:

> . . . *justice* looking at the sinner, not simply as the fit subject of punishment, but as existing in a moral condition of unrighteousness, and so its own opposite, must desire that the sinner should cease to be in that condition; . . . righteousness in God craving for righteousness in man, with a craving which the realisation of righteousness in man alone can satisfy.[13]

To the strictly logical mind this statement may suggest a failure to adhere to precise definitions, thus allowing love and righteousness to express the integrity of God's relation to us. The righteous God can hardly be thought to act towards the world without being influenced by the love which covets righteousness for it; so that the righteous God may truly be said to desire the sight of righteousness in human affairs fully as much as to demand the punishment of sinners. The love of God is not therefore to be regarded as the source of our salvation against or apart from righteousness. To speak of 'a just God and a Saviour' must mean that *because* God is just God is a Saviour.[14] Thus, though recognizing a sense in which God's righteousness is a barrier to forgiveness, Campbell claims that in a more fundamental sense the righteousness of God belongs to the divine love which provides a pardoning atonement.

The God of love both demands and yearns for a filial righteousness.

In working towards the fulfilment of this end God will not compromise himself by relaxing those demands. It is this very one who, 'without respect of persons, judgeth every man's work' and expects them to reverence him.[15] It is this God who demands that justice be rendered to his fatherliness, even though it involves him in the sacrifice of his Son to purge rebellious children. He shows no easiness, no 'soft accommodating indulgence,' that in weak tenderness would bend the divine requirement to what we are.[16] We can only be received when coming to the parent God as sons and daughters rightly relating ourselves to God and to one another – not otherwise. Campbell thus contends that it is utterly false to associate moral weakness with the nature of the divine love which includes righteousness. So clear a founding of atonement on the 'fatherliness of God' seemed novel for the time, yet Campbell believed that he was only tracing out a doctrine implicit in the New Testament which had kept re-emerging in the long story of the church.[17]

2. The Atonement Contemplates God's Prospective Purpose that Humanity Shall Be As Sons and Daughters

Having favoured interpreting the atonement by first 'ascending' to its source in God's love, Campbell likewise urged the importance of 'descending' again past the work of Christ as such to consider its intended results, the fruit of Christ's atonement. 'We cannot stop between,' says Campbell.[18] Why? Because while the atonement has an infinite excellence in itself, its results must surely have a special value in God's sight. Therefore the work of Christ is to be seen in the light of its results in humanity.

These objects to which the atonement bears reference are of two types. The first may be called the retrospective purpose of the atonement, having regard for the sin and consequent guilt in which people are found. The atonement is God's provision for the past as it were, both in forgiveness of the guilt of sin and in deliverance from the evil power of sin and death. The second purpose is prospective, referring to the blessings bestowed whereby to be engaged in the new relationship of eternal life.

Every view of the atonement takes these two aspects of atonement into account in greater or less degree. As to the way they had been traditionally handled, however, Campbell felt obliged to register a few complaints. In the first place, he felt there had been a tendency to over-emphasize the retrospective aspect by drawing conclusions as to the nature of the atonement exclusively from this standpoint, while treating the prospective element simply as the outcome of the forgiveness of sins or as the 'next step' in the Christian life. Campbell sought to alter this imbalance by showing that his prospective aspect of the atonement also sheds light on the nature of the atonement.[19] The two belong together. In fact, if either has priority it should be the prospective. Says Campbell: 'The pardon of sin is seen in its true harmony with the glory of God, only when the work of Christ, through which we have 'the remission of sins that are past,' is contemplated in its *direct* relation to 'the gift of eternal life.'[20] So it becomes characteristic of Campbell's writing that the prospective purposes of the atonement are always brought into clear view as determinative of its nature.

Further, when theologians did touch upon the prospective aspect of the atonement they seemed to Campbell to point people to 'an unknown *future happiness* instead of being the meditation on, and the welcoming of the present gift of eternal life.' He believed it to be more important to show what God wants us to be, what the atonement is meant to achieve in our actual existence, being open to them now, – participation in eternal life' which in itself is one and the same here and hereafter, – however it may be developed in us hereafter.[21]

Finally, he saw need for giving more communicable content to the phrase 'eternal life.' How shall it be characterized? For Campbell, since the God who wills to give us eternal life is Fatherly, no description of that proposed condition of life more highly commends itself than that expressed in the New Testament; namely, that it is 'the life of sonship to the heavenly Father.' We are to live as 'God's offspring.' Nothing could be conceived as more vital to humanity than to feel at home with the parent-God; and nothing could be conceived as more satisfying to God.

Herein lies one of Campbell's major objections to founding a view of atonement on the concept of justice – whether distributive or rectoral. Both systems visualize what he calls purely legal atonements, that is atonements, the whole character of which is determined by our relation to divine law. The real problem of atonement, however, is not merely to discover a way in which we may stand reconciled to God as a law-giver. The question contemplated in scripture and to which the Gospel is an answer is not how we can be pardoned and receive mercy, but how it could come to pass that the estranged can be reconciled. God's intention is, as St. Paul declared, 'to redeem those who were under the law, so that we might receive adoption as sons.' (Gal. 4:5). The relation between a judge or a governor and the accused subjects is vastly different from that of a parent to erring children. To distinguish the former from the latter is to move from an artificial atmosphere of impersonal display of benevolence to a warm and living relationship of love, Campbell therefore could not rest in any conception of the atonement which involved, as he says, 'the substitution of a legal standing for a filial standing as the gift of God to men in Christ.'[22] This is not to say that Campbell denies the truth of a legal standing any more than he denies the inexorable demands of divine justice. Just as justice is brought within the concept of God as love, so the validity of a legal standing is brought within that of a loving relationship. Justice has its ultimate source in the love of God. When the loving God is honoured, justice is honoured also.

The atonement is thus revealed retrospectively as God's way of putting right the past, and prospectively as introducing us to a life marked by a filial relation to God eternally. Both are celebrated by believers, both must be included in their thought concerning the nature of the atonement.

3. The Atonement Presupposes the Incarnation of God in the Humanity of Jesus the Christ

Having pointed up axioms belonging to the source of the atonement and to the ends contemplated thereby, attention should be focused on the central figure who is the mediator of atonement; namely, the incarnate Son of God. Here too Campbell has something to say by way of presupposition. It concerns the relation of the atonement of Christ to the incarnation.

What has priority: the incarnation or the atonement? Is the incarnation to be thought of as God's answer to human alienation and the need for atonement? If so, the atonement has a certain controlling interest, for the incarnation must be such as to achieve the end visualized by atonement. Western orthodoxy, Roman and Protestant, has tended towards this way of thinking. The centre of interest has been the atoning death of Christ. The incarnation is treated as necessary only in relation to that end. Some of the early Greek Fathers, however, laid stress upon the incarnation as such, tending to regard the death of Christ as an incident, albeit final and important, of the incarnate life. Students of the history of dogma point out that this emphasis was sometimes sufficiently strong to give the impression that the incarnation might be regarded as itself the atonement. By the very act of becoming flesh Christ redeemed the flesh from the taint of corruption and brought immortality to mankind. Thus Irenaeus (Ob. c.200 A.D.) wrote: 'Jesus Christ did through his transcendent love become what we are that he might bring us to even what He is Himself.'[23] Athanasius wrote in a similar vein: 'As the Lord, in putting on the body, became Man, so we men are made gods by the Word, being taken into Him through His Flesh, and from henceforth inherit eternal life.'[24] Taken in isolation these passages illustrate the tendency of Greek thought to stress the incarnation. But in reality the death of Christ was never lost to view. Irenaeus had a distinct conception of the death of Christ as the way of human deliverance from sin and the devil. So also did Athanasius. The difference between East and West then was not absolute. It was rather a matter of relative emphasis.[25] Campbell had been nurtured in the Western tradition, and in the final outcome he remained in that tradition. At the same time he did serve correctively to bring the incarnation into closer association with the atonement as the basic fact determining its nature:

> My attempt to understand and illustrate the nature of the atonement has been made in the way of taking the subject to the light of the incarnation. Assuming the incarnation, I have sought to realise the divine mind in Christ as perfect Sonship towards

God and perfect Brotherhood towards men, and, doing so, the
incarnation has appeared developing itself naturally and necessarily as the atonement.[26]

Campbell, however, never suggests that the incarnation was itself the
atonement. Nor does he speculate (as some have done) on whether the
incarnation would have taken place if sin had never happened. He deals
throughout with the fact of sin and the necessity for atonement on that
account – though he does this in the light of the incarnation, in order that
the atonement may be seen in proper perspective. In this way Campbell's
thought about the atonement is guided along certain lines. In the first
place, constant reference to the incarnation served to remind him that
God, in speaking and acting towards the world was not represented by
mere proxy. In Christ, God as God *is* confronts us with pardon, and grace
to engage in God's way. Campbell saw that all discussion of the
atonement should be informed by the fact that the whole process of
redemption is God's own action. When therefore it is said that Christ
'represents' God to us it can only be in the sense that in and through
Christ God is present to us *as God really is*. At the same time, and this
was fundamental with Campbell, the atonement is wrought out by God *in
humanity* by the man Jesus Christ. The atonement is not an ethereal
divine event. It is a truly secular one.

For Campbell also, to see the atonement as a development of the
incarnation means emphasizing the importance of the life as well as of the
death of Jesus. The details of that life are fully consonant with the
purpose of God in Christ, and they shed light on the nature of a divinely
provided atonement. 'In no view of the atonement,' he says, 'can the
crucifixion be separated from the previous life of which it was the
close.'[27] Campbell's study of the boyhood, temptations, teaching and
ministry of Jesus show them to be in full harmony with the death he died.
The death is the necessary outcome of that life in a sinful world. This
means that whatever view is taken of the atoning death of Christ, it must
be confirmed by an examination of the outward events of his life among
people.

Campbell's interest in the details of Jesus' life was shared in the latter
half of the nineteenth century by a widespread interest in the Jesus of
history. Yet his emphasis should not be confused with the general one.
There was in him no disposition to study the life of Jesus in isolation from
the Christ of faith. He only emphasized the congruity between the two.

One further comment is in order. While regarding the incarnation as a
presupposition of the atonement, Campbell did not think it necessary to
discuss the question as to *how* he is *who* he is – how the Son is related to
the Father in the Godhead or how the Word is made flesh. These
questions he set aside for the time being, along with a number of other
matters surrounding the atonement. For example, the mystery of human
freedom, how persons who derive their existence from God can yet
oppose their wills to God's will, could be passed over, as well as the

doctrine of election, how the sovereign freedom of God relates to ultimate human destiny. All these indeed are mysteries which have a bearing upon the atonement; but they are not thought by Campbell to be so related to it as to require a solution before the atonement itself can be understood. He felt it better to begin by exercising faith in the actual condition of things as revealed by the gospel, which commend themselves to conscience and are confirmed in experience as true. Then in that knowledge and experience one may contemplate the attending mysteries. This approach again reflects Campbell's predilection for spiritual and practical interests, a tendency he had always freely acknowledged. He certainly does not despise anyone's effort to say something intellectually meaningful about the manner of the incarnation. He simply delimits the area of study, and feels the procedure justified. To withold an effort to understand all that is meant by the doctrine of the incarnation does not prevent faith in the incarnation, does not deprive us of its results or even lose the importance which the incarnation has for understanding the atonement.

4. The Atonement is Mediated by Christ as Representative of a New Humanity

While the significance of the incarnation for the atonement can be discussed without dealing with the manner of the incarnation, Campbell can hardly avoid saying something about how the man Christ Jesus bore a relation to humanity in a manner which rendered their salvation possible. In what relation does Christ stand as being human? Campbell's answer to this question has sometime been criticized as obscure even by his most sympathetic readers.

Interpretations as to the sense in which Christ is related to humankind range between two extremes. At one end of the scale is an atomistic view, in which case the individuality of Christ's humanity is stressed. Campbell could not move in this direction because he could not think of Jesus Christ as merely an individual among others even though he be the perfect person; for then there would be no ground for a real connection between him and others. Christ's righteousness would then be of no avail to humanity as such. He might be a moral example for them to emulate, but he would not thus be a saviour to the race in the true sense of the term. Or he might be looked upon as a substitute for all other individuals, their guilt and his righteousness being artificially exchanged by imputation. But Campbell had already given up that view of Christ's relation to humanity as a legal fiction. He was searching for what he believed must be possible, a more personal and moral relation.

At the other end of the scale there is the possibility that in some way Christ is Humanity in a collective or corporate sense. All people everywhere are summed up in him. A good sample of this view appeared later in R.C. Moberly's concept of Christ as 'inclusive humanity,' an idea which he felt provided the basis for a connection between Christ and others which appeared to him to be lacking in Campbell's view. Campbell suspected that the several ways of regarding Christ as collective Man submerged the individual and obscured the personal character of the faith whereby the believer freely participates in Christ. There must be sufficient identity of persons as distinct from Christ to preserve both the believer's awareness that Christ died for him or her individually and personally, and the consciousness of freely deciding to participate in Christ's atoning death.

At the time of writing *The Nature of the Atonement*, however, Campbell had not clearly thought out the implications of all these possibilities. The problem was first actually posed for him when James Martineau wrote a critical review of the book shortly after its publication. Martineau held that Campbell was proposing what might be called a 'realistic' view of Christ as containing all humanity in himself, and that this stood over against the modern individualistic conceptions.[29] By way of response to this claim Campbell endeavoured to look back upon what had in fact taken place in his mind at the time of writing. His reply to Martineau appears in notes appended to the second edition of *The Nature of the Atonement*.

> I have felt that the 'individualism' and the 'realism' of which he speaks have been to me a Scylla and a Charybdis, between which I have steered in the *dark*, unconsciously, while I trust safely. I have had no conception of an 'individualism' which made my personality so cut me off from Christ that I could not, except by a moral or legal fiction, represent Him to myself as under the pressure of my sins, both confessing them before the Father, and pleading with the Father on my behalf. I had no conception of a 'realism' which represented humanity as one whole in such a sense as would have lost to me my personality.[30]

Not having considered all the refinements of the case, Campbell had simply fastened onto the New Testament conception of Christ as the second Adam in passages such as Romans 5:11-12 and I Corinthians 15:45-49. St. Paul had said: 'For as by one man's disobedience many were made sinners, so by the obedience of one shall many be made righteous.'[31] In other words, whatever connection people have in sin, as set forth in the biblical figure of Adam, this same ground of connection exists between all people and Christ in his righteousness. 'As we have borne the image of the earthly, we shall also bear the image of the heavenly.'[32] Here is the authority for Campbell's various descriptions of Christ's relation to us. He is the 'sinless root of humanity,' the revelation of a 'hidden preciousness.' 'There must be,' says Campbell, 'a relation between the Son of God and the sons of men, not according to the flesh only, but also according to the spirit, – the second Adam must be a quickening spirit, and the head of every man be Christ.'[33] None of these notions is thoroughly developed, but all of them show Campbell's straining for a way of expressing the closeness of the relationship between Christ and humanity. At the same time he wants to preserve the individuality and integrity of men and women.

At this point it is fitting to acknowledge that every theologian experiences great difficulty in finding a substantive for expressing the relation of Christ to the human scene in the atonement. Each possibility has its own values and limitations. There is not even a completely adequate New Testament substantive. **Archegos**, for example translated variously as Captain, Prince, and Author has the value of emphasizing the idea that someone takes responsibility for us. But it lends itself also to the notion that Christ is a leader or example to be obeyed and followed, which does not do justice to the complete idea of salvation. Non-biblical substantives such as Substitute and Representative likewise have strengths and weaknesses. Campbell had grown up at a time when artificial and even mathematical interpretations of Christ as 'man's substitute' were being made. It seemed to be suggested that Christ took the place of sinners in such a way as to exclude them from the action, only to be re-introduced through an arbitrary exchange of guilt and righteousness by way of imputation. The thought of Christ as our representative commended itself to Campbell as taking into account the fact that we, because of Christ's identification with us, are included in Christ's work. But even this figure is not entirely satisfactory, since the common notion of a representative implies that those who are represented ultimately control the terms of reference; also that the representative acts in their behalf in their absence. Yet precisely the opposite of these implications is affirmed by those who think of Christ in representative terms. A. S. Peake chooses to avoid both the substitutionary and the representative idea in favour of speaking of Christ's identification with us.[34] Campbell, however, means to take this very thought of Christ's identification with us as included in his representative role.

Some theologians have sought to assess the comparative validity of all these terms.[35] In British theology there is perhaps a preference for the representative idea, especially if it be remembered, as P.T. Forsyth once said, that 'it is representation by One who creates by His act the Humanity He represents, and does not merely sponsor it.'[36] In any case, Campbell speaks of Christ as our representative, though the actual terminology appears more in his sermons that in *The Nature of the Atonement*. He is representative because he is most truly human. He *is* as men and women are meant to be under God. There is a difference between Christ and ourselves in his sinlessness, but this confirms rather than destroys his representative character. He alone can offer God the filial life we are meant to offer, and he is so identified with us by the incarnation and through his sympathy with us that we are included in the offering of himself. Campbell believed that Christ did not suffer only as a private person, but as the head and representative of the race. His death was therefore in one sense our death, his rising our resurrection and his life our life. His righteousness counts in the sight of God as the righteousness of us all. Therefore every person has what may be called 'an interest in Christ' or a 'standing in Christ.' One has only to enter by faith into one's heritage in Christ. We are invited to share in the fellowship of Christ who is our true life, to participate in the remission of sins and eternal life which Christ has for us.

Though the terms 'representative' and 'substitute' are not New Testament words, many passages call each of them to mind. Perhaps the closest to the representative idea is the concept of Christ as our advocate. But no single word seems best suited to express the New Testament portrayal of the intimate relation between Christ and his people. St. John records Jesus to have said: 'I am the vine, you are the branches: He who abides in me, and I in him, he it is that bears much fruit: for apart from me you can do nothing.'[37] These words suggest a description of Christ's representative character which both Erskine and Campbell used: 'the sinless root of humanity' – every fibre of a root bearing an intimate relation to the branches and even to the fruit of a plant. Their figure of Christ as the Head of a new humanity is likewise founded on a New Testament concept, that of Christ as Head of the Church which is his body.[38] No statements could witness more clearly to the believer's involvement with and dependence upon Christ; yet they carry no suggestion whatever that the individual is swallowed up in some kind of impersonal absolute. On the contrary, Christ's work as our representative, and the degree to which we are included in his work, are contemplated as the very ground of life and freedom for us all.

VIII

CONSTRUCTIVE STATEMENT:
THE NATURE OF THE ATONEMENT

It may have been Campbell's love for preaching which led him to choose a text (Hebrews 4:4-10) as a point of departure for expounding the meaning of Christ's atonement. The passage declares that what the old sacrifices could not do for our salvation has in fact been achieved by the sacrifice of Christ. It further declares that Christ's work may be characterized by the words of Psalm 40, 'Lo, I come to do your will, O God.' From the context of the two sources Campbell gathers that 'the *will* of God contemplated is that *will* which immediately connects itself in our thoughts with what *God is*' in holiness, righteousness and love.[1] The incarnate one is God in the world, manifesting the divine nature among men and women and seeking to bring them to God: his doing of God's will in humanity (that is, his love both to the parent God and to all people as his brothers and sisters) inevitably involved him in bearing the burden of human sin and bringing us as children to our home in God. Campbell proposed to develop a doctrine of the atonement by tracing out Christ's fulfilment of this purpose.

According to Campbell, Christ as the mediator of salvation may be considered to have had dealings with both God and humanity, first, representing God to us; secondly, representing us to God. Each phase of his work had, as we have seen, both a retrospective and a prospective aspect depending on whether the reference is more particularly to the remission of past sin or to participation in newness of life under God eternally. Thus the whole subject readily lends itself to division for study as follows: In the *manward* direction: (1) Christ's revelation of the loving God. (2) Christ's revelation of what it is to be human. In the 'Godward' direction: (3) Christ's confession of human sin. (4) Christ's offering sonship to the Father. Each of these involves the others in a natural unity; so it is impossible to speak of any one of them without in some sense assuming the others. Yet there is an advantage in separating them for examination in favour of further understanding the living fact of Christ's atonement.

Christ's Revelation of the Loving God

The initial thing to say about the work of Christ is that he came to reveal God to the world. Apart from him there is no true knowledge of God and therefore no true conception of God's redemptive activity.

89

As the Word made flesh, Christ had the authority to say: 'He who has seen me has seen the Father.' (John 14:9). His faithful following of God's will in humanity found him perfectly fulfilling the second great commandment, which is like the first, to be for all others, thus manifesting God's nature as in essence love. This was not ordinary human love which, no matter how refined and honourable, seeks self-fulfilment by grasping at the beauty, goodness, or utility seen in others. Divine love is just the reverse. It moves towards the unlovely and unworthy with a powerful desire for their good.[2] It is utterly gracious and trustworthy to take upon itself whatever burden another may carry, including those which derive from sin, and to do so regardless of cost to the self. So with Christ, the human burden became his: 'an occasion for sorrow' as Campbell puts it.

At the same time Christ's doing the will of God and being in perfect harmony with God meant that he would be, in Campbell's phrase, 'in full sympathy with God's condemnation of sin.' So he was bound to come across as confronting people with the contradiction between what they actually were and what they were meant to be. This could only excite their embarrassment, their rejection of him, and even his death at their hands. Thus manifesting both a godly sorrow for the wrongness in human existence and the divine condemnation of that state it was necessary that 'the Son of man must suffer.' God could not become incarnate in this kind of world, could not reveal a boundless love, except by way of suffering which turned out to be the way of the cross.

One of the most common objections to the very idea of atonement is raised by those who ask: 'If there is forgiveness with God, if God's love really does reach out to us in spite of our alienation, then why should he not simply find a way of communicating this knowledge and a way to a restored life without requiring an atonement through such sufferings as Christ endured? If God is so infinitely wise and powerful, why should he not have achieved his purpose by indicating favour towards us in some less painful and costly fashion?' Campbell (in common with so many before him) believed that such questions arise from ignorance of what God's holiness and righteousness involve, and from failure to understand the extremity of the human situation. Those who thus question the necessity of atonement do not realize how wide is the gulf between what we are and what we are meant to be under God, how deeply entrenched sin is and how binding its power. When this is not comprehended, it is easy both to acknowledge sin and to expect remission at little or no real cost.[3]

Campbell believed that when we listen receptively, and by the Spirit, to the record of God's revelation, we find the realities of good and evil laid bare. In his presence we see ourselves for what we really are.

Now the fact is that those who have been most awakened to a sinful condition have been able, in the light of Christ's sacrifice of himself, to believe both that God really does forgive the past and that he does give a new life. Why? Because forgiveness and reconciliation given at such cost are infinitely enhanced. But this is by no means easily come by. Whoever persists in standing aside from it will continue to think it unbelievable. Yet the witness of those who draw near is that it registers itself in conscience as just and true. It is simply paradoxical that the features of atonement which might appear to cause the greatest intellectual difficulty are the very reasons of its power to bring peace and hope to the believer.

The question still remains as to what is involved in that which is spoken of as costly. Campbell looks to the New Testament again. St. Paul, for example, declared that 'God commends his love toward us in that while we were yet sinners Christ died for us.' (Rom. 5:8) In commenting on the context of this passage, which includes the figure of one person laying down life for another, Campbell claims the whole point of the argument is that the love which Christ manifests is none other than God's own love, and hence the underlying assumption that in the most fundamental sense Christ is God. Campbell never tires of telling how the gospel declares that God himself is involved in our salvation. The phrase 'he gave his Son' is to be understood as the offering of *himself* – the Divine Word made flesh – and nothing less. Says Campbell: 'thus is the atonement not only what was rendered possible by the incarnation, but (is) itself a development of the incarnation.'[6]

Campbell wanted to show that the sufferings of Christ involved in the incarnation were coherent with holy love as revealed in Christ. They were not to be understood as punishment meted out and accepted on the grounds of imputed sin as would be implied by strict Calvinism, or 'as if' guilty as the modified Calvinists might say. Incidentally, Campbell was immensely gratified that representatives of both groups sometimes, as it appeared to him, forsook their own logic as to the penal character of Christ's sufferings and pointed to the love of Christ as their chief ground.[7]

Moreover, the atoning element is not to be found in suffering as such, but rather that holiness and love taking the form of suffering in the face of what sin is and does are themselves the atoning elements: 'The sufferer suffers what he suffers *just through seeing sin and sinners with God's eyes, and feeling in reference to them with God's heart.*[8] We see in Christ's humanity what our waywardness means to God, and it is not merely that divine love is willing to suffer in the face of it but that it is precisely the nature of divine love to suffer with humanity.

Where there is suffering for sin it should not necessarily be assumed that the sufferer must either be the sinner or have sin imputed to him or her. A godly mother suffers sorrow over a wayward child; so also does holy love grieve. In the agonies of Christ we are confronted by one whose love brought him into the midst of a wilfully mixed-up suffering humanity. Campbell asks whether this kind of suffering can possibly be counted as the suffering of punishment, and responds to his own question: 'I find myself . . . being shut up to the conclusion, that while Christ suffered for our sins as an atoning sacrifice, what He suffered was not – because from its nature it could not be – a punishment.[9] Campbell thus takes the position that Christ's very revelation of God renders a penal atonement impossible in the ordinary sense. The suffering of Christ is undergone in and for humanity on account of human fault, but it arises from God's nature as love and is seen to be a revelation of that love. As Campbell says: 'God is revealed *in it* and not *merely in connexion with it*; God's righteousness and condemnation being in the suffering and not merely what demands it, – God's love also being in the suffering, and not merely what submits to it.'[10] In seeing Christ doing the will of God, loving God in and by loving humanity even unto death, we have seen God as God is.

Christ's Revelation of What it Means to be Human

It has been shown that Christ's work of representing God to the world involved the revelation of the holy loving God for all humanity. Campbell's next step was to remind his readers that this revelation was given as the Son of God lived the life of sonship *in* humanity, constantly pointing to God as the source of all good, associating himself with the divine will, and in all things giving glory to God. 'The Son can do nothing of his own accord, but what he sees the Father doing;' (John 5:19). Campbell keeps emphasizing that 'it was in humanity that he was having all this experience.'[11] Christ was human as God means the rest of us to be, children of God glorifying the creator and sustainer of our life.

This revelation of our true humanity has two aspects. First, by way of contrast as it were, we are shown the greatness of the gulf which exists between what we are and what we are meant to be. Confronted by the Son of God, we sense the dis-ease of our condition. Second, in the life of Christ in humanity our possibilities are set forth. In Campbell's words, Christ is:

> the revelation of an inestimable preciousness that was hidden in humanity, hidden from the inheritors of humanity themselves, but not hid from God, and now brought forth into manifestation by the Son of God. For the revealer of the Father is also the revealer of man, who was made in God's image.[12]

This means that in Christ we recognize that we can be made capable of love to both God and neighbour in spite of all appearances to the opposite. Jesus knew that even those who reject their life in him were redeemable. So he maintained a hope for them that he might bring them to God. He even prayed that the Father might forgive his crucifiers, as those cut off from any real knowledge of what they are doing. Thus Christ continued to the end, living the life of sonship by which he declared the divine name in order that the love which the Father held for him might be in them and he in them. (John 17:26).

This conception of Christ in humanity living out a filial relationship to God is a pivotal point in Campbell's thought. He believed that to see Christ as a human being maintaining a legal righteousness in relation to God is not to envision humanity as God wills them to be. So also, an atonement contemplating chiefly a new legal standing in the sight of God would misconstrue God's purpose in reconciliation. There is a vast difference between being awarded merely a new legal standing before a judge at law and being welcomed into a warm and accepting relation with a loving parent. Thus for Campbell God redeems us in Christ by bringing us into that filial relationship to God which is our true life. In our receiving that life by faith God is well pleased.

What has been said about the revelation of both God and humanity in Christ belongs to what Campbell calls the 'manward' side of Christ's work, which he regarded as fundamental to any view of the atonement. So strongly, indeed, did he express himself on this point that he has sometimes popularly been supposed to have stood in the tradition of Abelard. That this supposition is false will presently become apparent. Neverthelss, Campbell was prepared to acknowledge the partial truths in Abelardian views. He admitted both the purging effect which vicarious suffering has upon our feelings, and the drawing power exercised upon us by divine love 'lifted up.' These features of Christ's activity towards us cannot provide the whole basis for a true conception of the atonement, but they do belong to the reconciling process. Moreover, they are of special importance for shedding light on that other side of Christ's work in which he represents humanity to God in an act of reconciliation. For whatever else may be said about the death of Christ it must be seen as manifesting God's steadfast suffering love. To neglect this manward side of the atonement would involve not only losing its own inherent truth but would also risk a false notion of the 'Godward' side. Campbell was determined to preserve the values of both. It becomes appropriate therefore to turn to the Godward side of the atonement.

Christ's Confession and Repentance of Human Sin

Western orthodoxy, Roman and Protestant alike, has characteristically emphasized the Godward side of the atonement. It has been generally believed that sin is best described as an offence against God, though descriptive analogies have varied as to whether the offence is against God's honour, justice, or other. In any case, God could not be thought to ignore the offence without as it were denying himself. So sin occasions the wrath of God, brings humanity under condemnation and shuts them out from fellowship with God. The problem of reconciliation, therefore, was thought to involve some kind of redress, an act of atonement in the sense of a price paid to restore humankind to God's favour. This act must in the nature of the case be sufficient to satisfy the requirements of the divine honour or justice, re-establish fellowship and open the door to eternal life. But the gravity of sin and the helplessness of sinners in bondage render them unable to offer a sufficient atonement. God therefore provided the means in the man Jesus Christ. By his obedience unto death Christ rendered the honour due to God, and by his enduring the punishment due to man he fulfilled the requirements of divine justice.

God was thereby satisfied, and was 'freed up' so to speak to forgive.

There was no doubt in Campbell's mind (as in Luther's) about the reality of God's wrath. He agreed, moreover, that while Christians may often have erred in their understanding of how that wrath is to be 'appeased', the idea of satisfaction in some form belongs to the theology of the atonement. To that extent Campbell belongs generally to the Western tradition in atonement theory. But this adherence was qualified by a decided difference. He insisted that the meaning of satisfaction be interpreted in the light of who God is and who we are, and what is our true relation to God as revealed by Christ. It was at this point that Campbell found something helpful in the writings of Jonathan Edwards. The latter, in his concern to show the necessity of God's righteousness being vindicated, had fleetingly suggested a hypothetical alternative to the principle of punishment for sin – an alternative he apparently assumed to he quite impossible. He had said that justice must be vindicated by punishment 'unless there could be such a thing as repentance, humiliation and sorrow for this (viz. sin), proportionate to the greatness of the majesty despised.'[14] Theoretically, in other words, an equivalent sorrow and repentance would satisfy the demands of justice. Edwards was aware, however, that it is impossible to repent while under bondage to sin. Moreover, having begun with the assumption that remission of sins came by Christ's bearing the punishment of imputed guilt in order that righteousness might be imputed to believing persons, Edwards missed the possible implications of his passing thought of 'an equivalent sorrow and repentance' and proceeded to develop his own characteristic position. It remained for Campbell to pick it up, but it would be misleading to say that Edwards was really responsible for the direction of Campbell's thought. The fact is rather that, in coming upon Edward's comments, he had simply been encouraged to know that his great predecessor had been as Campbell put it 'on the verge of that conception of a moral and spiritual atonement which was occupying my own thought.'[15]

Campbell recognized as much as anyone the inability of people to offer an adequate repentance. Their efforts to repent tend at best to be a self-centred striving for personal security. In genuine repentance the sinner would see sin as God sees it; feel sorrow on its account and acknowledge the righteousness of the divine condemnation of sin; would stand as it were on God's side in condemnation of sin. Now Campbell held that what men and women were unable to do the man Jesus Christ was able to do for them. In his oneness with God he did see sin for what it is and did condemn it. At the same time it must be remembered that it was *in humanity* that Christ confessed the true character of sin and somehow shared the human need to repent. In other words, says Campbell, 'This confession as to its nature, must have been a perfect Amen in humanity to the judgement of God on the sin of man.'[16]

What does this confession involve? It has already been shown that

Christ's humanity and his contemplation of their condition as his burden brought him only rejection at their hands, and a measure of suffering beyond comprehension. Certainly Christ's confession could not be made apart from such great sorrow. But Campbell is more immediately concerned with the nature of what took place through Christ's confession than with the intensity of his suffering. The question is how this Amen to God's condemnation can meet the demands of divine wrath. In an important passage meriting full quotation Campbell offers his answer:

> He who so responds to the divine wrath against sin, saying, 'Thou art righteous, O Lord, who judgest so,' is necessarily receiving the full apprehension and realization of that wrath, as well as of that sin against which it comes forth into His soul and spirit, into the bosom of the divine humanity, and, so receiving it, He responds to it with a perfect response, – a response from the depths of that divine humanity, – and *in that perfect response He absorbs it*. For that response has all the elements of a perfect repentance, and that in absolute perfection all, – excepting the personal consciousness of sin; – and by that perfect response in Amen to the mind of God in relation to sin is the wrath of God rightly met, and that is accorded to divine justice which is its due, and could alone satisfy it.[17]

Along with this, of course, the reality of the incarnation of Christ as the Head of humanity is assumed, so that God deals with Christ as representing every human being. Indeed, the expiation of sin through Christ's confession not only 'became possible through the incarnation of the Son of God,' but the incarnation 'caused that it must be.'[18] Christ could not be the true humanity without confessing human sin, even though not conscious of individual sin. He could not bring to God those with whom he was utterly identified without confessing their evil, the rightness of God's wrath against them and his own sorrow on their account. All this Campbell regards as rightly due from him as the representative of a humanity which could not otherwise render repentance unto God. Christ in humanity is their living voice. So he was able to make their confession of sin and offer their repentance. With this response God is well pleased . . . 'satisfied' if you will.

Campbell's conception of Christ at this point differs from, though it is meant to serve the purpose of, both Luther's thought of Christ as 'the one sinner'[19] and Edwards' view of him as the one to whom all sin is imputed. Even for meeting the requirements of God's righteousness Campbell believed that Christ's confession and repentance for humanity provided a more adequate vision of the atonement than juridical views. In the final analysis a righteous God really desires righteousness in the world. The endurance of punishment as such does not make one righteous, but to be truly repentant is in fact to stand on the side of righteousness and in that sense to be as God requires one to be. 'There would be more atoning worth,' says Campbell, 'in one tear of true and perfect sorrow which the memory of the past would awaken . . . than in endless ages of penal woe.'[20] Thus Campbell presses for a representative repentance as a more truly moral and personal understanding of atonement than a substitutionary punishment. The notion of Christ's repentance bears difficulties which demand assessment at a later stage.

Christ's Intercessory Praying

Closely associated with Christ's confession (and repentance) from within humanity was his constant intercession before God on behalf of others. This was the case during his ministry, whether in prayer for intimates that their faith would be made firm (Lk. 22:32) or his enemies, that they might be forgiven in their ignorance (Lk. 23:34). It continues through the risen Lord in constant advocacy (Romans 8:34; I John 2:1; Hebrews 4:24). This praying is a natural development of his desire to redeem and reconcile. It is not an endeavour to effect a change in God's disposition towards us, but rather to utilize the purpose for us which is already in God. Thus, while in confession, the man Christ Jesus stood on the side of God's condemnation of sin, in intercession he grasped for us the love in God which is deeper than the wrath (though it gives rise to wrath) – saying an Amen in humanity to the yearning of the divine love for sinners, and laying hold of God's pardon.[21]

In short, we must have (and do have) a Mediator sufficiently identified with our need as to be able to plead for us according to that need, and at the same time sufficiently identified with God as by intercession to take full advantage of God's will for our good. Mediation of the kind contemplated here could not be accomplished apart from Christ's witness for God in the world, living the life of love which necessarily involves the condemnation of sin and the sacrifice of himself. This proves the completeness of his doing God's will and the measure of his acceptance with God: 'You are my beloved Son; with you I am well pleased.' (Mark 1:11)

Christ's Offering of Sonship to the Father

Campbell regards Christ's confession of sin on our behalf, and God's acceptance of that confession, as a transaction relating to the remission of past sin; but it is entered into with the prospective purpose that this same confession may be reproduced in everyone. That it *can* be arises from the fact that it took place in humanity and is therefore for all human beings.[22] What Christ has done constitutes both a permission and an invitation to come to God in the fellowship of Christ. We are invited to share Christ's confession and repentance by coming to God in his name and in his fellowship. 'In the faith of God's acceptance of that confession on our behalf,' says Campbell, 'we receive strength to say Amen to it, – to join in it – and, joining in it, we find it a living way to God.'[23] This is what it means to draw near with faith to the throne of grace, trusting that, as

Christ is given to be our life and as his confession for us is accepted, we ourselves are accepted. This is what it means to be justified by grace through faith.

At this point Campbell asks his readers to consider what is involved in expiation on an even higher spiritual level. He is thinking not only of an expiation due to a righteous God (as achieved by Christ's confession of human sin) but of the expiation due to God as love. To use Campbell's characteristic phrasing: Is it not a Father's heart which is to be satisfied? Christ indeed offered the confession due to the righteousness of the Father; yet he made that confession within the context of offering himself in perfect sonship which alone utterly satisfies the Father. It was this offering and its acceptance that determined the character of the reconciled relation in which we now stand. Divine law is after all only the formal expression of a moral constitution of things which has its roots in a loving God. It is '*First* spiritual, and *then* as a *consequence*, legal.'[24] Campbell observes that this happens to be the order in John 5:24 which says that the believer has life and shall not come into condemnation.

Campbell admits that these thoughts will sound strange, for theology does not customarily associate the notion of satisfaction with a loving God. Nevertheless he presses the claim that 'We must see that the *filial* spirit that was in that confession, and which necessarily took into account what our being rebellious children was to the Father's heart constituted the perfection of the expiation.'[25] Campbell believed that this is borne out by the New Testament account of Christ's work. Christ was declared to be the Son at baptism. The resurrection also fixes attention on the filial character of his work, for by the resurrection he is declared to be the Son with power over all flesh. Again, when his righteousness is declared to be our righteousness, 'that righteousness is *NOT the past fact of legal obligation discharged*, but the mind of sonship towards the Father.'[26]

Christ the Son, incarnate and raised up, is given to be our life. The full prospective purpose then is that by the Spirit we may enjoy the fellowship of what Christ is as the Son – a filial relation thus being reproduced in us. This is what Christ asks in interceding for everyone. He is justified in so doing, for it is a prayer according to God's will, since it is God's good pleasure to *give* eternal life. We are invited to draw near with faith in the fellowship of Christ, enabled by the Spirit to say with him 'Abba, Father.'[27] The significance of Christ's filial relation to God is thus the crowning and most inclusive feature of Campbell's understanding of Christ's work, and one too frequently overlooked by those who interpret Campbell's thought.

Campbell believed that his statement of the nature of the atonement faithfully reflected the facts of revelation, while at the same time it seemed to him that penal conceptions of the atonement presented a contradiction in terms. The New Testament records an unbroken testimony to God's pleasure in Jesus Christ, while Christ as Son never ceases to trust him. Under these conditions, how could it possibly be thought that God lays a punishment upon the Redeemer? In the deepest possible sense God is the Redeemer.

Moreover, Campbell claimed for his view certain advantages in relating the atonement to the Christian life. The notion of Christ enduring suffering strictly as a substitute is artificial. The sufferings of a substitute can hardly be of the sort in which others are intended to share, and the righteousness related to such suffering can only be arbitrarily imputed to others. Campbell believed that the scriptural account of Christ's work allows for what he called a more 'natural' connection between Christ's suffering on behalf of humanity and their participation in his life. We are not to be counted righteous by imputation or by virtue of transferring the effects of Christ's righteousness to us to provide legal ground for our adoption as children of God. On the contrary, God gave the Christ to be ours in humanity. From within our humanity and under the conditions of the 'enmity of the carnal mind to God' the man Jesus offers an adequate confession and repentance for our past, and intercedes for the gift of eternal life. As human beings therefore we find ourselves in 'a new space' as it were, – one of reconciliation. In faith we may participate in what Christ has done and is still doing for us. This is our part in the atonement whereby the Spirit draws us, and we freely enter, into an evangelical repentance, not a legal one, and share in God's own hope for us, which is more than merely our own striving for spiritual and moral excellence. Through the man Jesus Christ we are enabled to say as might a child, 'Abba, Father'; thus acknowledging ourselves as belonging. Therein is God well pleased, and therein we are called to mature.

IX

A CONTINUOUS LINE OF INFLUENCE IN THE THEOLOGY OF ATONEMENT

The publishers of *The Nature of the Atonement* naturally had high hopes for its success, but they were not without misgivings as to its difficult style. Campbell's father had long ago remarked: 'Man, you have a queer way of putting things.' The sentences are long and involved, with qualifying words and clauses placed in an unusual order whereby the reader may easily miss the thread of a thought, though a slight pause for examination lays bare a consistently logical argument. The publisher thought that 'it required on the part of the readers a combination of seriousness and intelligence that would be found in comparatively few.' The author himself expected no wide readership, and hoped at best for 'only a gradual getting into the hands of earnest minds.'[1] True enough, the book did not at first find a ready sale. However, some 'earnest minds' soon did realize its unusual worth, particularly in university centres. Principal Shairp, of United College, St. Andrews, wrote of it in the most glowing terms to Thomas Erskine.[2] That the book would have more than a momentary effect upon Shairp is testified to by the fact that some years later he sent a book of his own authorship to Campbell with a note appended saying: '. . . you know how much I prize your work on the Atonement as the only one I ever met with, which enabled me really to think and see some moral light through that mysterious fact and truth.'[3]

Campbell was further encouraged when Dr. John Tulloch recommended *The Nature of the Atonement* as a text for his students and included in his regular lectures two sessions on Campbell's thought.[4] The book was thus getting a foothold in institutions of higher learning, and the thoughts of the deposed minister were being entertained by the minds of the coming generation of clergy, at least in Scotland.

Mr. Macmillan had also said at the outset, 'if anything would help Scotch Calvinists to come into a larger place it would be such a book as this.'[5] He predicted well. Yet on the other hand the very Scottish character of the work was a matter of concern to the publishers, since they were interested in a possible English market. Many a reviewer since that day has claimed that Campbell had weakened his case by failure to take account of some traditions more familiar to Anglicans and of importance to Christendom in general.[6] For Campbell, however, the choice had been quite deliberate. To begin with, he felt himself in some degree driven to address the Church which had deposed him from the ministry. He also freely admitted his own limitations in some fields of study, as for example, in patristics.[7] On both counts, Campbell was aware that many readers, especially among Anglicans, would be disappointed.[8] Yet succeeding events proved the book to be generally better received in England than in Scotland.

It is just possible that publication in London by Macmillan and Company gave the book a better start in England than would otherwise have been the case. Promotional notices would be widely circulated, and major journals would carry reviews; but by a strange turn of events the first recorded response to *The Nature of the Atonement* came from a young scholar, F.J.A. Hort, who happened upon the manuscript at the publishers. Hort wrote to a friend about its power, more than any book he had yet seen, to draw out thoughts on the atonement.[9] This episode was prophetic of the ready reception Campbell's thinking was to gain in England where many a young theologian was waiting for someone to give form to new intuitions. One of these was C.E. Prichard, a Fellow and Tutor of Balliol,[10] who later wrote a full discussion of *The Nature of the Atonement* for the *North British Review* in which he accorded it the highest rank as a theological work.[11] Campbell was greatly heartened by such support. He said that this article had shown more insight into his understanding of the atonement than had yet been displayed in any review.[12] This was followed up by correspondence between the two men, personal meetings and a warm friendship.

Another important friendship cultivated in England was with Canon D.J. Vaughan. About six years after Campbell's death the Canon wrote an article for the *Contemporary Review* on the influence of Scottish theology upon English thought.[13] Of the four theologians singled out for review he declared Campbell's influence to have been the deepest and most lasting. He remarked in particular on the charitable spirit of Campbell's writing, as well as on his method of argument, as doing much to reconcile old ideas to new ones in the revolution of Christian thought which pervaded the latter part of the century.

Vaughan claimed for Campbell the advantage of what he called 'book influence.' By 1867 a second Edition of *The Nature of the Atonement* had been required, and still further editions appeared every few years thereafter. The sixth edition of 1886 was later reprinted a number of times, even into this century. It is of no little significance that it was published again in 1959 through James Clarke of London more than a hundred years after its original appearance. A publication record of this kind contributes to the conclusion that the book has become a classic in modern Protestant theology.

A casual coverage of literature on the atonement running up to our time yields a constant flow of witnesses to what J.K. Mozley identified as Campbell's 'solitary eminence' in Scottish contributions during the nineteenth century, and of his marked influence in the twentieth century at least in the English-speaking world. To list testimonials here would only be repetitious, and perhaps even question-begging.[14] I consider it more fitting to demonstrate Campbell's actual influence by a study of some representative theologians in both centuries. Some are well-known for their views on the atonement, while others are scarcely remembered today. Some obviously possible names for consideration are omitted by virtue of the limitations of space. In each case under review, there will be no attempt to describe general opinions of a writer except as his thoughts point up an interesting relationship to Campbell. Nor will emphasis rest on differences which these persons entertained in relation to Campbell, or on points where each may have sought to improve on his contribution, though a few of the latter may be held for subsequent consideration. It will be impossible, however, to avoid a certain repetition of ideas, since each of the men involved will doubtless have agreed with some others in choosing elements in Campbell's thought deemed important.

J.J. Lias

The Hulsean Lectures for 1883-4 given by J.J. Lias, vicar of St. Edwards, Cambridge, were published under the title: *The Atonement Viewed in the Light of Modern Difficulties*. Both the man and the book have long since been virtually forgotten, but they had a measure of importance at the time; and for us in particular, they demonstrate how Campbell's ideas were taken up by a younger contemporary. Lias was known in his day for contributions to the general field of Bible commentary, and for a book entitled *The Nicene Creed* which was used as a manual of study by candidates for the priesthood in the Church of England. His work on the atonement does not give so full a treatment of the subject as many others, but extensive appended notes reveal a rich background of knowledge in the field. The lectures themselves gained a good hearing and the book had a favourable press.

As the title suggests, Lias' primary purpose was corrective rather than creative. He says that his purpose was to forestall the notion that the Christian faith is to be identified with the strictly substitutionary doctrine of the atonement with which Protestant orthodoxy had so long associated itself. At the same time he wanted to take full account of the scriptural conceptions of the divine abhorrence of sin and of the necessity for reconciliation precisely in the face of that fact. Lias searched for a moderating stance which would avoid the difficulties attending the idea of Christ as a penal substitute. As to the sense in which he agrees that the sufferings of Christ were substitutionary, he says that Christ bore on our account the natural consequences of human sin in a manner which 'saved us from undergoing something which otherwise we should have been compelled to endure.'[15] But he denies that these sufferings are in any way equivalent in kind or degree, or that they are to be regarded as punishment in the ordinary sense of the term.

Lias warns against accepting any theory as it stands, yet he attempts to bring together a few fundamental thoughts which should be included as elements in any comprehensive view of the atonement. In so doing, Lias draws heavily upon Campbell. He even makes Campbell's framework his own: 'The Mediator between God and Man,' says Lias, 'acts toward man on the part of God and toward God on the part of man.'[16] Immediately following this he puts the very proposition which Campbell had set at the beginning of his exposition of the manward aspect of Christ's work, namely (in Lias' words), 'The one essential object of His Mission was to reveal the Father.'[17] This basic principle includes, of course, the idea that the pain and suffering consequent upon sin and felt as the wrath of God are themselves expressions of the divine love. Furthermore, Christ's suffering shows up sin for what it is, demonstrates God's condemnation and has for its purpose that we ourselves shall enter into the divine reaction to sin. The whole section is sharply reminiscent of Campbell.

On the Godward side there is no doubt in Lias' mind that a satisfaction is offered to God. It is not an external one provided by a substitute but is offered by Christ as representative of humanity. His passion is the 'Amen in humanity' to the righteous judgement of God. In Christ as human, therefore, the righteousness of God is satisfied as only it can be when men and women are righteous. Lias is prepared to follow Campbell in thinking of the content of this Amen as repentance, a change of mind and purpose within the human condition.[19] Lias admits that from one point of view the work of Christ is something done *for* humanity. It is *his* triumph over sin. It is also, however, something done *in* humanity, the Holy Spirit creating in them the same mind which answers to the divine condemnation of sin. Salvation is thus centred in Christ by the Spirit. This is God's doing, yet paradoxically, persons are called to exercise faith, to join themselves to Christ that they may share his abhorrence of sin and his loving obedience.

In both the pattern and the content of his thought, as well as by actual phrases, Lias displays a constant awareness of Campbell's ideas and manner of expression. This is doubly attested by notes on Campbell attached to the lectures upon publication.[20] He was manifestly impressed by Campbell's contribution to a moral and spiritual understanding of the atonement. Through Lias, therefore, the stream of Campbell's ideas merged further with the main flow of British theology in an unremembered way.

John Caird

Dr. John Caird was an able Scottish preacher who became a professor of divinity at Glasgow University and ultimately its Principal in the latter part of the nineteenth century. He was influenced by Hegelian idealism without losing his sense of the historical concreteness upon which Christian faith is founded.[21] Dr. Caird was the Gifford lecturer for two consecutive terms, the material being published in a two-volume work in 1899 under the title *The Fundamental Ideas of Christianity*. Four chapters are devoted to the atonement and immediately related matters.

Whoever reads Caird's pages on the atonement will be reminded of Campbell. Traditional penal views are set aside. Much is made of personal categories. Emphasis rests on the love which includes justice, on the divine sympathy in Christ and on the incarnation which provided the ground for faith-union with him.

Caird examines both Anselm's classical use of the debt analogy and the later penal view, finding in each a measure of truth but also finding them wanting in the task of enunciating a view of atonement which takes account of the truly moral and personal relations between God and humankind. His approach breathes an atmosphere with which we have become familiar in Campbell. Like Campbell, Caird seeks to find what truth there may be in the idea that suffering for sin provides ground for divine satisfaction. In what possible way can the divine justice so connect suffering with sin that it becomes the condition of forgiveness? Caird's answer, which he says is given by 'some thoughtful modern writers,' is followed by a footnote referring to a section of Campbell's *The Nature of the Atonement.* [22] It is quite evident that Campbell himself is the chief of the 'thoughtful writers' to whom Caird has referred. Indeed, from this point on Caird deals with the very problems which had been highlighted by Campbell. There is, for example, the impossibility of the sinner repenting. 'Our very repentance must be repented of.' [23] At the same time only a sinless person could really know sin for what it is or possess a godly sorrow for it. This is the dilemma; that the sinner who must render satisfaction is unable to do so, while only one who is free from personal sin could give satisfaction to God. Again Caird mentions the answer of theologians whom he does not specify; yet one has only to listen to him with Campbell in mind:

> The difficulty has been met and solved in the person and life of
> Christ. For here is presented to us, in one who is a partaker of
> our nature, that infinite sorrow for sin which is the perfect
> response to the divine condemnation of it . . . here, too, is one,
> in whose pure and perfect nature the presence of sin creates a
> moral recoil, a pang of nameless pain and grief, such as the
> sinful can never experience for themselves. [24]

Caird is quite aware of possible criticisms: two in particular with which we must deal later as the criticisms most frequently directed against Campbell. How can a sinless person repent? And, even if that were possible, how could the virtue of such repentance be transferred from the sinless to the sinful? Our immediate interest in these questions is that Caird proposes answers which again show that he has Campbell mainly in mind. In doing so, incidentally, he cites only two other modern writers, both of whom can be shown to have a distinct bearing upon Campbell. One is a reference to Jonathan Edwards in which Caird quotes a passage which Campbell had found helpful in interpreting the sufferings of Christ, and comments after the fashion of Campbell. [25]

> . . . along with and underneath all this experience of the effects
> of sin, there was in the consciousness of Christ a recognition of
> them as in themselves the just and righteous expression of the
> divine condemnation of sin, a profound response to that con-
> demnation as just and righteous.[26]

Caird follows this statement immediately with the only other direct
quotation he employs on the subject of the atonement, a comment from
James Orr which Caird cites with approval and which, it should be
observed, is the very passage with which Orr concludes his own
favourable review of Campbell.[27] In every use of a modern author then,
Caird moves distinctly with Campbell and in dependence upon him.
Even Campbell's characteristic phrases are scattered throughout the
lectures: 'the Father of Spirits,' 'the nature of the atonement and its
relation to remission of sins,' 'pain as pain possesses no atoning virtue,'
'prolonged for ages,' 'legal fiction.'[28] In spite of the fact that only one
open reference is made to Campbell, and this only a footnote, there can
be no doubt whatever that Campbell's ideas run through the whole of
Caird's treatment of the subject.

This conclusion is not too surprising in view of Caird's admission
elsewhere of his great personal admiration for Campbell. It was as a
young professor that he had nominated John McLeod Campbell for the
Glasgow honorary D.D. degree in 1868,[29] asking the university to
recognize 'one of the most able and original thinkers of the day.'[30]

John Caird's interest in Campbell is a splendid illustration of how the
latter found his way into the minds of others. His thoughts quietly took
possession of their thoughts, and then quite properly found further
expression in terms of their own experience. In Caird's case it was a
philosophical idealist who had had prior commitments to the fundamental
tenets of Christian faith and who sought a harmonious utterance of the two
in the field of atonement theory. Caird knew that Campbell was his teacher.

B.F. Westcott

Bishop B.F. Westcott is another theologian who found the views of
John McLeod Campbell particularly helpful. Westcott became known
not primarily for any contribution to systematic theology, but for his
achievements in biblical studies, and his duties as a leader in the Church
of England. In regard to the doctrine of atonement Westcott witnessed
(both in essays and in correspondence) to a dilemma.[31] On the one hand,
he felt the problem of understanding the atonement to be so tremendous
that he despaired of finding any theological statement which could
adequately set forth its meaning. That is, he tended to agree with those
who would settle for a simple witness to the fact of Christ's reconciling
work without trying further to elaborate on the fact. On the other hand,
Westcott found himself continually called upon, both by personal
interest and official duty, to say something about the meaning of our
redemption.

The best source of Westcott's thoughts on the atonement is *The Victory of the Cross* (1888), a series of passion week addresses delivered at Hereford Cathedral. Though small in size, the volume has sometimes been cited by historians of doctrine as an important contribution.

The preparation of these addresses evidently involved Westcott in a great struggle to find a satisfying utterance. In a letter some years later to the Archbishop of Canterbury he commented that he had taken more pains on these lectures than anything he could recall and added that the only books he had found helpful at the time were those of Dale and Campbell.[32] This debt he had generously acknowledged in the preface to his own book.[33] Indeed, one gains ground for guessing a considerable dependence on Campbell by looking at the marginal checking in Westcott's personally inscribed copy of *The Nature of the Atonement* (1886 edition) located today in the cathedral library at Durham.

It must be acknowledged that long before coming to Campbell's book Westcott had shared a number of affinities with him. Each in his own way had a prior interest in the people to be addressed. They also shared a common concern for a scriptural as against a philosophical basis. Both approached the subject in a clearly devotional spirit as persons who had long contemplated the meaning of St. Paul's notion of faith-union with Christ; and of course Westcott's great familiarity with the ancient church fathers would lead him to welcome Campbell's emphasis on the incarnation.

The homilectic character of *The Victory of the Cross* made it desirable to avoid much quotation in delivery. This renders a reader's analysis less certain; yet (as in John Caird's case) anyone thoroughly familiar with Campbell's thoughts, and especially with his characteristic phrases, may confidently recognize some of the 'many suggestive thoughts' which Westcott acknowledges he derived from Campbell: they centre around the familiar Campbell emphasis on the fatherly love of God who deals with humanity in warmly personal terms, and on Christ as a representative of humanity taking on himself from within humanity the burden of sin and bearing us up before God in intercession, thus carrying us and rendering possible our own proper response of filial love and obedience to God.

We have strong reason to believe then that through the Anglican Bishop Westcott Campbell's thoughts and feelings further penetrated the church at large.

R.C. Moberly

R.C. Moberly (1845-1903) was an Anglican High Churchman, and for some years Regius Professor of Pastoral Theology at Oxford. He is best remembered for his great book *Atonement and Personality* published in 1901. Moberly's views on the atonement are almost invariably brought into relation to Campbell in any historical survey of the subject. On every hand it is asserted that he 'continued the line of

McLeod Campbell' and that 'the core and centre of Moberly's theory is inherited from Campbell.'[34]

Whoever reads Moberly will constantly be reminded of Campbell. The two men share a common concern that the nature of the atonement should be enunciated in fully personal and moral terms. Campbell had urged: 'We have here to do with PERSONS, – the Father of Spirits and His offspring.'[35] Moberly's very title symbolizes this desire to take the nature of persons and personality into account in order that they may not be over-ridden by mechanical and legal conceptions. Moberly also declared himself favourable to the first principles detailed by Campbell such as the 'Fatherhood of God as the fundamental truth of life'[36] and that 'the root cause of the atonement is not the anger, but the love of God.'[37] Like Campbell, too, he sees the importance of the idea of satisfaction to God as long as it is interpreted in a truly moral sense. We even find a similar pattern of argument at this point. God can be satisfied, says Moberly, only if in some real fashion humanity fulfills the conditions of the moral life, which for the sinner means the offering of a true repentance. Moberly defines repentance in a manner specifically reminiscent of Campbell, involving, says Moberly, 'personal identity with righteousness in condemnation and detestation of sin.'[38] But men and women cannot offer a true repentance (i.e. be truly penitent) because of the disabling taint of sin 'which has blunted the self's capacity for entire hatred of sin.'[39] Hence the dilemma of necessary yet impossible repentance. In fact, only the perfectly holy person can appreciate the true nature of sin. Only a sinless being could really stand with God in condemnation of sin. The problem then is how to make repentance possible, how to yield the fruit of penitence in persons. It is just here, Moberly believes, that Christ is found to be the relevant answer. As both divine and human in the fullest possible sense, he fulfills the conditions of a perfect oneness with righteousness in the condemnation of sin which is in fact a perfect penitence in relation to human sin.

Christ's complete identification with sinful humanity, bearing the burden of human sin, necessarily involved him in suffering. How is this suffering to be understood? Moberly joins Campbell in protesting against mechanical and quantitative estimates of Christ's suffering. He also believes that the sufferings are not to be regarded as punishment in the ordinary sense of the term but as a personal consciousness as to what sin is by virtue of Christ's full identification with human nature.[40] The death of Christ, for example, cannot be isolated from his life – the death being 'the necessary climax of the life.'[41] Nor can Christ's death be rightly interpreted apart from his resurrection whereby the Spirit of Christ is made available to all men.[42]

In view of such obvious commonality it somewhat surprises Moberly's reader that in the main body of his text he never specifically acknowledges a debt to Campbell. In fairness to Moberly, it must be said that his habit of writing allows for only the rarest reference to *any* authors. This is somewhat compensated for by a supplementary chapter on *Atonement in History*. Here the importance of Campbell to Moberly may be judged by the comparatively large space afforded to him. Only Dale receives as much attention, and that largely in recognition for his having stemmed the tide of thought represented by Jowett.[43] Apart from this, Moberly's treatment of Dale is mainly negative. Campbell, on the other hand, is introduced as one who, though belonging to an earlier time, is considerably in advance of Dale in his grasp of the meaning of Christ's atonement. Moreover, after quoting numerous extracts from Campbell, Moberly says by way of appreciation: 'To me it seems difficult to estimate too highly the debt which Christian thought owes to this reverent spirit.'[44] There is here at least tacit admission of his dependence upon Campbell. It becomes clear that Moberly has Campbell often in view as the one to whom he must relate himself whether by way of agreement or correction. When, for example, he says that Campbell's theory 'in its real completeness is a very grand one'[45] he means that there is something yet to complete and that he intends to show the way. This is not ungracious on Moberly's part. Being preoccupied with next steps, he simply failed to say explicitly that much of his own progress was due to the work of his predecessor.

Moberly does criticize Campbell at several points, and endeavours to carry the subject-matter farther at others. Yet he proposes correctives to Campbell founded on a basic philosophical outlook of his own which I believe to be flawed, and less useful than Campbell's, as suggested below (pp. 131f). My purpose here has been only to show how some of Campbell's thoughts and feelings about Christian reconciliation fanned out still further through the English-speaking world. Many a reader of Moberly's widely circulated work has turned back to savour Campbell himself.

A.B. Macaulay

Dr. A.B. Macaulay of Trinity College, Glasgow, must certainly be cited among thinkers of the twentieth century who have drawn heavily from McLeod Campbell. Macaulay's views on the atonement found expression in the Cunningham Lectures of 1937 published under the title *The Death of Jesus*. For anyone interested in classifying theories of the atonement Macaulay proves to be a difficult case. Thomas Hughes places him, perhaps awkwardly, along with William Manson, F.C.N Hicks and others in a chapter headed *Back to the Bible*.[46] Actually Macaulay wrestled with a variety of traditional views and found himself unable fully to accept any one of them. His strength seems to lie in showing how various interpretations of the atonement contribute to the unity and truth of the doctrine. He was concerned to uncover those elements which should be included in any adequate approach, and it was in the pursuit of this aim that he made abundant use of Campbell who had written in the same city (Glasgow) some eighty years before.

Macaulay's references to Campbell are frequent, carefully discussed and usually related to the more important issues. Only one other theologian ranks so highly in Macaulay's mind, and both are acknowledged generously. 'Readers,' he says, 'will easily perceive who my masters have been: Dr. J. McLeod Campbell and Principal James Denney.'[47] Of Campbell's *The Nature of the Atonement* he continues: 'A nobler book on the death of Jesus . . . has in my judgment never been written in any age or language.'

In his chapter on *Postulates and Methods* Macaulay commends Campbell's delineation of the work of atonement as covering *both* 'Christ's dealing with men of the part of God' and 'Christs dealing with God on behalf of men.' Macaulay uses this distinction to emphasize, in opposition to certain popular conceptions of the atonement, that there is a Godward reference in the doctrine which cannot be ignored. He claims that this Godward reference appears in the New Testament 'wherever the terms 'ransom' and 'propitiation' are mentioned, and whenever, though the actual term is not used, the idea of 'satisfaction' occurs.'[48] Macaulay also adopted Campbell's clear distinction between 'retrospective' and 'prospective' aspects of the atonement as a means of bringing the passive and active obedience of Christ into proper relation with one another. The intimate connection between the believer's justification and sanctification is similarly shown.[49] In short, the main elements of Campbell's framework for a view of the atonement are taken over with little alteration.

It is characteristic of Macaulay too that at crucial points in his argument he pin-points as axiomatic some principle which we have discovered to be one of Campbell's presuppositions. For example, instead of approaching the doctrine of atonement via an historical study of various views, as so many writer do, Macaulay places himself beside Campbell who had insisted on beginning by 'studying the atonement by its own light.'[50] Again, consider Macaulay's treatment of the idea of a costly forgiveness. He cautioned against taking it to mean that forgiveness must be won from God at great cost – Christ paying that cost. That would miss the real truth of costliness, for God himself is involved in the cost of forgiveness. God initiated the sacrifice by coming in Christ the Son. The truth must be protected, according to Macaulay, by Campbell's insistence that 'forgiveness precedes atonement' and that the forgiving love of God is manifested in the form of Christ's atonement.[51]

Macaulay was also much impressed by Campbell's interpretation of the sufferings of Christ. Christ's ordeal consisted not so much in dreadful physical endurances as in a two-fold spiritual temptation: First, the testing of his love for others and his faith in the redemptive possibilities of others. Second, testing his filial trust that his own mind of forgiving love was in fact the mind God. In other words, while the incarnation involved Christ in bodily suffering to the greatest degree, the real ordeal was that of enduring and being tempted by every possible evil in the midst of the world. Thus Christ endured, in words which Macaulay several times repeats after Campbell, 'a perfected personal experience of the enmity of the carnal mind to God.'[52]

Macaulay was no slavish follower of his acknowledged teacher. He readily differed when he thought it necessary. Yet his work provides an illustration of how Campbell's views remained alive and helpful in the first half of the twentieth century.

Vincent Taylor

The thought of John McLeod Campbell has an important place in the writings of Dr. Vincent Taylor, for many years the Principal of the Methodist College at Headingly, Leeds. Dr. Taylor is known primarily as a most competent New Testament scholar. Fortunately for systematic theology, however, he made a particular study of those aspects of the New Testament which provide the foundation for a doctrine of the atonement, and published the results over a period of twenty years. Taylor's combination of biblical scholarship and doctrinal interest lends a common pattern to his books on the atonement, the initial and major parts of each being allotted to scriptural background, while the final sections draw out the doctrinal implications.[53]

Vincent Taylor's major contribution to atonement theory was to bring the language of sacrifice into prominence as a suitable means of expressing the meaning of the atonement. To do this he felt that he must first clarify the idea of sacrifice itself, as did others of his contemporaries. He desired to be rid of the popular notion that the basic ideas connected with sacrifice are those of substitution and the need for a propitiatory offering to appease an angry God. Emphasis should rest rather on sacrifice as a means whereby the worshipper renews fellowship with God.[54] Taylor shows how the sacrificial element in the right sense of the term appears in every part of the New Testament – in the passion sayings, in the primitive preaching of Acts and in the Epistles. A review of Old Testament sacrifice is required for an understanding of the New, but is not entirely sufficient; for Jesus introduced something utterly unique by combining the several conceptions of Messiahship, Son of Man and Suffering Servant.

Taylor sees some elements of truth in all historic views of the atonement.[55] He elaborates the sacrificial conception not to displace former theories but because he believes that it provides a scriptural means for gathering them together. The idea of sacrifice is able to express the several aspects of Christ's work. His work is *vicarious* in the sense that Christ did something for us which we could not do for ourselves. But this 'for us' must be interpreted in harmony with New Testament terminology to mean that what he did for us he did as human 'on our behalf.' Therefore the deed of Christ is *representative*. But how does he represent us? Clearly by the sacrifice of himself. The deed is *sacrificial*, and as such it includes both vicarious and representative aspects. On several occasions Taylor places these categories in this ascending order.[56]

My purpose here is not to describe Taylor's distinctive views in any detail, but only to create a setting in which to show how he employs Campbell's thoughts to advantage.

In common with many other theologians since Campbell's time, Taylor credits him with performing a major role in rejecting the penal view in its grosser forms. After quoting Campbell's well-known denial that the sufferings of Christ could not be in the nature of a punishment, Taylor concludes: 'In these burning words all theories of vindictive punishment are utterly consumed; they have no vitality, either in the words' of Jesus or in his thought about God.'[57] At the same time, he qualifies his statement by associating himself more than Campbell allows with those who feel that the sufferings of Christ cannot be entirely separated from the penal consequences of sin.[58] But when Taylor touches on the representative character of Christ's work he cites without qualification how Campbell, in the language of an 'older day' expressed the view that 'the suffering of Jesus is indeed representative and vicarious, but, in relation to men, it is neither crudely substitutionary nor automatic in its action, but something which is owned and appropriated.[59] This includes Taylor's adherence to Campbell's emphasis on faith-union with Christ. He agrees that while it is true to say that the deed of Christ is an objective fact, the atonement is not comprehended in its wholeness apart from considering the manner by which we enter into the fruits of Christ's saving work. Taylor identifies Campbell as one who pressed for an awareness of faith-union with Christ as the most intimate and deeply personal religious experience.[60] Thus he finds that his study of sacrificial concepts confirms a point which Campbell had already worked out.

When Taylor writes on what he calls the 'content' of Christ's saving deed the reader realizes even more strongly the importance of the place which Taylor gives to Campbell in his own conclusions. In *The Cross of Christ* Taylor briefly summarizes the position he had taken in his former works. In a chapter entitled 'Towards a Modern Statement,' he italicizes four basic propositions considered essential to a true understanding of the nature of the atonement. Their force as related to Campbell is best felt when quoted verbatim:

> First, the saving deed of Christ is the supreme revelation of the love of God for men.[61]

This will immediately be recognized as the first also of Campbell's propositions.[62] While Taylor only puts the idea as one that 'no Christian will deny,' (and as one which represents the truth for which Abelard stood, though not the whole truth of the matter). It must be remarked as interesting that an idea for which Campbell had been obliged to argue should now be so readily taken for granted.

> Secondly, the saving deed of Christ is an act of obedience to the Father's will.

While other writers have also highlighted the New Testament figure of the obedient Christ, it is not without significance that in discussing this same proposition in an earlier book Taylor shows a clear link with Campbell by referring to him by way of illustrating the representative character of Christ's obedience.[63]

> Thirdly, Christ's saving deed was an act of submission to the judgement of God upon sin.

This proposition as it stands runs parallel to Campbell's similarly italicized statement of Christ's 'perfect Amen in humanity to the judgment of God on the sin of man.'[64] Campbell of course was careful to divest the description of Christ's relation to sin of all penal conceptions. Taylor would not go quite so far, though he does give Campbell credit for taking the critical step necessary to a more positive construction.

> Fourthly, the saving deed of Christ issues in a ministry of intercession in which He voices our inarticulate penitence and desire for reconciliation.

No words could more clearly echo Campbell's constantly reiterated themes of Christ's confession and intercession. Here Taylor relies on the same passages of scripture to which Campbell's attention was drawn, wherein the risen Christ is pictured as an advocate before God for all humanity: Romans 8:34; I John 2:1; Hebrews 9:24. Here also he openly aligns himself with Campbell and Moberly on the question of vicarious penitence. He admits that their view is not specified as such in scripture, but he claims that if the death of Christ is to be understood in sacrificial as well as in representative terms, as he believes it must be, then Campbell's way of putting it is very acceptable. Over the years Taylor urged theologians to look past the surface criticisms of Campbell's statement of the case in order to appreciate its deeper psychological levels.

Altogether it is impressively interesting that in The Cross of Christ (1956), published exactly one hundred years after The Nature of the Atonement, Campbell's mark should be so clearly visible.

I have drawn attention to a few theologians and church leaders who clearly acknowledged Campbell's considerable role in shaping their understanding of Christian atonement. He founded no school of thought as such, yet by such persons Campbell found his way as it were into theological class rooms, pulpits and published works. In some places the trail is clearly marked. Elsewhere one is left to make an educated guess, as in F.R.M. Hitchcock's Donellan Lectures given at the University of Dublin in 1911,[65] and H.A. Hodges in The Pattern of Atonement, (1955)[66] where passage after passage offer reminders of Campbell's phrasing. Still others leave us with more questions than answers until harder evidence is laid bare, as in the case of Donald Baillie whom Prof. John McIntyre once suggested as a good subject for research in relation to Campbell.[67]

X

A MORAL AND SPIRITUAL CORRECTIVE IMPACT ON TRADITIONAL VIEWS

In tracing John McLeod Campbell's influence on subsequent thought concerning the atonement, it seemed important first to show how his positive doctrines found a broad measure of acceptance. It must be remembered, however, that much of Campbell's work was done in a critical vein. He had been aroused by the disabilities of a theological system, defects he felt called upon to expose. It was therefore to be expected that some people would rise to defend that system. Of greater interest, however, were those who, while holding to the more traditional view, willingly listened to Campbell's criticisms by way of correction. It is fitting to focus briefly on a few such thinkers even at the risk of repeating some elements of Campbell's approach.

In his initial criticism of the Calvinist (not Calvin's) doctrine of atonement Campbell had been in a position similar to Athanasius in the Arian controversy of the ancient church. Campbell held that no use of logic or language should drive a separating wedge between the first and second persons of the trinity. It is God *as God is* who (in Christ) acts to reconcile the world to himself, not some agency other than God, less than God, a substitute for God. The Fourth Gospel reveals a struggle to say this is the language of the *Word* which in the beginning was 'with God' and indeed 'was God' prior to the fleshly manifestation of the Word in the man Jesus Christ. So God the Creator and judge is also the Redeemer; but if we are to know the nature of the sovereign God we take our cue from the revelation of that God in the incarnate one, the Redeemer.

From this base, for Campbell, so much else stemmed. He had to say a firm 'no' to speculative arguments about atonement, and even to cherished creedal statements which seemed to cut across the revelation of God in Christ. Sydney Cave identifies Campbell's insistence on beginning with the given and not with the preconceived as his most important contribution to atonement theology.[1]

As to specifics, the most obvious was the priority Campbell gave to the love of God as providing the atonement in Christ and determining its nature.

The love of God is *not* secondary to the justice of God. Rather it has primacy; and as such includes justice. So God's justice, as well as God's love, is a ground for human hope. God acts to put things right! Righteousness makes righteous, and justice justifies.[2]

This means that God must not be understood as withholding love until the demand for righteousness is somehow satisfied. Nor is Christ's work in any sense to be looked upon as somehow to change God's disposition towards humankind. He came not to change God's mind, but to reveal it.

It meant also for Campbell that he had to dispel the notion that the sufferings of Christ arose from the fact that God was venting anger against the man Jesus Christ as a necessary sort of scapegoat, or that in any sense his sufferings could be regarded as punishment. Precisely the opposite! God was (in Christ) taking the consequences of human folly upon himself. The Cross of Christ thus shows up the suffering love of God. Campbell had not been the first of those raised in the Calvinist tradition to question the concept of Christ's punishment. Rather, it was the timing and effectiveness of his protest.[3]

Campbell's overall approach to the atonement involved him in rejecting a legalistic (let alone mechanistic) working out of a divine decree regarding human destinies in favour of recognizing the livingly personal good news of divine grace. Even as a young man in the Row pulpit he had lifted up such thoughts:

> You have made God's law a lifeless thing . . . but *God's law* is God's own *heart come out in the shape of law* . . . you have to do not with rules, or precepts, or opinion, but with a person, a real person, a living God.[4]

In other words God calls for and enables us to live by a filial relation not a legal one. For Campbell the good news of God could best be expressed through what we have come to call the 'category of the personal.' Knowledge of a person is gained not by objective analysis (as of a thing or a principle) but by the distinctive process of personal encounter through an I-Thou relation. Said he of the atonement: 'We have here to do with PERSONS, – the Father of spirits and His offspring. *These are to each other more than all things and all circumstances.*'[5] In Christ, God himself meets humankind with holy love. God wills that men and women shall be in fellowship with him. God has provided a way which need not first be won by them but is unconditionally free, and wills no other alternative. However, since God offered persons a moral and spiritual choice, there can be thrust upon him as it were an alternative he does not will; namely, that those who refuse love and persist in their ways can only experience the wrath which must proceed from a holy love which cannot abide denial. In this respect Campbell was in accord with Luther's thought, as he would also be with the revival of this element of Reformation theology in contemporary Protestant thought.

Thoughts of these sorts by the end of the nineteenth century were being taken as axiomatic, even by those who had not (and could not) go all the way with him. For example, when *Lux Mundi* came out in 1890 with the express purpose of relating the Christian faith to current intellectual and moral problems, the author of its chapter on the atonement thought it necessary to emphasize that the death of Christ was not the cause but the revelation of God's love. A footnote refers to Campbell as having aptly stated the principle.[6] In the first series of lectures under the Kerr Foundation (1891) Dr. James Orr drew attention to a tendency of the times: 'the endeavour to give a spiritual interpretation to the great fact which lies at the heart of our Redemption; not necessarily to deny its judicial aspect . . . but to remove from it the hard legal aspect it is apt to assume when treated as a purely external fact . . .'[7] Orr then proceeded to illustrate this by reference to Campbell and to claim for him a place of major importance in the development of this more 'spiritual' view of atonement.

It is not generally recognized how many well-known writers on the atonement, then and for forty years, shared Orr's feeling about Campbell. The doubts which Orr and others did have about his use of the phraseology of repentance,[8] and their suspicion that he had over-stated his case in opposition to penal conceptions, have prevented the general reader from recognizing their overall debt to Campbell. R.W. Dale is an excellent example of this. Dale is too often regarded as having held firmly to a penal view of the atonement in reaction to the tendencies represented by Campbell. This estimate is quite misleading. Dale believed that his real mission was to preserve the objective character of the atonement against the enticements of subjective views and to interpret the older theory in terms which would apply to his day. This meant that he, like Campbell, emphasized the love of God as the ultimate motivation for redemption, and the unbroken unity of the Father-Son relationship as the determining factor in the nature of the atonement. Similarly he sought to show the natural relation existing between Christ and humanity, and declared himself opposed to the traditional doctrine of imputation of sin to Christ as a 'legal fiction.'[9] A.M. Fairbairn's essay on *Dale as a Theologian* claims for Dale a clear sympathy with the approach of Erskine and Campbell while his 'mind was still in the forming, . . . a spirit less legal and more personal, less concerned with abstract ideas of law and justice, and more concerned with the concrete ideas of fatherhood and forgiveness.'[10] It is unfortunate that in Dale's famous Congregational Union Lecture of 1875, published under the title *The Atonement*, his only reference to Campbell is of a critical nature. While he did make a passing comment on Campbell's book as a valuable treatise,[11] his main purpose at the time was to criticize what he felt to be a limitation in Campbell's thought. Readers were thus left with the impression that Dale was not particularly favourable to Campbell. Dale later sought to correct this unfortunate conclusion through his *Preface to the Seventh Edition*. Here one finds him declaring agreement with Campbell in matters of major importance, though critical of some points. He seems to have regarded Campbell almost with awe:

> An objective element in the Atonement is so distinctly recognized
> in Dr. Campbell's theory, that I did not care to make any
> elaborate statement of the grounds on which his theory seems to

me defective and unsatisfactory. And those who have read his
book will understand me when I say that there is something in it
which makes me shrink from criticism . . . I feel in no mood to
argue with him; it is better to sit quiet, and to receive the subtle
influence of his beautiful temper and profound spiritual wisdom.[12]
This is a remarkable admission when one considers the vigour and
confidence which marks the manner in which Dale stated his own case.

John Scott Lidgett is another author who displays obvious sympathies
with Campbell. His very titles remind one of Campbell's emphasis: *The
Spiritual Principle of the Atonement* (1897) and *The Fatherhood of
God* (1902). Lidgett remarks on Campbell's service in attempting to
rescue the atonement from Calvinistic explanations,[13] and freely
acknowledges that Campbell's book 'puts us on the high road to a true
conception of the matter.'[14] This does not mean that Lidgett felt himself
limited by an special obligation to Campbell. The fact is that in a much
later work he credits F.D. Maurice more than others with restoring the
truth of the Fatherhood of God to its primacy in Christian thought.[15]
Even so, and this is an important point at the moment, Lidgett's view of
the atonement is worked out with a high degree of sympathy for the
principles for which Campbell had argued long before. Much of what he
has to say is a distinct, though indirect, vindication of Campbell.

The name of P.T. Forsyth, an outstanding British theologian of the
early twentieth century, is not often associated with Campbell's ideas.
The two men were of vastly different temperaments, and on some points
their thoughts are best studied by way of contrast. Forsyth's primary
focus was on the Cross of Christ both as a means of victory over all evil
powers and as rendering in the deepest sense satisfaction to God as holy.
Yet he must also be placed among those who had a special appreciation
for Campbell's achievement in clearing the ground for a truer approach to
the atonement. In a series of talks to a ministers' study-conference in
1909 Forsyth declared: 'I hope you have read McLeod Campbell on the
Atonement. Every minister ought to know that book, and know it well.'[16]
He then indicated his 'one criticism' – Campbell's emphasis on Christ's
confession of human sin instead of his confession of God's holiness in
judgement. Yet Forsyth's writings on the work of Christ proceed on the
assumption that there can no longer be a debate on a variety of ideas
which are known to have been enunciated by Campbell. Many a
statement is reminiscent of Campbell. For example, 'there can be no
talk,' says Forsyth, 'of any mollification of God, or any inducement
whatever, offered by either man or some third party, to procure grace.
Procured grace is a contradiction in terms. The atonement did not
procure grace, it flowed from grace.[17]

Forsyth had participated at the turn of the century in a symposium for
The Christian World designed to assess the situation in atonement
theory to date.[18] There he listed in point form, both negatively and
positively, a number of basic ideas not previously accepted which he
believed had been clearly established in the recent past. It is highly

interesting that his list can be matched very closely with points made in Campbell's book. This does not prove that Forsyth had Campbell specifically in mind. The importance of the reference lies rather in the fact that early in the twentieth century Forsyth could identify at least a dozen currently accepted ideas on behalf of which Campbell had previously been obliged to dispute at length. Also it must be noted as a plain statistical fact that in the whole of that particular symposium Campbell's name was relied upon for support more often than any other – by Dean Farrar for instance, and by W.F. Adeney who says: 'Now it is quite clear that the critical work of the earlier part of this century was most potent and final, especially when it was based on moral and spiritual grounds, as in the case of McLeod Campbell.'[19]

A mere enumeration of names can be exercised to the point of tedium. But since the case for Campbell should be sufficiently reviewed, perhaps one more example would be in order. James Denney wrote as often and as fully as any theologian in favour of holding to, though revising, a penal concept of the atonement. Some observers detect a change over the years not only in his attitude but in the content of his thought. However this may be, his most mature thinking on the atonement appears in the Cunningham Lectures for 1917 which Denney's final illness prevented him from delivering but which were published posthumously under the title *The Christian Doctrine of Reconciliation*. At several points in these pages Denney turns to Campbell as a pioneer in the search for a satisfying view of the atonement. After recounting some of Campbell's basic emphases – the divine love, an interest in the life as well as in the death of Christ, the desire to exchange an artificial 'scheme of salvation' for a view which takes account of the requirements of personality, Denney concludes:

> The questions once so fiercely debated about the extent of the atonement have no meaning. The humiliating sophistries with which the Scripture was tortured to make it mean the very opposite of what is written broad upon its face, need vex us no more. Of all books written on the atonement, as God's way of reconciling man to Himself, McLeod Campbell's is probably that which is most completely inspired by the spirit of the truth with which it deals . . . no one who has ever felt its power will cease to put it in a class by itself.[20]

These estimates of Campbell by Dale, Lidgett, Forsyth and Denney, have been given particular citation for several reasons. First, each made a significant contribution to the theology of the atonement in his own right. Second, all are frankly critical of Campbell's thought at points which they regard as fundamental to closer adherence to a penal view. Third, they lived through the period when the implications of Campbell's work were being most thoroughly assessed and absorbed. It is especially significant, therefore, that these theologians, while diverging from Campbell, credit him for contributing to their own struggle for a more moral and spiritual view of the atonement.

PART THREE
CRITICAL ASSESSMENTS

XI

A PERCEIVED LIMITATION IN
INTERPRETING THE SUFFERINGS OF CHRIST

I have suggested that in his understanding of atonement Campbell adhered to the Athanasian concern that whatever distinctions may properly be made between 'the Father and the Son' Christian experience could allow no separating wedge as to essence to be driven between the two; and hence no faulty tension could be entertained as between justice and love in God's redemptive action through Christ. It had been an equally important concern of Athanasius and the Nicene party that neither should there be any faulty separation between the Redeemer's humanity and our own. The incarnate Christ is not someone subtly more than human or in any way other than human. No awareness of his life of obedience to God, and his apparent sinlessness in that respect, should be interpreted as preventing him sharing fully in our humanity. Nor does our own alienation from God and our failure to be what we are meant to be in any way set us apart by nature from Christ's humanity. This has always been the bottom line of orthodoxy. Naturally enough Christians have been teased again and again to give a satisfying rationale for the manner in which the divine and human natures have been joined in the man Jesus Christ yet none has succeeded in avoiding a suspicion that he has somehow been partitioned off from a real humanity. Witness the lengthy Christological debates of the fourth and fifth centuries which yielded the declaration at Chalcedon (451 A.D.) that in him we are confronted by 'the same reality as ourselves as far as his humaness is concerned.' In the face of their perception of heretical attempts to express the meaning of the New Testament witness to the 'Word made flesh,' the councils of the ancient church had employed the more rigorous terminology of essence and substance. Campbell, however, reverted to those phrases of biblical thought more suited to express personality and personal relationships. Thus Jesus Christ is understood not only to have come to be with us and to be for us, but in a complete sense to be human as we are, and to share experience at every level of our existence.

Insofar therefore as sin (whether regarded as transgression of the moral law, a state of lostness, despair and alienation, or by prideful assertion a refusal to let God be God) brings humanity into the realms of consequential suffering, Christ's humanity involves him in freely entering into the same arena. Indeed, St. Paul, desiring to emphasize the depth of Christ's association with us, acknowledges it as an implication of the incarnation that, while in harmony with God as a person, he somehow also shares our sinful state (II Cor. 5:21); and Martin Luther, more as preacher than as theologian blurts it out bluntly that Christ can be regarded as 'the greatest sinner.' Thus by virtue of Christ's identification with humanity, by his entry into their life he shared also the pains which stem from the divine judgement on a deliberately wayward humanity.

It happens, however, that Campbell's language sometimes seems to possess a quality which leads the reader to suspect that in his view Christ did not enter fully and completely into the arena of sin and suffering. He continually describes Christ as 'seeing' sin with God's eyes and as 'confessing' human sin. By these words Campbell meant much more than simply that Christ was a spiritually-minded observer who could acknowledge the sins of people while standing somewhat aloof, but such words do not make it unequivocally clear in what sense Christ did more than that. Even where Campbell says that Christ 'absorbs' the wrath of God against sin, the degree of involvement is described as a 'response' in which he receives full 'apprehension and realization' of God's wrath into his 'soul and spirit.'[1] These words show the persistence of a language which fails to specify that Christ actually experienced the sinner's experience. Whatever the moral difficulties of the Calvinistic conception of penal substitution, that position was able to communicate the fact that somehow Christ was able *to be* in the place of sinners. He suffered humanity's just deserts and in reality died the sinner's death.

R.C. Moberly, who has been shown to owe much to Campbell, assessed Campbell as having 'discerned with more complete success the nature of the relation of Christ to God, than that of the relation of men to Christ.'[2] Certain of Campbell's key phrases are taken as symptoms of this weakness. A good sample is the oft-repeated reference to 'the Son's dealing with the Father in relation to our sins.'[3] To Moberly this seemed to suggest that Christ was a third party, neither God nor fully human, who interposed between the two. This hardly involves Christ with humanity in the biblical sense that he was 'made sin.'

A.B. Macaulay, a sympathetic interpreter of Campbell who repeatedly used Campbell's phrase descriptive of Christ's suffering as 'a perfect personal experience of the enmity of the carnal mind to God,'[4] felt that Campbell had failed to amplify its meaning adequately. When it is indicated for example that this is the manner of Christ's 'confession' of human sin, Macaulay wonders whether Campbell's words suggest that the ordeal of Christ would only be 'the trial of his assent to a proposition,' to which he had to continue to say 'Amen' in spite of all he had to bear.[5] To him also Campbell seemed too much to have looked upon Christ as one whose filial relationship to God included a knowledge of all that was to take place as a resource for meeting his sufferings in a manner which blunted their full onslaught. In technical phrase then, Macaulay suspected Campbell of slipping into a measure of docetism.

It is sometimes pointed out that towards the end of his book Campbell is more successful in relating Christ to the human condition. In some lengthy passages Campbell contemplates the biblical concept of death in relation to sin as its 'wages,' and by his death Christ had somehow to meet not simply the mind of God towards sin, but 'an existing law with its penalty of death'; moreover that Christ alone ever truly tasted death.[6] James Orr, for example, welcomed these sections as proving that in Campbell's view Christ 'really bore in His own Person the penal evils which are the expression of the wrath of God against sin.'[7] Orr felt that the gap between his own thinking and Campbell's was closing at this point, and that the remaining difference was only one of nomenclature. This was perhaps the direction in which Campbell's thought was moving, but did he actually go as far as Orr believed? When the above statements by Campbell are examined more closely in their context they reveal that Christ is not conceived to have tasted death in the same dimension as that death which is due to humanity. Campbell says that what men and women shrink from in death is either the loss of the world of experience which they have known or else those fears of the future which attend an accusing conscience. Neither of these factors was present to Christ, but Campbell claims that these conditions do not in any case represent the real character of death:

Death, *as death*, is distinct from such accompanying consider-ations as these, and our Lord tasted it in truth for what it is.
For, as He had truly lived in humanity, and possessed and used the gift of life according to the truth of humanity, so did He also truly die; death was to His humanity the withdrawal of the gift of that life which it closes. As men in life know not life as God's gift, neither realize what it is to live; so neither do they in death know God's withdrawal of that gift, nor consciously realise what it is to die.[8]

In other words, since Christ alone knew what true life in God is, so also could he alone know what death is – the 'withdrawal of the gift of life which it closes.' He desired to retain that gift but was willing to give it up through love for humanity. Emphasis here rests upon the difference between death as Christ submitted to it and death as the sinner must finally experience it. After further illustration of the subject, Campbell actually speaks of 'the difference between death coming as the wages of sin, and passing upon all men, for that all have sinned, and death as tasted by the Son of God.'[9] On the whole, Christ's death seems to be regarded as a death somewhat other than that endured in the reality of sinful human existence. If so, then Campbell has failed to show a fully adequate relation between Christ and humanity.

The point in Campbell's writing where this weakness has usually been observed is in his treatment of the cry of dereliction from the Cross: 'My God, my God, why hast thou forsaken me?' (Mark 15:34 and Matthew 27:46) The words are drawn from an Old Testament setting in Psalm 22. Traditional Protestant theology, especially under Luther's influence, and only slightly less so under Calvin's, has found in the cry an expression of Christ's forsakenness and utter desolation. Said Luther: 'Look at Christ who for thy sake has gone to hell and been abandoned by God as one damned forever.'[10] Protestant scholasticism cherished this interpretation as an essential feature of its penal substitutionary view of Christ's work. Campbell, however, interpreted the cry otherwise. He agreed that the circumstances of crucifixion would naturally have called Psalm 22 to the mind of Jesus, but he contended that the words of the cry should not be isolated from the rest of the psalm. They should rather be interpreted in the light of the whole psalm. While the psalm opens with a prayer of complaint to God, God is still the psalmist's God; and the psalmist's faith, though severely tried, never gives way. In utter weakness he continues to trust God, and at last is led triumphantly to praise the God who has never hidden his face from the suppliant. To Campbell this means that the cry from the Cross witnesses not to forsakenness as evidence of God's wrath come upon Christ, but to the Son's unbroken trust in the Father. The man Jesus was aware of God's presence through every test. The cry is an extension of his earlier testimony in the face of impending forsakenness by his disciples' flight from disaster: 'I am not alone, because the Father is with me.' (John 16:32) Campbell concludes that there is no trace or suggestion of the idea that Christ was cut off from the Father or tasted death under his wrath.[11]

The history of Psalm 22 in the Hebrew-Christian tradition yields some evidence for Campbell's position. Long before the time of Christ the Jews had learned to read it in time of trouble. The despairing cry followed by expressions of triumphant faith brought courage and assurance to people under trial. In view of this fact Martin Dibelius claims that Christ's utterance of the first words of the psalm could never be taken to mean either that God had forsaken him or that he could have imagined it so. 'No pious Israelite dying with those words on his lips,' says Dibelius, 'could be thought – or could have thought himself – to be abandoned by God.[12] It is also known that Christians early recognized the special relation of this psalm, even in its details, to the death and resurrection of Christ. The evil and the darkness which enveloped the Cross are followed by the victory of the resurrection morning. Moreover, it may be significant that some Christians were embarrassed at the suggestion that Christ had been forsaken of God. This is reflected in the softening down of the cry in the non-canonical Gospel of Peter by the substitution of the words 'My power, my power,' for 'My God, My God.'[13] Similar signs are discernible in Western texts of the Greek where the word 'reproached' replaces 'forsaken.'[14]

We are not called upon here to discuss the authenticity of the cry itself. Even if the words were considered to have been drawn by the Church directly from the psalm, and thus seen to be a reflection of her faith rather than an utterance of Jesus, it would still not be ruled out as material for understanding the experience of Christ. At many points the scholar must interpret the apostolic witness as a reflection of the mind of

Christ. Authenticity is not therefore the final question, though it may be fair to say that biblical criticism largely favours the authenticity of the cry of dereliction.

It must nevertheless be stated that biblical scholars do exhibit unusual caution when asked for a judgement on what these words meant on the lips of Jesus. Rawlinson says that 'on the assumption that our Lord really uttered the words it is better to say frankly that we do not know exactly what was in His mind.'[15] In the *Interpreter's Bible*, Sherman Johnson comments in a similar vein.[16]

It would appear that the theologian should take great care not to draw too much from a passage of such uncertain meaning to the exegetes. In any case no single verse of scripture should be made to bear the whole weight of so important a doctrine. Interpretation of the passage should perhaps be controlled by two lines of approach. There is wisdom first in beginning with the statement as it stands rather than with a theological conclusion about it. The cry does express a feeling of utter desolation, a sense of abandonment and an experience of defeat. It is temporary but real. The second line of approach is to step aside from the cry as such in order to ask a theological question: What does the doctrine of the incarnation, which is by no means dependent upon any single portion of scripture, really imply for the man Jesus Christ? Does not the incarnation involve an entry into the human situation which is something more than identification with the sinner through sympathy? A complete incarnation would mean that in some incomprehensible way Christ became the sinner and died the death which belongs to the sinner. This question of incarnation thus turns into the traditional question of atonement; namely, as to how far God is willing to go in meeting the situation of fallen humanity. In helplessness and need humanity requires an atonement which they cannot themselves offer and for which they must depend upon God to provide, whereas God, who brings down upon humanity the judgement of a deserved death, at the same time gives himself over through Christ to the human lot. Thus, as A.E. Garvie puts it: 'God's complete answer to sin is not the judgment on it which falls on man alone, but the share in all that judgment involves which he takes upon himself.'[17] Traditionally, theologians fastened upon the cry from the Cross as signifying that final thrust of the divine life into the human situation, the culmination of the incarnation and the answer to the problem of atonement. But the cry is not the sole evidence of that thrust. The interpretation of the incarnation and atonement which runs through all the New Testament points to some such experience as the cry of dereliction has commonly been taken to suggest. This may explain why the traditional interpretation of that cry has become so deeply rooted.

It has sometimes been thought that, while Christ underwent the experience of desolation on the Cross, he was in fact not really forsaken but only seemed to have been so. This position can imply serious difficulties. When Stopford Brooke offered it as a solution to the problem he drew a strong objection from Dale who declared that this would make our Lord's cry unreal.[18] Upon this question too, however, the paradox of the incarnation throws light. It implies that from the standpoint of Christ as a man the cry witnesses to the reality of his complete forsakenness and utter desolation. At the same time, when the event is viewed from God's side, there is a true sense in which Christ was not forsaken; for God was in Christ reconciling the world unto himself. 'We who are Christians,' William Temple once said, 'remember that the Godhead never shone forth in Christ so effulgently as in the moment when He felt himself forsaken of God.'[19]

It is well nigh impossible to discover a language adequate to express the paradoxical relation of the Father to the Son at the moment when the Son is most completely identified with humanity. Moberly speaks of it as 'that two-sided, that incompatible cry – so spiritually desolate, yet so tranquil in spirit.'[20] Forsyth, with perhaps a more profound sense of the terror and rightness of the cry, speaks of it as 'desertion by the Father in sympathy with the complete fulfilment of their common task.'[21] The struggle to express it is unending and to those standing outside the faith must sound contradictory in the extreme, but such apparently contradictory expressions arise from faith in the paradox of the incarnation and the inevitable impulse to set forth that faith. As H.E.W. Turner emphasized: 'In any approach to the doctrine of the Atonement, the double solidarity of our Lord with God as well as with ourselves must be fully utilized.[22] It is a question of ensuring that a statement concerning the nature of the atonement meets the requirements of a full Chalcedonian Christology.

I must add a comment from the pastoral side of Christian existence which occurred to me upon hearing Jean Vanier speak of the very worst possible human experience known to the poor, the weak and the marginalized person – being utterly without a sense of trust in anyone, human or divine. Does not our faith in atonement as presupposed by the incarnate life imply that somehow Christ shares even so desolate an experience as the absence of trust?

We should remember also that the cry of dereliction was never received by the church either in isolation or as the last word from the cross. On the other side of desolation was that other and final word: 'Father, into thy hands I commend my spirit.' (Luke 23:46)[23] – a word of unbelievable trust in God's way with the world to which even the most desperate person may be found to cling as by a miracle.

Campbell's preoccupation with the filial trust so thoroughly evident in Jesus Christ seems to have led him too readily to assume that an expression of complete forsakenness would necessarily mean a denial of trust in an ultimate, final and irretrievable sense. Further, his recoil from unfortunate images traditionally associated with the cry of desolation may have prevented Campbell from appreciating any revision of its meaning short of the reversal he proposed. Finally, there may be clues to gather from the character of Campbell's own Christian experience. His personal story was one of quiet flowering out of faith in a home where his father (who had to play the role of mother as well) related to him with constantly loving trust. Whatever turmoil of spirit Campbell may have known by virtue of his own frailty, whatever awareness he had of the bad news of life before he sensed the good news of the gospel, it seems not to have breached the canopy of trust under which he dwelt from the first. By whatever miracle he was nevertheless enabled to be a pastor who could get next to others in their deepest spiritual anxieties, it seems that in theological formulation he occasionally allowed the impression that Christ remains at a little distance from the place where he wills to be, namely and always, in the actual space where people are.

XII

CHRIST'S CONFESSION AND REPENTANCE
INSIGHTS WITH STAYING POWER

One of John McLeod Campbell's distinctive contributions to a study of atonement was that the work of Christ included an offering to God from within humanity which may be described as confession and repentance for their sin. While some other elements of Campbell's doctrine have been heartily accepted, the notion of Christ's 'confession' has been only when clearly qualified, and that of his 'repentance' has often been rejected. Account, therefore, must be taken of these responses.

It is important at the outset to examine the degree to which Campbell, in describing the work of Christ, actually may or may not have depended upon the two terms in question. The crucial statements on this begin where Campbell recognized the difficulty of expressing Christ's approach to God on behalf of humanity in such a way as to fulfill those elements of truth which do belong to the traditional idea that satisfaction was due to God's justice. According to him, Jesus Christ met the divine wrath by 'according to it that which was due,'[1] namely, towards humanity a condemnation of sin and towards the creator God a perfect confession of human sin. But since Jesus himself had been utterly obedient to God, what was the *nature* of such a confession? Campbell replies that it was 'a perfect Amen in humanity to the judgment of God on the sin of man.'[2] Through his complete identification with the human race Christ thrust himself into the arena of human folly, realized the exceeding evil of alienation from God, and himself suffered its consequences as a witness to the righteousness of the divine judgement. This is what Campbell means by saying that Christ confessed human sin, and this way of expressing that confession, as a kind of witness to the terrible character of sin, many a reader would accept. Yet it is of this confession that Campbell further asserts: 'That response has all the elements of a perfect repentance in humanity for all the sin of man – a perfect sorrow – perfect contrition – all the elements of such a repentance . . . .excepting the personal consciousness of sin.'[3] Observe carefully that Campbell has not yet spoken of this action of Christ's as 'repentance.' He has only said that it has all the *elements* except one. And this something which is not repentance as such is deemed to be entirely sufficient to meet the situation. To be sure, Campbell proceeds to his well-known reference to Edwards' alternative – 'either an equivalent punishment or an equivalent sorrow and repentance.'[4] Edwards, for his part, had been thinking at the time not of Christ's offering but of what should happen to humanity. He knew, as Campbell knew, that men and women could not offer repentance. Therefore only the penal option remained for Edwards, while Campbell laid hold of Edwards' other phrase to describe the view he himself had long been cogitating. So Campbell does indeed take the further step of assuming that Christ by virtue of his identification with the whole race could 'experience in reference to their sin, and present to God on their behalf, an adequate sorrow and repentance.'[5] Nevertheless, in his very next discussion of what this repentance means, Campbell reverts to his earlier language. Once again he is speaking not of repentance as such but of the elements of repentance except guilt:

> Without the assumption of an imputation of our guilt, and in perfect harmony with the unbroken consciousness of personal separation from our sins, the Son of God, bearing us and our sins on His heart before the Father, must needs respond to the Father's judgment on our sins, with that confession of their evil and of the righteousness of the wrath of God against them, which were due, due in the truth of things, due on our behalf though we could not render it . . .[6]

Campbell no doubt thought of this as Christ's repentance, but he does not in this instance actually call it that. With the element of guilt being absent there seems to be some awkwardness in insisting that Christ's action be labelled 'repentance.'

The term 'confession' on the other hand is used more readily. Christ confesses the sins of humankind. It is constantly shown that in standing on God's side as it were in condemnation of their evil he did what no other person was able to do. He thus endured the suffering and death which stem from the divine judgement, and with this offering of himself God was well pleased. By virtue of Christ's representative character all people have an 'interest' in the fruit of his death, and by saying amen by faith to his condemnation of sin in the flesh they enter into their repentance and their deliverance. Beyond this point there is perhaps a measure of limitation in Campbell's manner of expression, for he seems to place more emphasis upon deliverance from the power of sin than upon forgiveness of the guilt of sin. However, Campbell intends no imbalance. In spite of a tendency here to deal more with sin's power than with its guilt he never forgets the latter. Christ's repentance for human guilt continues to be an essential element of Campbell's thought even though the term 'repentance' is used less frequently. Indeed, one reason for an impression to the contrary may be that repentance is often subsumed under the more general concept of confession. Christ's confession of human sin includes his repentance for it, which thus remains a central element in his work on behalf of humankind.

It is not at all surprising that Campbell's talk of Christ's repentance met at first with a mixture of puzzlement, incredulity and outright rejection. To the ordinary church member, employing the language of confession and repentance in the commonly accepted sense, such an idea would be quite foreign. Nor had biblical scholars normally detected images of Christ along these lines.

Serious minds, even among the unschooled, were bound to ask: 'How is it possible either psychologically or morally for one person to repent for another?' That one individual may be punished for another does seem possible to illustrate from a wide variety of experiences. For example, parents are held responsible by law and subject to penalty for their child's breach of a law. Again, a business person must answer along with a partner for the partner's mistakes. It is commonly acknowledged also that when through sympathetic identification, one person voluntarily undergoes the evil consequences due to another for wrong-doing, the action can possess power for good both for the guilty party and for others who may see or hear of it. It may have redemptive consequences, including even a measure of repentance in the guilty one. Yet this can hardly be called repentance in the volunteer unless perchance he or she feels guilty for something done or not done in relation to the other and repents of that, as when a mother feels some reponsibility for her son's destructive behaviour. In common usage then the idea of repentance is regularly regarded as having a direct reference to actual individual misconduct and guilt. If this be so, then it would hardly be possible to envision Christ as a repentant figure.

When simple considerations of this sort were taken up by theologians already fixed in a judicial view of atonement, Campbell met with outright opposition. How could anyone, while maintaining a difference between a sinless Christ and sinful humanity, conceive of him as coming into relation with sin without employing concepts of imputed guilt and substitutionary punishment? Campbell had accused them of promoting a 'legal fiction.' Surely in visualizing repentance by an innocent one Campbell had landed himself in a moral fiction even worse than a legal one. Those whose theology differed from Campbell's in a major way sometimes dismissed this repentance then in an atmosphere of ridicule. One theologian dubbed it 'the eccentricity of a devout author . . . very like an absurdity.'[7] Another (as late as the mid-twentieth century) gathered up all of Campbell's themes, including this one, as completely heretical, before which: 'The penal, the forensic, the judicial aspect of the great transaction was spirited away. It melted into the thinnest of thin air.'[8]

Campbell's difficulty in gaining acceptance for his ideas was underlined by his own anticipation of questions which he attempted to answer in advance as he wrote *The Nature of the Atonement*. In speaking of the difference in personal identity between the guilty and the righteous he had said:

> To one looking at the subject with a hasty superficial glance,
> this difference may seem to involve all the difficulties connected
> with imputation of guilt and substituted punishment. Yet . . .
> this adequate sorrow for the sin of man, and adequate con-
> fession of its evil implies no fiction – no imputation to the

sufferer of the guilt of the sin for which he suffers; but only that He has taken the nature, and become the brother of those whose sin He confesses before the Father, and that He feels concerning their sins what, as the holy one of God, and as perfectly loving God and man, He must feel.[9]

In other words, for Campbell the identification of Christ with humanity which renders him their representative does away with the problem of imputation, leaving open only the question as to which is more conceivable as a moral action satisfying to God – punishment or repentance? He argued for the latter. An offering of confession and repentance from within the human condition constitutes a truly personal and moral means of reconciliation as against the endurance of punishment in fulfilment of legal requirements.

Moreover, this action of Christ precludes the possibility that his repentance could be substitutionary in the traditional sense of the term. The first critic in print had made just that suggestion, bringing a rejoinder from Campbell that he had missed the point.[10] The idea of penal substitution means that Christ relieved others of the punishment which was their due by taking it on himself. The idea of Christ's representative repentance, on the other hand, is conceived to be exercised entirely with the prospective purpose that they shall themselves be brought to repentance. The one absolves people from punishment. The other involves them in repentance. This is a distinction which too few of Campbell's critics took into account. They created a false impression of his meaning by flatly saying that he had simply put a doctrine of vicarious repentance in place of vicarious punishment. Indeed, I believe that Campbell would not entertain the use of the designation 'vicarious repentance' if it appeared to bear the substitutionary ideas which had been affixed to the word vicarious.

It is highly important to observe that much of the argument for the negative has stemmed from a dissatisfaction with Campbell's terminology which is nevertheless accompanied by admissions that he was actually dealing with facts vital to an understanding of the atonement. It was said, for example, that the idea of a repentant Christ is 'the faulty expression of a great truth,'[11] that it was 'an objectionable name for the indubitable and essential facts.'[12] Even so enthusiastic an admirer of Campbell's doctrines as H.R. Mackintosh found his terminology at this point inadmissable, not having 'even a faint allusion' in the New Testament, yet agreed that Campbell's description of Christ's sympathetic iden-tification with humanity does refer to a dread reality which enabled him to make in our name a worthy acknowledgement both of our sin and of the holiness of God. Once we take this point of view there is not a Pauline phrase about Christ in our place that sounds too strong.'[13] These writers would seem also to be saying that words be used in accordance with their generally accepted meaning, and that analogies should not be stretched beyond the bounds of common experience. But this is precisely what cannot always be done when dealing with the facts of the revelation. The old phrases become invested with new meanings. There are no exact analogies to express, for example, the doctrines of the incarnation or the conception of God's nature as agape. Indeed there is no human experience completely analogous to the atoning work of Christ as such.

Account must be taken also of the long experience of the church in arriving at doctrinal statements as implied by the scriptures, even though not expressly stated therein. The doctrine of the trinity is a case in point, a doctrine which took many years to develop as an implication of the biblical witness. Another is the concept of 'satisfaction' itself which in one way or another most theologians include in their broad understanding of atonement.

It is just possible that Campbell's very devoutness, acknowledged even tangentially by some who dismissed him, impressed others as grounds for giving him a second and more sympathetic hearing. Something of this sort had happened after his deposition for heretical views of the *extent* of atonement. The church had subsequently eased the official wording of clergy subscription to the Westminster Confession. Perhaps similar factors operated with respect to his views on the *nature* of the atonement, disposing critics to listen more carefully to an odd notion, oddly put.

In the face of a reluctance to accept his thought that one person's repentance can possibly avail for others (which arises from limiting discussion to ordinary experience) Campbell had pleaded for a clearer response to the question: What does it mean for God to deal with people as sinners who must be brought to repentance? Could it just be that something unique in Christ's identification with us made him able to repent on our behalf? An affirmative reply to this question has worked its way into Christian thought and devotion with a strange persistence. In one of his sermons John Henry Newman speaks of Christ's passion as follows:

> He cries to his Father as if He were the criminal, not the victim, His agony takes the form of guilt and compunction; He is doing penance; He is making confession; He is exercising contrition with a reality and a virtue infinitely greater than that of all the saints and penitents together; for he is the one victim for us all, the sole satisfaction, the real penitent, all but the real sinner.[14]

Are these expressions best accounted for as due to homiletical enthusiasm, or would they represent the serious claim of Newman the theologian? The latter is more likely to be the case.

R.S. Franks refers to some German discussions on the possibility that Christ was so identified with humanity as to be able somehow to share their guilt and repent of their sin. In summing up his account of German Protestant theology of the nineteenth century, Franks remarks:

> The most difficult problem that emerges is that of Christ's

identification with us in the consciousness of guilt, which Schleier-macher and Ritschl deny, but the mediating and Erlangen theology affirm. This is a question still awaiting a complete theological solution. On the basis of the concrete conception of personality as the union of opposites, however, the advantage appears to lie with the latter group of theologians.[15]

It is significant that in 1918 so able a man as Franks was thus leaving the question of Christ's representative repentance an open one, although he did finally close it against Campbell in his own work on the atonement in 1934.[16] Meanwhile, Emil Brunner had been affirming that Christ must repent for us, since we find it utterly impossible ourselves to repent:

We only really repent when we know that we can never be penitent enough, that we do not feel the seriousness of the situation sufficiently to be penetrated with the intense earnestness which such repentance demands, when we realize that Christ must repent for us. If we could repent as we should no atonement would be needed, for then repentance would be atonement. Then the righteousness of God would have been satisfied. But this is precisely what we cannot do. We can only do this where we can 'be righteous', for to be 'righteous' and to repent mean the same thing. The point or 'place' at which this happens is Christ.[17]

Brunner's concluding comment is a statement of faith. Yet an enquiring mind persists in asking: 'How can any person be so connected with *all* other persons as to be in a position to act for them at any deep level of existence, of which repentance may be only one sample?' James Martineau, in reviewing Campbell's book in 1856 pointed directly to a difficulty in making the connection. 'We are firmly convinced,' he said, 'that the doctrine of *mediation*, – in the strict sense implying transactions with God on behalf of men, *as well as* in the opposite direction, – cannot be harmonized with the modern *individualism*.'[18] If persons are conceptualized as utterly discreet individuals then indeed there could be no adequate saving connection between Jesus the Christ and humanity.

This problem has accordingly led some theologians to search out a rationale more adequate to the situation. R.C. Moberly, for example, under the impulse of philosophical idealism, relied on a different conception of the nature of personality as his starting point. In the last analysis no individual has a separate existence but is part of all others. The true idea of personality, whether in God or humanity, is not therefore to be understood as exclusive but inclusive. Moberly believed that this fact both warranted and provided for a stronger conception of Christ's humanity whereby he could be looked upon as relating to the race not in a differentiating, but in a consummating manner. This then is the nature of his representative character. As inclusive humanity Christ is perfectly in accord with the divine righteousness and therefore perfectly penitent for human sin. Christ's atoning work is an action which in *his* doing of it *mankind* somehow shares the doing. When Moberly speaks of Christ's confession it is by way of saying that he 'confessed the sin of humanity by being the very manifestation of humanity.'[19]

Moberly's concept of an inclusive humanity is of course not subject to empirical proof, though to some people it may be an attractive one; yet by describing Christ's humanity as 'an inclusive pervasive Spirit' he was in danger of an error the very opposite of the individualism he sought to avoid. He was pressing the identity of Christ to humanity to the point where both his and our separate identities are blurred and the mediator- ship *between* ourselves and God could be lost to view.[20]

One should not fail to notice other probings on the question of how Christ may be conceived as connected with humanity in a manner suited to his representative action in reconciliation. H. Wheeler Robinson is remembered for his laying hold of the anthropological grounds, especially in biblical anthropology, for the notion of 'corporate personality' in which, by virtue of origin and blood ties, an individual may be regarded 'realistically' as representative of the whole people.[21] Robinson finds a theological application of this in the Pauline contrast whereby in Adam all are involved in sin whereas in Christ all are liberated. He traces this theme through the recapitulation doctrine of Irenaeus and on into Augustine's Christian anthropology. Yet he admits the difficulty of transforming these concepts meaningfully for an age characterized by individualism; and in any case fails to suggest how any one individual may be uniquely representative of the race, unless it be by virtue of perceived moral and personal excellence which makes one the represen- tative of all by *'instrinsic right.'* Thus he says 'Christ is my representative in "all I could never be", simply by being Himself.' But this sounds like a witness after the fact of Christian experience rather than a rationale which makes that representation possible.

Professor John Macquarrie opened up a more challenging possibility in an article published during the centennial year of Campbell's death (1972). He pointed to the manner in which modern theologians from Schleiermacher through Reinhold Niebuhr and beyond have identified and examined the corporate nature of sin. 'To be truly in the human condition . . . is inevitably to be involved in the moral ambiguities of that condition. Only a total drop-out from society could be immune from the contagion of corporate sin. But such total withdrawal is impossible.'[22] Macquarrie boldy concluded that simply by living in human society as a man Christ must be regarded as participating in some ways in that 'disorientation of society which is corporate sin,' acknowledging his share in it and feeling its terrible weight upon his spirit. In some such way Macquarrie envisioned Christ as in a position to repent, himself the 'focal turning-point for humanity as a whole, the point at which a new humanity centered in Jesus Christ came into being.'

This need not I believe imply individual sin amounting to wilful transgression on the part of one who in all things willed to do the will of

God, who in fact 'learned obedience' (Heb. 5:8), and in whom God was well pleased. Yet his very existence in the flesh would mean a willing submission to live in a corrupt world and be implicated in sin merely by participating in society. To be thus responsible would be a burden upon the man Jesus Christ beyond our imagination; yet at the same time he would know himself to be under the unconditional pardoning love of God and thus be the pioneer in whose repentance we participate by faith. His repentance enables ours.

This may be a line of thought for theology today if we are to take the paradoxical character of the incarnation seriously *vis-à-vis* Christ in relation to sin, and perhaps in the process free ourselves of yet one more vestige of the docetism which has always lurked within orthodoxy.[23] Campbell, however did not lay hold of this conceptual tool, though he might well have done so through a form of it in his friend F.D. Maurice's thought. Moreover, and more importantly, he seemed to feel no need to keep on asking the Nicodemus-type question: 'How can these things be?' He was more concerned to express *what* had happened as known in the experience of faith than to explain *how* it had happened. To Martineau's question as to the nature of personality (whether individualist or 'realist') as preventing an adequate rationale for connecting Christ with humanity, Campbell had responded by witness to the personal union between Christ and the believer described in the scriptures and known to faith. He could sense neither a loss of individuality, nor a being swallowed up by impersonality in St. Paul's phrase: 'I live, yet not I, but Christ lives in me.' (Gal. 2:3), or in the Fourth Gospel's witness: 'I am the vine you are the branches . . . without me you can do nothing.' (John 15:5) Campbell's 'Row Companions', especially Henry Dormey's writings, had long since helped to found him firmly in that sense of intimate personal union with Christ which determined his style as a theologian. Under the impress of the gospel of the incarnation, the Word made flesh, who had taken on our nature, he somehow knew that Christ had come into a real connection with us in our need for repentance. In Christ's representing humanity to God he carried the repentance meant to be ours and to which in faith we can be thankfully joined.[24]

On that first occasion of responding to criticism Campbell might just as readily have turned again to the theme of Christ's sacrifice to make his point. Many years later Vincent Taylor did just that for him. After a thorough study of the meaning of sacrifice in the New Testament, including the paradoxical figure of Christ as both priest and victim, Taylor concluded that the nature of sacrifice portrayed there allowed for its further description representatively as Christ's confession and repentance by doctrinal influence, though not of course as explicit New Testament teaching.[25] In defending Campbell's concept of Christ's repentance, he says: 'It is easy to reply that no one but the sinner can repent and say that Campbell replaced a legal by a moral fiction, but it is certain that such retorts do little justice to the subtlety and truth of his thoughts.[26]

For two decades prior to Taylor's work, J.H. Leckie of Edinburgh had not ceased to warn that the debate on the question of Christ's repentance too often hinged on externalities rather than on a real desire to seek out Campbell's meaning. He pictured Campbell as 'subject to the disabilities of a pioneer.'[27] Eugene Bewkes was pressing the same point, though changing the metaphor by saying that Campbell had poured new wine into old bottles;[28] and as late as the 1972 centennial of Campbell's death John Macquarrie was claiming that much could be gained by considering in depth all that is involved in the idea of a deep sorrow, repentance, contrition for the sin of mankind, the moral and spiritual expiation . . . a remarkably pregnant idea.'[29] So at least for some perceptive people the truths beneath Campbell's terminology have yet to be fully expounded.

It is not necessary to press for the inclusion of this or that phrase of Campbell's in definitive statements of Christian doctrine. It may be enough to recognize their helpfulness in the interpretation of doctrine for faithful Christian practice. Consider, for example, the route followed by a member of the American Pastoral Counselling movement, Don S. Browning, in his work on *Atonement and Psychotherapy*.[30]

Beginning from the standpoint of a revelational theology (as did Campbell), Browning recognized the deeply personal character of God's dealings with humanity as essentially loving, and found in Christ's identification with humanity a basis for faith that God is unconditionally *for* us, never flagging in redemptive and restorative activity in the midst of our life. He thus fashioned a model of pastoral counselling grounded in what he believed to be an 'ontological structure for acceptance'.[31] The very possibility of a pastor accepting a person as he or she *is* rests back upon a prior 'intuition' that *both* are accepted by, and dependent upon, a transcendent resource present in the counselling process; and thus by analogy the Christian therapist performs 'a Christological function, limited and ambiguous as it is'[32] which witnesses to and affirms the unambiguous manifestation of God's love in the world of human experience through the man Jesus Christ.

Though not, as I believe, situating Campbell properly in atonement theology, Browning does find in Campbell's priestly motif a means of conceptualizing what Christ accomplishes in and for humanity. Moreover, he leaves something to be desired when he describes Campbell's view of Christ's engagement as 'a perfect participation in and subsequent confession of the sins of man'; also that 'the ultimate end of this confession was to confess man's basic created status as a son of God.'[33] I question the use of the word 'subsequent' to describe what must surely be a simultaneous action, and assume that 'the ultimate end' relates more than only to 'status' under God. Christ's participation in our life constitutes the way in which we may participate in his life and thus be what we are meant to be under God. Yet the reader is properly drawn to Browning's desire to show how the pastor can help persons to the point of participating in that confession, to allow Christ's confession to be one's own and thus to know pardon in the face of guilt and experience freedom from bondage.

A Christian therapist is thus seen to have studied the dynamics of Christ's priestly work in atonement, and to have developed a high degree of skill in helping people to share in it. Our immediate interest lies in Browning's initial effort at mutual translation of language as between atonement and psychotherapy relying on the model of our relation to God in Christ as enunciated by Campbell. The hope lies in the possibility that others may develop this in a more complete way to advantage for pastoral practice.

As for apreciating the significance of Campbell's terminology for an understanding of Christian worship, considerably more has been achieved. The Apostle Paul himself was a forerunner in offering to the church at Rome (and through them to all others) an account of the risen and ascended Christ constantly interceding for us in a saving manner (Rom. 8:34) This included the knowledge that even when we do not ourselves know how to pray, Christ by the Spirit takes our inner groanings and fashions them into prayers acceptable to God (Rom. 8:26-27). Campbell, in harmony with St. Paul's even more inclusive awareness of what it means to be 'in Christ', probed the further thought that Christ so makes himself one with us in our inability to repent as to offer a confession and repentance which by the Spirit we are enabled to recognize, and participate in, as our own. So Campbell contemplated Christ's continuing threefold priestly activity of offering confession, repentance and intercession in us and for us by way of atonement – done once and for all, and yet paradoxically still doing so for our sakes.

In his book *Christ the Bread of Life* (1851), written prior to his major volume on the atonement, Campbell had already suggested the bearing of these thoughts upon worship in general and the eucharist in particular. In his view worship is grounded in the vicarious humanity of Jesus Christ who bears us up with himself in *his* response to God (as we are meant to respond), so that we may share by the Spirit in the mind of the incarnate Son towards his God as our God. To know this, as Professor James Torrance so aptly says, is to regard worship not as something *we* do (often out of a sense of duty and to the point of weariness) but as the privilege of 'participating, in union with Christ, in what *he* has done for us once and for all in his life and death on the Cross, and in what *he* is continuing to do for us in the presence of the Father, and in *his* mission to the world'.[34] Yes, and I would add that insofar as his mission in the world may be conceived as having institutional and social purposes of his choosing, these also are shared in, not by our dutifully trudging towards uncertain ends, but in thankful awareness of ultimate providential outcomes through his fulfilling love. Thus all forms of worship and service, while truly ours, belong in the first instance to the grace whereby, through his humanity, Christ presents us together with himself to the God of our salvation.

XIII

APPRECIATION VIA THE CLASSIFICATION PUZZLE

It has been customary for theologians to speak of various systematic statements on the atonement as theories of the atonement, classifying them according to their similarities and differences. The word 'theory' is an unfortunate one which implies both too much and too little. In common parlance it tends to stand over against practice as an hypothesis which requires proof by experience, whereas many (if not most) so-called theories of atonement are systematic elucidations of the fact and experience of atonement. Put in another way, a theory is often set forth as a possible explanation of a phenomenon which otherwise remains a mystery whereas statements on atonement must acknowledge a mystery which can never be explained but only expressed. This is always so with the paradoxes of grace at the centre of the Christian faith. The term 'theory' seems also to imply a more purely conceptual aim whereas, as Campbell so pointedly remarks, the primary question is not What am I meant to think, or believe, regarding the nature of the atonement, but 'What am I called to be?'

At best then, we are dealing with views as perspectives, ways of expressing the meaning of, and responding to, Christian atonement. Even then, in the effort to classify these views we encounter difficulties – first as to the number of categories to employ. Some interpreters seem driven to accept divisions and subdivisions numerous enough to distinguish major authors from one another.[1] This procedure risks the danger of so emphasizing the unique feature of each person's view as to neglect those points held in common with others. Differences can thus be falsely exaggerated. Other scholars present a much simpler divison.[2] They are open to the opposite danger that, in the interests of demonstrating common tendencies, views are brought together in a somewhat forced fashion. In this way the variant elements of a given writer's position may be given less than rightful prominence.

Another difficulty in classification arises from the fact that so many analogies have been employed as suitable vehicles for expressing the meaning of atonement. They arise sometimes out of deeply private experience, sometimes from an historic cultural base. Figures such as the battlefield, the temple sacrifice, the law-court and the market-place come readily to mind. Each expresses a particular aspect of the atonement better than the others do. The very differences in the figures used tend to highlight points of contrast. The contrast can be overdone, however, for it is also true that into each analogical mould there has been poured as it were the whole content of a living and valid experience of the divine redemption. When therefore a theologian is charged with weakness at this or that point of a chosen analogy he or she may express surprise, pointing to some feature of the system claimed as already to have taken that criticism into account. The fact remains, however, that no one analogy possesses the magic quality of satisfying all sides of the question sufficiently to supplant the others.

What then shall be said in the face of so many differing views of the atonement, and the difficulty even of bringing them under some agreed scheme of classification?

Some thinkers have felt it best to give up the search for any adequate statement of atonement and settle for a simple witness to the *fact* of the atonement. Coleridge was one who felt that one cannot do better than to accept the revealed fact of God's redemptive act, including the incarnation of Christ to live a human life, and his death which conquered death for all who receive Christ. 'More than this,' he said, 'the mode, the possibility, we are not competent to know. It is a mystery by the necessity of the subject.'[3] Butler before him was generally sceptical of stating an adequate rationale: 'It is our wisdom,' he wrote, 'thankfully to accept the benefit by performing the conditions upon which it is offered on our part, without disputing how it was produced on His.'[4] For the most part, however, theologians continue trying for a meaningful statement of the atonement, with a growing willingness to appreciate the values which belong to any view which appears to have proceeded from honest meditation upon the life, death and resurrection of Jesus Christ. By the mid-twentieth century Leonard Hodgson spoke for many others when he claimed that the many images of the atonement should be considered not as rivals but as each contributing to an understanding of the whole. Even notions apparently inconsistent with one another can point to the same incarnate one, just as such various parables of Jesus all point to the one Kingdom of God.[5] This is not to suggest that the modern mood is an eclectic one whereby all threads of atonement thinking are drawn together. It would be impossible to do this without either relying on one of the alternatives as an exclusive organizing centre, or engaging in a process of mutual cancellations which sacrifices the legitimate values of each. The comparatively recent concern for wholeness of interpretation is better described as one of mutual witness, each person desiring to say to others something about the atonement of Christ, while also being willing in turn to listen receptively. This combination is wonderfully exhibited by Vincent Taylor. He spent twenty years searching out the possibility of expressing the meaning of Christ's atonement in terms of sacrifice. He believed in the advantages of the sacrificial mould. Yet he was prepared to admit the fragile character of any and every mould.[6] This approach does not mean intellectual compromise. Individual differences have been sharp. People have spoken and responded through clearly presented views. But their readiness to listen to each other has brought about an inward and spiritual coalescence.

Now this was precisely the attitude of mind maintained by Campbell long ago, though there were few like him at the time. He tried constantly to take account of an opponent's thought. He thankfully acknowledged taking over some of their ideas. Often he would give credit to others for implicitly holding views which he merely tried to make explicit. There is therefore an unusual quality of wholeness in the results at which Campbell arrived. This is particularly evident in his conceptual method. He reckoned both 'manward' and 'Godward' sides of the atonement as belonging to a complete understanding of the subject. Likewise he placed the prospective aspect of Christ's work alongside the retrospective as reflecting something of the nature of the atonement. Campbell's sense of continuity between the life and the death of Christ also makes for largeness of view, though his inclusion of the resurrection is less firmly worked out.[7] Finally, Campbell's spirit of inclusiveness is demonstrated by his bringing the atonement into relation with the doctrine of the incarnation on the one hand and justification on the other.

Campbell has little or nothing to contribute to the revival in our times of interest in the ancient thought of Christ as winning a victory over the Devil and the demonic powers. British and American theologians are familiar with Gustav Aulen's book *Christus Victor* in which he claims that this notion of Christ's victorious deliverance is the 'classic' view of Christ's work. He believes that the theme of Christ as Victor has often indeed been neglected, but that it has come forward again and again in the great climactic periods of Church history. Many theologians generally have appreciated the element of truth for which this book stands. Nathaniel Micklem[8] and Sydney Cave,[9] for example, have taken time to underline its importance, but none have adopted Aulen's position as he himself might wish. For the most part in Britain and in the English-speaking world generally it can only be said that this theme continues to have a meaningful place in the rituals of worship, especially public, with occasional illustrative use in preaching. It has no commanding place in atonement theory. That is where the matter stood with Campbell. He was not averse to the language traditionally employed to describe Christ's victory over the Satanic powers; for this appears often in his sermons and even occasionally in *The Nature of the Atonement*.[10] But he made no contribution to this view as such.

It may be observed that, while the orthodox statement of the atonement for a thousand years involved some kind of dealings with the Devil, the underlying thought of the early fathers was often moral and mystical. Witness the recapitulation doctrine of Irenaeus. His emphasis rested on the entry of the divine life into the human order to renew it, and on the mystical union which men and women have with Christ in the latter's obedience towards God and consequent victory over evil powers. This is not to be confused with that mysticism in which the human soul is regarded as striving to achieve the beatific vision, an approach which puts a premium on human effort and virtually denies the role of the Mediator. It is rather the New Testament idea of faith-union with Christ made possible through the incarnation. I have already suggested that a number of elements in Campbell's thought tend to place him alongside the Greek fathers – his stress on the incarnation as the presupposition of the atonement, his thought of the life of Christ shedding light on the nature of atonement and his emphasis on faith-union with Christ whereby he imparts his life to humanity. Dr. John Dickie remarks that Campbell's thought 'leads up to and merges in the mystical one, and no form of the mystical theory is likely to commend itself to present day believing theology unless it has room for Dr. Campbell's broad general principles and findings.[11] It is apparently no accident then that persons of a mystical strain, such as John Caird and B.F. Westcott, found in Campbell a kindred spirit.[12] Yet in the final analysis (for them and for him) the 'mystical union' label would be insufficiently descriptive.

Another understanding of the atonement with which Campbell had much in common is the sacrificial view. This approach has been brought into renewed prominence in the twentieth century by both Old and New Testament scholars. They have dispelled the notion that sacrificial offerings were always attempts motivated by fear to offset possible ill deserts from an angry god. Sacrifice is more characteristically a means of communion whereby the worshipper identifies the self with an offering in the belief of gaining acceptance through it. Sacrifice is thus a means to life. To the first Christians the idea of sacrifice would probably commend itself beyond all others as fitted to set forth the meaning of Christ's death. A study of the passion sayings suggests that Jesus himself prepared the disciples for such thoughts; and the Epistle to the Hebrews is founded on the conviction that Christ fulfilled the whole sacrificial system.

In Campbell's writing this sacrificial theme is evident at several points. The scripture text with which he opens his exposition is taken from a sacrificial setting. He is constantly aware of Christ's dual role as both victim and priest. Moreover, as many have acknowledged, Campbell understood the significance of a representative offering. Yet in spite of his inclusion of sacrificial ideas it would be inaccurate to place Campbell's total view under a sacrificial label.

There are several New Testament admonitions to tease one into thinking of Christ primarily as a moral example, in following whom one finds salvation. We are to do as he did in the footwashing of his disciples (John 13:15); 'Christ also suffered for you, leaving you an example, that you should follow in his steps (I Peter 2:21); you are to be 'imitators of God.' (Eph. 5:1). Campbell recognized the truth involved here, but he believed it to be the true wisdom of the gospel to avoid any suggestion of independence on the part of the believer in the imitation of Christ. As an elder brother Christ pioneered a filial relationship with God in humanity as a pattern for us and as that to which we are invited to join ourselves.

We may be caught up to participate in his life as vines to branches without whom we wither (John 15:1-6). So Campbell could not go the route of thinking that salvation comes by an external imitation of the man called Christ.[13]

I have shown also that Campbell cannot correctly be classified as a member of the 'moral influence' school associated with the name of Abelard. Yet that judgement was qualified by saying that Campbell did appreciate the truth for which Abelard contended, and that his own treatment of the atonement gave due place to the power of divine love to melt human hearts and draw them to God. Indeed, Campbell's language has continued to lead some interpreters mistakenly to place him among Abelard's followers, so reads A.H. Strong in the nineteenth century, and F.L. Paton in the twentieth.[14] A.B.D. Alexander veers in this direction when he says that in Campbell's thought 'the sacrifice of Christ effects salvation by its moral power over men in example and inspiration.'[15] And Hastings Rashdall, an avowed twentieth century Abelardian, gives his reader the distinct impression that what is best in Campbell belongs to this tradition.[16] But all this, it must be repeated, is quite misleading. Campbell's sympathy with the partial truths of the moral influence theory gives no ground for attaching his name to the school itself. For Campbell, what God did in Christ was not only more than we could do for ourselves but was also independent of our changing responses. It was in reality a work done by God objectively for us and paradoxically achieved through God's Son in humanity though the issue from atonement may be subjectively felt. In one of his letters Campbell comments on the fluidity which exists between the objective and the subjective elements: 'In the light of the nature of the atonement the transition from objective to subjective religion, and back from subjective to objective, is necessary and constant.'[17] It may be in order to consider whether Campbell in some degree compromises the truly objective character of the atonement. But certainly, his is not a subjective view, even though he takes its values into account.

While there is an inclusiveness in Campbell's treatment of the atonement, it may still be rightly claimed that he bears affinities to the typically Western type of thought, though with a distinct difference. The central question around which his discussion turns is how, while taking full account of the divine condemnation of human sin, men and women can be reconciled to God. True, Campbell emphasizes a number of elements neglected by traditional views. He sets forth the essential character of God in different terms. He sees that the life of Christ, as well as his death, sheds lights on the meaning of the atonement; and Christ is regarded as representative humanity rather than as a substituted individual. Moreover, the subjective features of the whole process are brought into firmer association with an admittedly prior objective fact. But beneath all these differences lies the general concept of satisfaction rendered to God the Father by the Son as the means of our redemption.

C.E. Prichard, whose review of *The Nature of the Atonement* Campbell felt was the first to give a clear estimate of his meaning, wrote appreciatively about the several major changes in perspective which Campbell had brought to the subject, yet felt forced to conclude that it would be startling to find that we were called upon to suppose that the Church had been essentially in error on so cardinal a point as the ground of our acceptance with God in Christ.[18]

Campbell's struggle was to show the truly personal and moral lines upon which any idea of satisfaction should be conceived. His position has sometimes been called a theory of ethical (or moral) satisfaction in contradistinction to that of penal satisfaction.[19] If, however, the notion of satisfaction to God is to be taken up at all, I believe a more inclusive personal phraseology should be employed in order to reflect the scriptural declaration as to the 'son' in whom God is well pleased (Mk. 9:11 *et al*). A deeply personal parental satisfaction over a filial offering includes the highest possible ethical satisfaction and more.

Campbell's fully developed view of atonement led him to describe Christ's filial offering as a confession of, and repentance for, human sin, together with intercession from within humanity for their complete restoration. Hence the frequent classification of his view as a theory of vicarious repentance.[20] Yet to stress only the central element of a trilogy drawn together naturally within Campbell's loftiest notion of Christ's filial offering may itself be somewhat limiting as to the rightness of Campbell's way of putting the case. Moreover, the word vicarious itself needs to be used with care by virtue of its long association with substitutionary ideas. Even the adjective 'representative' which seems so fitting a designation of Christ's relation to us is open to faulty understanding if taken only in the common parlance as one who represents people in their absence, or in the concise Oxford Dictionary usage: 'fill the place of, be substitute or deputy for.' Campbell and others with him are endeavouring to express a more intimate relation than that may suggest. Even the word 'identification' which Campbell sometimes uses, and which Professor John McIntyre employs so helpfully in exploring the doctrine of the divine love,[21] has its problems in the hands of a purist mentality bent on protecting the separate identities of God and humanity. This is why these men rely ultimately on personal and biblical language which come across as expressing meanings not open to a more precise and rigorous terminology. Be that as it may, the terms 'identification', 'representative' and 'vicarious' have all been helpfully descriptive of Campbell's doctrine of Christ's work.

All this has a bearing upon the fact that beneath Campbell's concern for conceptual wholeness in responding to the theological tradition to which he belonged lies the conditioning of his home and pastorate towards a devotional approach to any Christian doctrine. No one who reads *The Nature of the Atonement* can fail to recognize its quality of worshipful witness to the reconciling and liberating power of Christ as experienced by himself and perceived in others. It seemed therefore natural for him to rely most on portions of the Bible wherein the intimacy between Christ and believers is most clearly expressed: notably the Fourth Gospel (including the prayer life of Jesus), the dual images of priest and victim in the Letter to the Hebrews, and St. Paul's dwelling on what it means to be 'in Christ.' All this yielded a multiplicity of thoughts and images which make it so difficult acceptably to classify Campbell's view. Thomas Hughes, for example, who places him in the 'Ethical Satisfaction' chapter might also have included him under the heading 'Mystical Theories' alongside his choice of Caird and Westcott who, as I have shown, owed much to Campbell.[22]

No doubt many other authors on the atonement are likewise difficult to classify in the traditional manner. It may be significant in this regard that F.W. Dillistone, in *The Christian Understanding of Atonement* (the most complete English-language book on the subject to have been circulated over the last couple of decades), abandons the older style of classification. Even the word 'atonement' as an overall caption is used only after recognizing its somewhat dated character, its double meaning primarily as the 'at-one-ment' which belongs to reconciliation, and secondarily relating to the notion of a costly payment relating to the Cross; and only after claiming that it can be thought to bring under its umbrella the most characteristic human disability of our times: alienation in all its many facets. Dillistone (who happens to have a profound appreciation for Campbell's way of putting things) deals with Christian atonement under four analogies and four parables in which Campbell properly relates somewhat to a few and is appreciated as pivotal only in the third parable, namely, 'the All-inclusive Forgiveness.' Dillistone's work is also a healthy reminder that no matter how inclusive a thinker may be in expressing the meaning of atonement, he or she cannot approximate the inclusiveness which proceeds from Christ's work. Nor is it possible, even desirable, to escape the marks of one's own time and place. This kind of perspective is required if we are to assess Campbell rightly, and to accept the fact that others would take the contemplation of the atonement beyond his immediate sphere. They would move, for example, beyond an individualistic age to ask about the implications of Christ's work for institutional and social salvation; and in our time also ask about the meaning of atonement from the particular standpoint of women's experience.

Yet, of John McLeod Campbell it remains true as a person of his time, and as reflected upon by someone many generations thereafter: 'With the patience of a man of science, and the fervour of a saint, he thought and lived and prayed his way to the heart of the atonement, and he speaks as one who stands at the centre.'[24]

A REFLECTION

Language twists and turns in a change of metaphor to tell a person's story. The image of an enriched soil gives place to one of sowing and reaping.

Of the little parish church where John McLeod Campbell began his work, only a partial arch today remains. In the present larger sanctuary a memorial window depicts the Psalmist's account of those who go out to plant in the rough hard places, yet one day return rejoicing in the bounty of their yield.

It seemed much like that for Campbell in his closing years at Rosneath. Gazing across the waters of the Gareloch towards the towns he had once served, and contemplating events throughout the land he loved, he would not only recall the time of sowing in painful isolation, but also savour the first fruits of his labours, and sense the promise of a fuller harvest which others in due season would gather for their good.

While so many of Campbell's thoughts and feelings have become part of our heritage, his name is little known today. He would be satisfied to have it so, for it was his desire in his own time and place only to explore the meaning of God's humanity in Jesus Christ – suffering and triumphant for all – and to share the Apostolic experience of being found in him. Ours can be the same desire in a different day.

NOTES

CHAPTER ONE

1. Testimonials run through most standard Scottish church histories such as *The Church in Late Victorian Scotland 1874-1911* by Andrew L. Drummond and James Bulloch, (Edinburgh), St. Andrew Press, 1978. Yet one can find them further afield. See, for example, Otto Pfleiderer's late 19th century reference to Thomas Erskine and to Campbell as having made 'the best contribution to dogmatics in the century' (*The Development of Theology in Germany Since Kant and its progress in Great Britain Since 1825*, p. 382); also Bernard M.G. Reardon as a twentieth century representative looking back to the nineteenth: 'In Scotland the century was largely one of movement away from the more or less strict Calvinism of the past, a movement in which the most prominent figure was John McLeod Campbell' (*From Coleridge to Gore: A Century of Religious Thought in Britain*, p. 20). Elsewhere in the same work Reardon speaks of Campbell as a man in Scottish theology which evokes the memory of a cause célèbre of a kind unparalleled in England, at least in modern times.
2. See *Prophet of Penitence: Our Contemporary Ancestor*, a lecture by Dr. John McIntyre published by St. Andrew Press, Edinburgh, 1972.
3. Professor James Torrance, in a paper read to the Edinburgh Theological Club, New College Edinburgh, Feb. 6, 1972 and published that same month in the Scottish Journal of Theology. Prof. Torrance counts Campbell's book on *The Nature of the Atonement* (1856) as one of the classics alongside that of Athanasius (*De Incarnatione*) and St. Anselm (*Cur Deus Homo*).
4. My first effort to research and write on the subject took the form of a graduate dissertation entitled *The Place of John McLeod Campbell in British Thought Concerning the Atonement*, Emmanuel College, Victoria University, Toronto, Canada, 1961.
5. John McLeod Campbell, *Reminiscences and Reflections*, ed. by his son Donald Campbell, London, Macmillan and Co., 1873, p. 7 (here called *Reminiscences*).
6. R.B. Lusk, ed. *A Full Report of the Proceedings in the General Assembly of the Church of Scotland, in the Case of the Reverend John McLeod Campbell*, Greenock: Lusk, 1831, p. 177 (here called *Proceedings III*).
7. In the light of the changing roles of women and men in our time many people employ an inclusive language in general speech, and insofar as possible in theological language. Quotations of course must follow the usage of a given author; so also in the expression of certain ideas fundamental to the author.
8. Shairp, John C., *Portraits of Friends*, Boston, Houghton Mifflin and Co., 1889, p. 169: cf. Donald Campbell, ed. *Memorials of John McLeod Campbell*, D.D., Vol. II, p.344 (here called *Memorials*).

9. Norman McLeod, ed., *Good Words, 1872*, London, Strahan and Co., p. 353.
10. Campbell, *Memorials*, Vol. I, p. 313.
11. *Ibid.*, Vol. II, pp. 1-2.
12. *Ibid.*, Vol. I, pp. 239 and 269.
13. A competent student of Campbell's theological methodology, Donald L. Faris, has done more than others to demonstrate the place of the 'Row Companions' as a formative element in Campbell's life and work. See his doctoral thesis *The Nature of Theological Inquiry* . . . undertaken through Edinburgh University, 1967.
14. The *Spectator*, Vol. 42, No. 2127, p. 420 – book review on *THE COMMUNION*, author not given, yet naming Campbell as 'about the most completely and profoundly Protestant of our living theologians.'
15. T.F. Torrance, *Theology in Reconciliation*, (London) Geoffrey Chapman, 1975.
16. John T. McNeill, *The History and Character of Calvinism*, New York, Oxford University Press, 1954, p. 398.
17. Philip Schaff, *The Creeds of Christendom*, Vol. III, 4th ed. New York, Harper and Bros., 1905, p. 676.
18. Campbell, *Reminiscences*, p. 54.
19. *Ibid.*, p. 219.
20. See, for example, Campbell, *Sermons*, Vol. I, pp. 442-3.
21. Campbell, *Memorials*, Vol. II, p. 11.
22. Campbell, *Reminiscences*, p. 126; and *Memorials*, Vol. II, p. 293.
23. See Campbell, *Reminiscences*, p. 115.

CHAPTER TWO

1. Westminster Confession VI, 2 and 4. See Philip Schaff, *Creeds of Christendom*, 4th ed., New York, Harper and Bros., Vol. III, p. 615.
2. Donald J.M. Corbett, focusing on the moral aspect of the atonement, effectively describes the tensions between the gospel and legal strains throughout the history of Scottish theology, and deals sympathetically with Campbell as part of that story.
3. Campbell, *Memorials*, Vol. I, p. 20.
4. From Professor Edgar Dickie's Introduction to the 1959 edition of Campbell, *The Nature of the Atonement*, p. XV.
5. J.M. Campbell, *Sermons and Lectures*, 2 Vols., Greenock, R.B. Lusk, 3rd ed., 1832. After criticism had brought Campbell to some notice, arrangements were made to record a number of his sermons by shorthand for publication. He was aware by this time that everything that could be said on a few central issues must be said. Hence there is much repetition, along with a certain controversial tone which he himself mentioned with regret in later years (*Memorials*, Vol. II, p. 166). They also exhibit less palatable elements of theology which he was later to abandon. Witness the revisions appearing in some of these sermons published under the title *Responsibility For the Gift of Eternal Life*, through Macmillan and Co., 1873. Our references are confined to the early sermons as delivered.
6. Westminster Confession XVIII, 2. See Philip Schaff, *op. cit.* p. 638.

7. Westminster Confession XVIII, 3. See Philip Schaff, *ibid.*

8. Campbell, *Reminiscences*, p. 17.

9. Campbell, *Sermons*, Vol. I, p. 285.

10. Campbell, *Reminiscences*, p. 176.

11. Campbell, *Sermons*, Vol. I, p. 128.

12. *Ibid.*, p. 331.

13. *Ibid.*, p. 59.

14. *Ibid.*, p. 45.

15. Campbell, *Reminiscences*, p. 19.

16. *Ibid.*, p. 154.

17. Campbell, *Sermons*, Vol. II, pp. 189-90.

18. *Ibid.*, p. 25.

19. *Ibid.*, Vol. I, p. 189.

20. Campbell, *Memorials*, Vol. I, p. 65.

21. Campbell, *Sermons*, Vol. I, p. 320.

22. *Ibid.*, p. 332.

23. In sermon number XVIII, Vol. I, Campbell traces his theological position of the time more fully, using Acts 20:27 as his text: 'For I have not shunned to declare unto you all the counsel of God.'

CHAPTER THREE

1. See Hector Macpherson, *The Intellectual Development of Scotland*, London, Hodder and Stoughton, 1911, p. 25.

2. William Dunlop, *The Uses of Creeds and Confessions*, Edinburgh, James Watson, 2 Vols., 1719-22.

3. A.J. Campbell, *Two Centuries of the Church of Scotland, 1707-1927*, Paisley, Gardner, 1930, p. 36.

4. A.J. Campbell, *Two Centuries of the Church of Scotland*, p. 163. Cited from Inglis, *Vindication of Religious Establishments*, p. 232.

5. Geddes MacGregor, 'The Row Heresy', *The Harvard Theological Review* XLIII, No. 4, p. 284. Cf, Sir William Hamilton's sneering comment in 1836: 'Now for nearly two centuries *Scotland* compared with other countries may be broadly said to have been *without a theology*,' as reported by Donald Macmillan, *The Life of Robert Flint*, London, Hodder and Stoughton, 1914, p. 62.

6. Campbell, *Memorials*, Vol. I, p. 43.

7. Drummond, Andrew L. and Bulloch, James, *op. cit.* p. 17-18.

8. Campbell, *Memorials*, Vol. I, p. 55.

9. Lusk, *Proceedings I*, p. vi.

10. *Ibid.*, p. 1.

11. The careful student of these years will find many attacks on Campbell in periodicals of the time, some of which were circulated also as pamphlets now held by the library at New College, Edinburgh. They include: Buchanan of North Leith (letter to Mr. Erskine); Barr of Glasgow (a sermon on *Peace in Believing*); Hendry of Ardrossan (*Serious Enquiry*); Brotherston of Allen (*Essay on Saving*); Hamilton of Strathblane (Remarks on Certain Opinions Recently Propagated, Respecting Universal Redemption) etc. Perhaps the most closely reasoned and widely circulated by Dr. Robert Burns of Paisley: *The Gairloch Heresy Tried in a Letter to the Rev. John M.*

Campbell, of Row, and a Sermon Presented at Helensburg (Paisley), Alex Gardner 1830. There were also some written in defence of Campbell, notably two responses to Hamilton and Burns, anonymously signed: 'A Lay Member of the Church of Scotland.' This turned out to be Campbell's legal counsel at the trial to follow, a certain Thomas Carlyle. He claimed support for Campbell in point by point consideration of earlier confessions of reformed faith and by quotes from Luther and Calvin.

12. Possible levels of censure in order of seriousness were as follows: Admonition, Rebuke, Suspension, Deposition, Excommunication. A last minute move by some of the Moderates to amend in favour of suspension was lost.

13. C.L. Warr, *Scottish Sermons and Addresses*, London, Hodder and Stoughton, 1930, p. 69.

14. Lusk, *Proceedings I*, p. xxix.

15. G.D. Henderson, *The Church of Scotland: A Short History*, Edinburgh, Church of Scotland Youth Committee, 1939, p. 119.

16. J.H. Leckie, *The Expository Times*, Vol. XL, No. 5, p. 199.

17. H.F. Henderson, *The Religious Controversies of Scotland*, (Edinburgh), T. & T. Clark, 1905, p. 148.

18. The impression is a persistent one that Campbell may be called a 'disciple' of Edward Irving, witness H.C. Whitely in *Blinded Eagle*, London, S.C.M. Press, 1955, p. 25. Campbell was indeed a beloved friend. He admired Irving's spirit, agreed with some of his ideas, allowed him to occupy the Row pulpit occasionally; but he never did join the group and distinctly differed from his friend whom at several points he considered extreme and even bordering on the fanatical. Cf. R.H. Story, *Memoir of the Life of the Reverend Robert Story*, London, Macmillan and Co., 1862, p. 138.

19. *Doctrinal Attitudes in the Church of Scotland in the Pre-Disruption Era*, Journal of Religious History, Vol. 8, 1974 (Australia).

20. *Presbyterian Review*, Vol. I, p. 127.

21. See also Geddes MacGregor, 'The Row Heresy', *The Harvard Theological Review*, XLIII, No. 4, p. 291. The records of the trial reveal a sensitivity to the importance of the Westminster Confession as a symbol of the Scottish Establishment. Cf. Lusk, *Proceedings III*, p. 85.

22. Reardon, *From Coleridge to Gore: A Century of Religious Thought in Britain*, London, Longman, 1971. p. 405.

23. Campbell, *Reminiscences*, p. 32.

24. Lusk, *Proceedings I*, p. 94.

25. Robert Story, *Memoir of the Life of the Reverend Robert Story*, London, Macmillan, 1862, p. 190.

26. Lusk, *Proceedings III*, p. 125. See further W.M. Hetherington, *History of the Church of Scotland*, 3rd American, from 3rd Edinburgh edition, New York, Robert Carter, 1844, pp. 344-5.

27. Campbell, *Memorials*, Vol. II, pp. 34-5.

CHAPTER FOUR

1. Lusk, *Proceeding I*, p. 16. Cf. Campbell's very similar statement in final defence before the General Assembly, *Proceedings III*, p. 50. Thoughts expressed in a lower court are often found in the proceedings of a higher

court. There was indeed a great deal of repetition by all the chief speakers.

2. Lusk, *Proceedings I*, p. 19.
3. Lusk, *Proceedings I*, p. 20. Cf. Campbell's statement at the General Assembly: 'Does the *world* then mean election? . . . If the use of any word be more fixed than another, it is the word 'world'; and once admit that it means all mankind, and this will decide the question as to whether Christ did or did not die for all men.' *Proceedings III*, p. 53.
4. *Ibid.*
5. Lusk, *Proceedings I*, p. 24.
6. *Ibid.*, p.25.
7. Lusk, *Proceedings II*, pp. 188-9.
8. *Ibid.*, p. 185.
9. Henderson, *The Religious Controversies in Scotland*, pp. 168-9.
10. Lusk, *Proceedings I*, xxiii.
11. *Ibid.*, xxiv.
12. *Ibid.*, xxix.
13. Lusk, *Proceedings II*, p. 249.
14. *Ibid.*, pp. 240-1.
15. *Ibid.*, p. 251.
16. *Ibid.*, pp. 204-206. Cf. John A. McHugh and Charles J. Callan, *Catechism of the Council of Trent for Parish Priests*, New York, Joseph P. Wagner Inc., Ninth Printing, 1945, p. 57.
17. Lusk, *Proceedings II*, pp. 205-206. Cf. John A. McHugh and Charles J. Callan, *Catechism of the Council of Trent for Parish Priests*, New York, Joseph P. Wagner Inc., Ninth Printing, 1945, p. 57.
18. *Ibid.*, p. 208. This Confession actually dates from 1558.
19. Lusk, *Proceedings II*, p. 210. Cf. Philip Schaff, *The Creeds of Christendom*, 4th ed., New York, Harper and Bros., 1905, Vol. II, p. 9.
20. *Ibid.*, p. 211.
21. Lusk, *Proceedings I*, p. 55. Cf. W.M. Hetherington, *History of the Westminster Assembly of Divines*, New York, Mark H. Newman, 1843, p. 84.
22. Lusk, *Proceedings I*, p. 56. Our source for the Anglican Articles is William Wilson, *The XXXIX Articles of the Church of England*, Oxford, J. Abrams, 1840. Capitalization does not occur here as in Campbell's quotations.
23. *Ibid.* Underlining Campbell's. Cf. Schaff, *Creeds of Christendom*, Vol. III, p. 518.
24. *Ibid., p. 57. Cf. Wilson, op. cit.*, pp. 119ff.
25. Westminster Confession, Chapter III, section 6. Philip Schaff, *op. cit.*, pp. 609-610.
26. Lusk, *Proceedings III*, p. 48.
27. Alex. F. Mitchell and John Struthers, (eds.) *Minutes of the Assembly of the Westminster Session of Divines*, Edinburgh and London, William Blackwood and Sons, 1874, p. 152.
Cf. John Macpherson, *The Confession of Faith*, Second Edition, Edinburgh, T. & T. Clark, 1882, p. 77.
28. Lusk, *Proceedings I*, p. 55.
29. *Ibid.*, p. 59. Quoted from Dunlop's Collection of Confessions, Vol. II. Cf. Schaff, *Creeds of Christendom*, Vol. III, p. 447.

30. *Ibid.*, p. 58. Cf. Schaff, *op. cit.*, p. 319. (Underlining Campbell's.)
31. Lusk, *Proceedings I, xxvii.*
32. Campbell, *Memorials*, Vol. II, p. 35.
33. Lusk, *Proceedings II*, p. 342.
34. Lusk, *Proceedings I*, p. 30.
35. Lusk, *Proceedings I*, p. 31; (bracketed words mine).
36. Lusk, *Proceedings II*, p. 260.
37. Lusk, *Proceedings III*, p. 110.
38. Lusk, *Proceedings II*, p. 340.
39. Leckie, *The Expositor*, Eighth Series, Vol. 21, p. 63.
40. Lusk, *Proceedings II*, p. 193.
41. Lusk, *Proceedings II*, pp. 275 and 346.
42. Campbell, *Sermons*, Vol. II, p. 448.
43. Campbell preferred the Confession of 1560 as being more explicit on the Scriptures as the supreme rule of faith.
44. Lusk, *Proceedings II*, p. 179; *Proceedings III*, pp. 39-41.
45. Lusk, *Proceedings II*, p. 214.
46. Lusk, *Proceedings III*, p. 40.
47. *Ibid.*, p. 47.
48. Lusk, *Proceedings III*, p. 111.
49. William Hanna, *Letters of Thomas Erskine of Linlathen*, Vol. I, p. 106.

CHAPTER FIVE

1. Hanna, *Letters of Thomas Erskine*, Vol. I, p. 137.
2. See further, William Adamson, *The Life of the Rev. James Morison*, London, Hodder and Stoughton, 1898.
3. Campbell found this 'modified' Calvinism of George Payne, Ralph Wardlaw and Thomas Jenkyn worthy of consideration when he turned to write on the nature of the atonement.
4. Robert Peden, *The Atonement of Christ*, (Toronto: Examiner Office, 1850).
5. *North British Tracts for the Times in Reference to the Controversy in the Scottish Churches on the Atonement*, edit. J. & A. Muirhead, 1846. Publisher not given.
6. J.K. Mozley, *Some Tendencies in British Theology*, London, S.P.C.K., 1952, pp. 145ff.
7. W.A. Curtis, *History of Creeds and Confessions of Faith*, Edinburgh, T. and T. Clark, 1911, p. 281. This is our general source for information on the Declaratory Acts.
8. C.G. McCrie, *Confessions of the Church of Scotland*, Edinburgh, MacNiven and Wallace, 1907.
9. Curtis, *op. cit.*, p. 282.
10. Henderson, *Religious Controversies in Scotland*, p. 178.
11. Macpherson, *Confessions of Faith*, p. 77.
12. *Minutes of the Sessions of the Westminster Assembly of Divines*, ed. A.F. Mitchell and John Struthers, London, William Blackwood and Sons, 1874, p. lvii.
13. R.H. Story, *The Apostolic Ministry in the Scottish Church*, London, William Blackwood and Sons, 1897, p. 308.

14. A.J. Campbell, *Two Centuries of the Church of Scotland*, p. 187. (Bracketed words mine).
15. *Ibid.*,pp. 284ff.
16. J.H. Leckie, 'John McLeod Campbell: The Development of His Thought, I.' *The Expositor*, January 1921, p. 55.
17. A.B. Alexander, *The Shaping Forces of Religious Thought*, Glasgow, Maclehose, Jackson & Co., 1920, p. 366.
18. A.J. Ross, 'Memorial of Alexander Ewing', London, Dalby and Isbister, 1877, p. 566.
19. See the documentation by Prof. A.C. Cheyne in *The Westminster Confession in the Church Today*, A.I.C. Heron (Edit.), Edinburgh, St. Andrew Press, 1982; also Drummond and Bulloch, *The Church in Late Victorian Scotland*, 1874-1900, p. 12. Louis Hodges' studies in historical theology appear to confirm the notion that Campbell played a special role in the turn-around from Federal Calvinism to a renewal of reformation theology. See his doctrinal dissertation *The Doctrine of the Mediator in Classical Scottish Theology (From John Knox to James Durham)*, University of Edinburgh, 1975.
20. So runs the opening sentence of Professor Dickie's introduction to *The Nature of the Atonement*, p. xiii.
21. William Hanna, *Memoir of the Life and Letters of Dr. Thomas Chalmers*, 4 vols., Edinburgh, Sutherland and Knox, 1881, Vol. III, p. 291. The use of the plural 'topics' arises from the fact that the Assembly had other cases before it as well.
22. John McNeill, *The History and Character of Calvinism*, p. 388.
23. Notably a letter in the Glasgow Herald, May 3, 1868, submitted by the Bishop of Argyll and the Isles, as referred to in Edward Caird's Memoir of his brother John Caird in the latter's work, *The Fundamental Ideas of Christianity*, Vol. I, p. xc.
24. Campbell, *Memoirs*, Vol. II, p. 299.
25. J. Caird, *The Fundamental Ideas of Christianity*, Glasgow, Maclehose, 1899, Vol. I, p. lxxxviii.

CHAPTER SIX

1. Campbell's understanding of the psychology of reproach, rejection and hatred in relation to love is of no little interest. See for example, *Sermons*, Vol. I, pp. 266-8, 326, 370.
2. *Movements of Religious Thought in Britain During the Nineteenth Century*, p. 156.
3. Campbell, *Memorials*, Vol. I, pp. 91 and 103.
4. *Ibid.*, p. 190.
5. See John Tulloch, *Movements of Religious Thought in Britain During The Nineteenth Century*, New York, Charles Scribner's Sons, 1885, p. 138.
6. See Erskine titles listed in bibliography.
7. See for example, George M. Tuttle, *The Place of John McLeod Campbell*, etc., The American Library Association Microtext Project, University of Chicago.
8. Andrew Thomson, *The Doctrine of Universal Pardon Considered and*

Refuted, Edinburgh, William Whyte and Co., 1830. See Preface and Appendices, esp. p. 471.

9. Vernon F. Storr, *The Development of English Theology in the Nineteenth Century 1800-1860*, London, Longmans Green, 1913, p. 355. See also Thomas McCrie, *The Story of the Scottish Church*, London, Blackie and Son, 1875, p. 529, and R.S. Franks, *A History of the Doctrine of the Work of Christ*, London, Hodder and Stoughton, 1918, Vol. II, p. 391.
10. Robert Mackintosh, *Historic Theories of the Atonement*, London, Hodder and Stoughton, 1920, p. 240.
11. Eugene Bewkes, *The Legacy of a Christian Mind*, Philadelphia, Judson Press, 1937, p. 7.
12. Campbell, *Memorials*, Vol. I, p. 27.
13. *Ibid.*, Vol. II, p. 270.
14. William Hanna, *Letters of Thomas Erskine of Linlathen* (2 vols.), Edinburgh, David Douglas, 1877, Vol. I, p. 129.
15. R.H. Story, *Memoir of the Life of Rev. Robert Story*, p. 152.
16. Campbell, *Memorials*, Vol. II, p. 273. See also Campbell, *Reminiscences*, p. 44, and Duncan Finlayson *Aspects of the Life and Influence of Thomas Erskine of Linlathen, 1788-1880* in Scottish Church History Society, 1980, Vol. XX, pp. 31, 36.
17. D.J. Vaughan, 'Scottish Influences Upon English Theological Thought,' *Contemporary Review*, XXXII, June 1878, p. 457.
18. Campbell, *Memorials*, Vol. I, p. 272.
19. Campbell, *Reminiscences*, p. 42.
20. Campbell, *Memorials*, Vol. I, p. 147.
21. *Ibid.*, Vol. II, p. 12.
22. *Ibid.*, Vol. I, p. 255.
23. F. Maurice, *The Life and Letters of Frederick Denison Maurice*, New York, Charles Scribners Sons, 1884, Vol. II, p. 150.
24. *Ibid.*, Vol. I, p. 183.
25. *Ibid.*, Vol. II, p. 298. See also Maurice's commendation of Campbell in the former's work *The Gospel of St. John*, London, Macmillan, 1894, 10th edit. (First published in 1857).
26. Campbell, *Memorials*, Vol. I, p. 274.
27. F.D. Maurice, *Theological Essays*, London, James Clarke and Co. Ltd., 1957, Chapter VII; See especially pp. 107-114.
28. Pfleiderer, *The Development of Theology in Germany Since Kant, and Its Progress in Great Britain Since 1825*, London, Swan Sonnenscheim and Co., 1890, p. 382.
29. See Vernon Storr, *The Development of English Theology in the Nineteenth Century*, p. 356.
30. H.R. Mackintosh and J.S. Stewart, trans., *The Christian Faith*, Edinburgh, 1928.
31. Richard B. Brandt, *The Philosophy of Schleiermacher*, New York, Harper and Brothers, 1941; see pp. 302ff.
32. William Thomson, *The Atoning Work of Christ*, London, Longman, Brown, Green and Longmans, 1853, pp. 199f and 305ff.
33. Campbell, *Memorials*, Vol. II, p. 201.
34. Further on the subject of vicarious penitence, below, Chapter XII.
35. Campbell used an edition of Luther's *Commentary* published in London by

Matthews and Leigh, 1810. The edition used here: Edinburgh, Thomas Turnbull, 1822.

36. Campbell, *Reminiscences*, p. 173.

37. Campbell, *Sermons*, Vol. I, p. 121.

38. *Ibid.*, p. 389.

39. *Ibid.*, Vol. II, p. 373.

40. *Ibid.*, Vol. I, pp. 387-9.

41. Campbell, *The Nature of the Atonement*, p. 32. Cf. Campbell, *Memorials*, Vol. II, p. 136.

42. Campbell, *The Nature of the Atonement*, p. 47.

43. *Ibid.*, pp. 390-7.

44. See Campbell, *Reminiscences*, Chapter IV, p. 158.

45. Geddes MacGregor, 'The Row Heresy', *Harvard Theological Review*, Vol. XLIII, No. 4, p. 289.

46. It is interesting to speculate on how R.B. Lusk, editor and publisher of the proceedings of Campbell's trial, may have contributed to the suggestion that Campbell had in some measure been basing his case on patristic studies. Lusk included some editorial notes which do raise the question of the Fathers: 'The Editor has no fears of being effectually contradicted by any one conversant with the writings of the Fathers of the Primitive Church, and of the Churches of the Reformation, when he asserts, that there was scarcely one of all these holy Confessors and Martyrs who ought not to have been libelled and deposed, if these doctrines, now condemned, are heretical.' Among those cited he names Clement, Cyprian and Augustine. *Proceedings III*, p. 181.

47. Campbell, *Memorials*, Vol. I, p. 244.

48. Henry Oxenham, *The Catholic Doctrine of the Atonement*, London, W.H.Allen, 3rd ed., 1881.

49. Cf. Campbell, *Memorials*, Vol. I, p. 244.

50. R.S. Franks, *A History of the Doctrine of the Work of Christ*, Vol. II, pp. 386-7.

CHAPTER SEVEN

1. See *The Works of John Owen*, William H. Gould, ed. (London and Edinburgh, Johnstone and Hunter) 1852.

2. Campbell's classification of Edwards as a strict Calvinist may be somewhat qualified. Stevens describes Edwards' main treatise on the atonement as 'a Grotian edifice built upon a penal basis, with Anselmic and other embellishments.' (*The Christian Doctrine of Salvation*, p. 421). Even so, the influence of Edwards has certainly been taken to be in the direction of strict Calvinism by others besides Campbell.

3. See Campbell, *The Atonement*, Chapter IV, 'Calvinism as Recently Modified', pp. 76-113. It should be mentioned that G.B. Stevens, whose book on the *Christian Doctrine of Salvation* is counted by J.K. Mozley 'far the best account of the work of American and English Divines since the Reformation,' named none of the men reviewed by Campbell. However, when Andrew Marshall sought to defend the traditional doctrine of limited atonement, he named these very people as his adversaries and dealt with them at length. See his posthumous work: *The Atonement: or, the Death of*

Christ the Redemption of His People, edited by John Forbes, Glasgow, Thomas Murray and Son, 1868.

4. Campbell, *The Nature of the Atonement*, p. 119.

5. *Ibid.*, p. 4.

6. In introducing the second edition of the book he discusses this procedure of approaching the atonement 'from the side of faith.' Campbell acknowledges that he is speaking mainly from within the so-called 'theological circle' to the believer, though he hopes that some impression may be made upon the interested non-believer who considers the facts, since 'Christianity has its highest and ultimate evidence in what it is.' See *The Nature of the Atonement*, pp. xxiiiff.

7. Campbell, *The Nature of the Atonement*, p. 20. See also p. 333.

8. Campbell, *Sermons*, Vol. II, p. 76.

9. Lusk, *Proceedings II*, p. 185.

10. Campbell, *The Nature of the Atonement*, p. 171 and p. 338.

11. *Ibid.*, p. 72.

12. Hanna, *Letters of Thomas Erskine of Linlathen*, Vol. II, p. 183.

13. Campbell, *The Nature of the Atonement*, p. 30.

14. *Ibid.*, p. 31.

15. Peter 1:17.

16. Campbell, *The Nature of the Atonement*, p. 188.

17. Campbell, *The Nature of the Atonement*, p. 190.

18. *Ibid.*, p. 334.

19. Campbell, *The Nature of the Atonement*, p. 28.

20. Campbell, *The Nature of the Atonement*, pp. 153-4.

21. *Ibid.*, p. 14.

22. Campbell, *The Nature of the Atonement*, p. 69.

23. Ireneaus, 'Against Heresies,' V, Preface, *Ante Nicene Fathers*, Vol. I, p. 526.

24. Athanasius, 'Incarnation of the Word,' *Nicene and Post Nicene Fathers*, Second Series, Vol. IV, p. 36. Cf. W.A. Brown, *Encyclopaedia of Religion and Ethics*, Vol. V, p. 643.

25. That the line should not be drawn too sharply between East and West regarding relative emphasis on the incarnation is further indicated by the fact that Latin theologians sometimes expressed themselves in terms ordinarily expected of the Greeks. Witness Hilary of Poitiers (Ob. 368 A.D.), 'The Son of God was born . . . that by His Incarnation he might take to Himself from the Virgin the fleshly nature, and that through this commingling there might come into being a hallowed Body of all humanity; that so through that Body which He was pleased to assume all mankind might be hid in Him, and He in return, through his unseen existence, be reproduced in all.' Hilary, 'On the Trinity,' Bk. II, *Nicene and Post Nicene Fathers*, Second Series, Vol. IX, p. 59. Modern theology in the West also exhibits its share of writing which bears the flavour of thought ordinarily associated with the Greek and eastern emphasis. See for example, Archdeacon James Wilson's Hulsean Lectures of 1899: 'Let us say boldly that the Incarnation, that is, the life and death of Christ, – for the life and death were equally necessary – is the identification of the human and the divine life. This identification is the atonement. There is no other.' In *The Gospel of the Atonement*, London, Macmillan and Co., 1901, p. 89.

26. Campbell, *The Nature of the Atonement*, xxv.
27. Campbell, *The Nature of the Atonement*, p. 203.
28. *Ibid.*, p. 246.
29. Martineau's review entitled 'Mediatorial Religion' appeared in *The National Review*, April 1856. It was reprinted in Martineau's *Studies of Christianity*, London, Longmans, Green and Co., 1879. Cf. Campbell, *Memorials* Vol. II, p. 342, and *The Nature of the Atonement*, pp. 397-404.
30. Campbell, *The Nature of the Atonement*, pp. 401-2.
31. Romans 5:19.
32. I Corinthians 15:49.
33. Campbell, *The Nature of the Atonement*, p. 160.
34. A.S. Peake, *Christianity, Its Nature and Truth*, London, Duckworth, 1935, p. 281.
35. See John Burnaby, *Christian Words and Christian Meanings*, New York, Harper and Brothers, 1955, p. 99.
36. P.T. Forsyth, *The Work of Christ*, London, Hodder and Stoughton, 1909, p. 182. This is not to forget that much has been said also in favour of the truth for which the substitutionary idea of the atonement stands, namely, that in Christ God did something *for* us which we could not do for ourselves. See the appreciative discussions in A.B. Macaulay, *The Death of Jesus*, London, Hodder and Stoughton, 1938, pp. 156ff., and in the much earlier work of James Denney, *Studies in Theology*, 3rd ed., Edinburgh, Hodder and Stoughton, 1895, p. 126.
37. John 15:5.
38. Ephesians 1:22-23.

CHAPTER EIGHT

1. Campbell, *The Nature of the Atonement*, p. 124.
2. See, for example, Campbell's *Sermons*, Vol. I, pp. 72-75. Incidentally, theologians who press the difference between Eros and Agape relating to the language of love could find Campbell a helpful source.
3. Campbell, *The Nature of the Atonement*, p. 21.
4. Campbell, *The Nature of the Atonement*, p. 16.
5. *Ibid.*, pp. 24-25.
6. Campbell, *The Nature of the Atonement*, p. 142.
7. See Jonathan Edwards, 'Of Satisfaction for Sin,' Ch. II, 9, 1. *The Works of Jonathan Edwards*, New York, Leavitt, Trow and Co., 1844, Vol. I, pp. 603-5. Noted by Campbell, *The Nature of the Atonement*, pp. 86-7. Also, John Pye Smith, *Four Discourses on the Sacrifice and Priesthood of Jesus Christ, and the Atonement and Redemption Thence Accruing*, 3rd ed., London, Jackson and Walford, 1847, p. 41. See also Payne, *Lectures on Divine Sovereignty*, pp. 181-2; and Jenkyn, *The Extent of the Atonement*, p. 292.
8. Campbell, *The Nature of the Atonement*, p. 116.
9. *Ibid.*, p. 117.
10. Campbell, *The Nature of the Atonement*, p. 141.
11. Campbell, *ibid.*, p. 167.
12. Campbell, *The Nature of the Atonement*, p. 160.
13. Campbell, *The Nature of the Atonement*, p. 171.

NOTES **155**

14. Edwards, 'On Satisfaction for Sin,' Ch. II, 1-3, *The Works of Jonathan Edwards*, Vol. I, p. 586. Cf. Campbell, *The Nature of the Atonement*, p. 137.
15. Campbell, *The Nature of the Atonement*, p. 400. Cf. G. Stevens,*The Christian Doctrine of Salvation*, p. 212.
16. Campbell, *The Nature of the Atonement*, p. 135. The conception of Christ having come into the world as 'the great confessor of its sin' had already been expressed in Campbell's preaching as a young man in Row. See, for example, *Sermons*, Vol. I, p. 238.
17. Campbell, *The Nature of the Atonement*, pp. 156-7.
18. *Ibid.*, pp. 138-9.
19. See further on Campbell and Luther. Note #24, p. 162.
20. Campbell, *The Nature of the Atonement*, pp. 145-6.
21. See Campbell, *The Nature of the Atonement*, p. 231.
22. Campbell, *The Nature of the Atonement*, p. 332.
23. *Ibid.*, p. 182. Cf. p. 225.
24. Campbell, *The Nature of the Atonement*, p. 206.
25. *Ibid.*, p. 183.
26. *Ibid.*, p. 174.
27. For an expression of this thought in the *Sermons*, see Vol. I, p. 45. In Christ's sacrifice we know it is consistent with God's character to receive us. By his resurrection the Holy Spirit is given us whereby we have the power to share his delight in God. This is not to forget that so to delight includes sympathizing with the condemnation of sin. The *Sermons* often dwell on this theme. See also Vol. II, p. 57.

CHAPTER NINE

1. Campbell, *Memorials*, Vol. I, pp. 267 and 271.
2. William Knight, *Principal Shairp and His Friends*, London, John Mac-Murray, 1888, p. 178. Actually it was in his student days in Oxford, 1845, that Shairp had first come to know both Erskine and Campbell through their anonymous work *Fragments of Truth*; also read with enjoyment by Charles Kingsley, see *Memorials*, Vol. I, p. 243.
3. *Ibid.*, p. 304.
4. Campbell, *Memorials*, Vol. I, p. 294.
5. *Ibid.*, p. 267.
6. Witness R.C. Moberly's pointed comment that if Campbell had been raised in the truest sacramental tradition of the Church 'he could hardly, in expounding the rationale of the atonement, have ignored so completely the relevance of all this side of Christian experience.' *Atonement and Personality*, pp. 409-410.
7. See above, pp. 73-75.
8. Campbell, *Memorials*, Vol. I, p. 295.
9. Arthur F. Hort, *The Life and Letters of Fenton John Anthony Hort*, London, Macmillan, 1896, Vol. I, p. 316.
10. Constantine Prichard, according to Principal Shairp, was a man of rare ability who never became as widely known as his talents warranted.
11. C.E. Prichard, *Modern Views of the Atonement*, in *North British Review*, March-June, 1867, p. 186.

12. Campbell, *Memorials*, Vol. II, pp. 127 and 248.
13. D.J. Vaughan, *Scottish Influence Upon English Theological Thought*, in *The Contemporary Review*, Vol. XXXII, June 1878, p. 458. See also Campbell, *Memorials*, Vol. I, p. 313.
14. For a few samples of testimonial statements see:
    J.K. Mozley, *Some Tendencies in British Theology*, pp. 149 and 179.
    William Adams Brown, 'Expiation and Atonement,' *Encyclopaedia of Religion and Ethics*, Vol. V, p. 648.
    R.S. Franks, *A History of the Doctrine of the Work of Christ*, Vol. II, p. 391: *The Work of Christ*, Nelson, 1962, p. 665.
    R.H. Culpepper, *Interpreting the Atonement*, Eerdman's, 1966, pp. 115-117.
    A.B.D. Alexander, *The Shaping Forces of Religious Thought*, Glasgow, Maclehose, Jackson and Company, 1920, p. 362.
    Sydney Cave, *The Doctrine of the Work of Christ*, London, Hodder and Stoughton, 1937, p. 235.
    B.M.G. Reardon, *From Coleridge to Gore*, London, Longmans, 1971, p. 404.
15. J.J. Lias, *The Atonement Viewed in the Light of Certain Modern Difficulties*, 2nd ed. London, James Nisbet, 1888, p. 66.
16. *Ibid.*, p. 71.
17. *Loc. cit.*
18. *Loc. cit.*
19. See Lias, *op. cit.*, p. 78.
20. See especially Lias, *op. cit.* p. 93, where he expresses surprise at A.B. Bruce's remark that Campbell's notion of Christ's repentance is merely 'the eccentricity of a devout author'; and p. 143, regarding supplementary ideas on a moral view of atonement.
21. Cf. Mozley, *Some Tendencies in British Theology*, pp. 117ff.
22. Caird, *The Fundamental Ideas of Christianity*, Glasgow, Maclehose, 1899, Vol. II, p. 205.
23. *Ibid.*, p. 208.
24. Caird, *op. cit.*, p. 209.
25. *Ibid.*, p. 216. Cf. Campbell, *The Nature of the Atonement*, p. 87.
26. Caird, *op. cit.*, p. 218.
27. *Ibid.*, p. 220. Cf. James Orr, *The Christian View of God and the World*, 3rd ed., p. 314. Cf. the 1st edition p. 362 which Caird had before him.
28. *Ibid.*, pp. 173, 186, 202 and 204.
29. Campbell, *Memorials*, Vol. II, p. 189.
30. Caird, *Fundamental Ideas of Christianity*, Vol. I, p. xci.
31. Arthur Westcott, *Brooke Foss Westcott Bishop of Durham*, London, Macmillan, 1903, 2 vols., Vol. I, p. 231; also especially p. 239 for Westcott's letter to his friend Hort questioning any possibility of an intelligible theory of atonement.
32. Arthur Westcott, *op. cit.* , Vol. II, p. 226.
33. Brooke Foss Westcott, *The Victory of the Cross*, London, Macmillan, 1888, p. vi.
34. Franks, *A History of the Doctrine of the Work of Christ*, Vol. II, pp. 428 and 435. Cf. Mackintosh, *Historic Theories of Atonement*, pp. 210ff; A.M. Ramsay, *From Gore to Temple* (The Development of Anglican Theology

1889-1939), Longmans, p. 47.

35. Campbell, *The Nature of the Atonement*, p. 212.

36. Moberly, *Atonement and Personality*, London, John Murray, 1901, p. 396.

37. *Ibid.*, p. 397.

38. *Ibid.*, p. 43.

39. *Ibid.*, p. 42.

40. See Moberly, *op. cit.*, p. 130. Cf. Campbell's *The Nature of the Atonement*, p. 138f.

41. Moberly, *Atonement and Personality*, p. 112. Cf. Campbell, *The Nature of the Atonement*, p. 203.

42. While both Campbell and Moberly declare the objective character of the atonement they agree that in an important sense the atonement is incomplete apart from the subjective appropriation of Christ's work, and that its nature cannot be adequately set forth apart from the awareness of actual reconciliation through Christ. Moberly, indeed, feels it a weakness in Campbell that he stops short with consideration of the doctrine of justification in traditional evangelical fashion. He would go several steps further by bringing Calvary into association with the outpouring of the Spirit at Pentecost, and with the Church and Sacraments. The gift of the Spirit at Pentecost completed the cycle as it were: 'It is the gift progressively transforming, it is the indwelling of the Spirit of Holiness, the Spirit of the Crucified, which is the transfiguring of personality.' (*Atonement and Personality*, p. 153) Thus in the light of Pentecost the atonement becomes more fully intelligible. It is also in and through the community of the Church and the sacraments as the appointed means of grace that Christ's presence is made progressively and effectively real. Some writers have chided Moberly for over-exercising his High Church predilections. The fact remains, however, that it has been all too possible to isolate Calvary, whether from Pentecost, Bethlehem or the heart of God's character, Moberly has performed a service in reminding us that the atonement is best understood in its broadest possible relations with the whole system of Christian faith and doctrine.

43. Benjamin Jowett, Master of Balliol, had attacked the language of sacrifice, satisfaction, atonement as expressing fundamentally immoral conceptions. See the essay 'On Atonement and Satisfaction' in Jowett, *The Epistles of St. Paul to the Thessalonians, Galatians, and Romans*, London, John Murray, 2nd ed., 1859, Vol. II, p. 547.

44. Moberly, *op. cit.*, p. 402.

45. *Ibid.*, p. 406.

46. Thomas H. Hughes, *The Atonement*, London, George Allen and Unwin Ltd., 1949, pp. 164ff.

47. Macaulay, *The Death of Jesus*, p. vii. It is an interesting coincidence that in their indices the publishers for both Denney and Macaulay treat the name McLeod as part of the surname.

48. *Ibid.*, p. 43.

49. *Loc. cit.*

50. Macaulay, *The Death of Jesus*, p. 63.

51. *Ibid.*, p. 176.

52. Macaulay, *op. cit.*, pp. 143, 145, 178. Cf. Campbell, *The Nature of the Atonement*, p. 289.

53. See *Jesus and His Sacrifice*, London, Macmillan and Co., 1955, in which the passion sayings of Christ provide the study background; also *The Atonement in New Testament Teaching*, London, Epworth Press, 1941. This book sprang from the author's feeling that his next step was to look at the New Testament as a whole for help in understanding the doctrine of the atonement. A quite different structure appears in *Forgiveness and Reconciliation*, Macmillan and Co., 1941, which treats of atonement in one chapter alongside others on a variety of closely related topics such as justification and sanctification. The original pattern is revived in Taylor's latest work, *The Cross of Christ*, London, Macmillan and Co., 1956. This little book has the advantages both of summarizing his former writings on atonement and of offering comments retrospectively concerning them.
54. See Taylor's Chapter VI on *Sacrifice* in *Jesus and His Sacrifice*, p. 49.
55. See, for example, the sympathetic treatment of authors so various as Rashdall, Aulen and Brunner in Taylor's article 'Best Books on the Atonement,' *The Expository Times*, Vol. XLVIII, No. 6, pp. 267ff. The same material with some alterations appears again in *The Cross of Christ*, pp. 73-85.
56. Cf. *The Atonement in New Testament Teaching*, pp. 173-179, and *The Cross of Christ*, pp. 54ff and p. 90.
57. Taylor, *Jesus and His Sacrifice*, p. 277. The reference is to a passage in Campbell's *The Nature of the Atonement*, p. 117, also referred to above, p. 189.
58. Cf. the view of Lidgett, Orr, *et al* below, p. 371.
59. Taylor, *Jesus and His Sacrifice*, p. 283.
60. *Ibid.*, p. 315ff.
61. Taylor, *The Cross of Christ*. This and succeeding propositions are found in pages 92-95.
62. See above, pp. 79-81.
63. Taylor, *The Atonement in New Testament Teaching*, p. 176.
64. Campbell, *The Nature of the Atonement*, pp. 136ff.
65. F.R.M. Hitchcock, *Atonement in Modern Thought*, London, Wells Gardner, 1911.
66. H.A. Hodges, *The Pattern of Atonement*.
67. See John McIntyre, *Prophet of Penitence*, *op. cit.,* p. 4f.

CHAPTER TEN

1. Sydney Cave, *The Doctrine of the Work of Christ*, London, Hodder and Stoughton, 1937, pp. 233 and 246.
2. Campbell's relating of justice to love (pp. 79-80 above) seems to be affirmed by biblical scholars. See Norman Snaith's article in Alan Richardson (ed.), *A Theological Word Book Bible*, London, S.C.M. Press Ltd., 1950, pp. 202-3. The words tsedeq and tsedaquah in the Old Testament, usually translated 'righteousness' (though occasionally 'justice'), originally referred to norms which in Hebrew religion rested back on the character of God as the deliverer from bondage, bearing with Israel in steadfast love. Norman Snaith points out that there was in the history of these words 'a steady tendency towards the idea of salvation.' This development may be seen in the eighth century prophets whose claims on behalf of the poor and needy

were grounded in the fact that a righteous God who demands that righteousness shall characterize relations among the covenant people will also act to vindicate a righteous will – especially in order that justice may be achieved for the needy and the helpless. God thus acts 'or the saving of the people. This is even more manifestly the case in the Second Isaiah where, says Snaith, 'the word tsedeq-tsedequah (righteousness) has come to mean "salvation". The Righteousness of God shows itself in a saving work.' The same theme can be traced with various alterations in the Psalms and on into the New Testament itself where the Greek *dikaiosune*, translated 'righteousness', though sometimes having an ethical reference, will often carry a distinctly soteriological meaning. Here indeed the righteousness of God and the forgiving love of God are seen to be *one* in the saving act of Jesus Christ. 'It is something new,' say the authors of the article on Righteousness for the Kittel series, 'when absolute justice is said to be shown in the atonement through the sacrificial death of Jesus (Rom. iii:26) and when God is called "faithful and just to forgive our sins" (I John 1:9), *dikaios* combining the ideas of judgment and salvation.' See Gottfried Quell and Gottlob Schrenk, *Righteousness*, London, Adam and Charles Black, 1951, (Manual IV, Bible Key Words from Gerhard Kittel's *Theologisches Wörterbuch Zum Neuen Testament*, trans. J.R. Coates, Stuttgart, 1935), p. 21.

3. Of previous attempts to re-examine the concept of Christ's sufferings as penal, a good example may be found in lectures by William Magee, Archbishop of Dublin, delivered in 1798-9 and in their published form reasonably familiar to Campbell's generation. See the fifth edition of *Discourses and Dissertations on the Scriptural Doctrine of the Atonement and Sacrifice*, New York, D. Appleton and Co., 1839, Vol. I, p. 314 *et al.*

4. Campbell, *Sermons*, Vol. I, pp. 316-317; See also Vol. II, p. 286.

5. Campbell, *The Nature of the Atonement*, p. 212. Italics Campbell's.

6. Arthur Lyttelton, 'The Atonement', Ch. VII in Charles Gore, *Lux Mundi*, 5th ed., New York, John W. Lovell, 1890, p. 256.

7. Orr, *The Christian View of God and the World*, 5th ed., Edinburgh, Andrew Elliott, 1902, p. 296.

8. *Ibid.*, pp. 311ff. Orr's writings generally demonstrate how much he himself came under Campbell's influence in this respect. In addition to many other passages in the Kerr Lectures, see Orr, *Sin as a Problem of Today*, London, Hodder and Stoughton, 1906, pp. 296-302, and *God's Image in Man and Its Development*, London, Hodder and Stoughton, 1906.

9. R.W. Dale, *The Atonement*, London, Hodder and Stoughton, 1875. Preface to the Seventh Edition, p. lxiii.

10. As quoted by A.W. Dale, *The Life of R.W. Dale of Birmingham*, 2nd ed., London, Hodder and Stoughton, 1898, p. 424.

12. *Ibid.*, p. lvi.

13. John Scott Lidgett, *The Fatherhood of God*, Edinburgh, T. and T. Clark, 1902, p. 272.

14. John Scott Lidgett, *The Spiritual Principle of the Atonement*, 3rd edition, London, Charles H. Kelley, 1901. p. 175.

15. John Scott Lidgett, *The Victorian Transformation of Theology*, London, Epworth Press, 1934, p. 38.

16. Forsyth, *The Work of Christ*, London, Hodder and Stoughton, 1909, p. 148.

17. P.T. Forsyth, *The Cruciality of the Cross*, 2nd ed., London, Hodder and Stoughton, 1910, p. 78.
18. This symposium was subsequently published in book form under the title *The Atonement in Modern Religious Thought* by F. Godet, *et al*, London, James Clark (Third Edition) 1907. Forsyth's article begins at page 51.
19. In Godet *et al.*, *The Atonement in Modern Religious Thought*, p. 151.
20. James Denney, *The Christian Doctrine of Reconciliation*, pp. 119-120.

CHAPTER ELEVEN

1. Campbell, *The Nature of the Atonement*, pp. 136-7.
2. Moberly, *Atonement and Personality*, p. 402.
3. Campbell, *The Nature of the Atonement*, p. 135.
4. Macaulay, *The Death of Jesus*, pp. 143, 145, 178. Cf. Campbell, *The Nature of the Atonement*, p. 289.
5. Macaulay, *op. cit.,* pp. 141ff. Cf. Dale, *The Atonement*, p. 424; also Moberly, *Atonement and Personality*, p. 405.
6. See Campbell, *The Nature of the Atonement*, pp. 301-303.
7. James Orr, *The Christian View of God and the World*, p. 314.
9. *Ibid.*, p. 305.
10. Cited by Taylor, *Jesus and His Sacrifice*, 159fn.
11. Campbell's full treatment of the cry from the Cross appears in *The Nature of the Atonement*, pp. 276ff. While there is nothing to show that he relied on others for his interpretation, some had previously held a similar opinion. See Franks, *A History of the Doctrine of the Work of Christ*, Vol. II, p. 249, for remarks on Schleiermacher, and J.J. Hess of Zurich before him.
12. Martin Dibelius, *From Tradition to Gospel*, London, Ivor Nicholson and Watson, 1934, pp. 193-4.
13. See M.R. James (trans.), *The Apocryphal New Testament*, Oxford, The Clarendon Press, 1924, p. 91.
14. The Gospel According to St. Matthew, a commentary by W.C. Allen (International Critical Commentaries), New York, Charles Scribners Sons, 1913, p. 295.
15. A.E.J. Rawlinson, *St. Mark*, with Introduction, Commentary and Additional Notes (Westminster Commentaries), London, Methuen and Co., Ltd., 2nd ed., 1927, p. 236.
16. Sherman Johnson, *Interpreter's Bible*, Vol. VII, p. 608.
17. A.E. Garvie, *The Christian Faith*, London, Duckworth Press, 1936, p. 160.
18. Dale, *The Atonement*, p. 473, in reference to Stopford Brooke, *Freedom in the Church of England*, London, H.S. King and Co., second edition, 1871.
19. William Temple, *The Nature of Personality*, London, Macmillan and Co., 1911, p. xxxi.
20. Moberly, *Atonement and Personality*, p. 131.
21. P.T. Forsyth, *Positive Preaching and the Modern Mind*, London, Hodder and Stoughton, 1907, p. 363.
22. H.E.W. Turner, *The Meaning of the Cross*, London, Mowbray Co., 1959, p. 18.
23. Mark 15:37 and Matthew 27:50 indicate the fact of Jesus crying with a 'loud voice.' Luke alone (23:46) records what was said, in words again drawn from the Psalms, this time Psalm 31:5.

CHAPTER TWELVE

1. Campbell, *The Nature of the Atonement*, p. 135.
2. Campbell, *The Nature of the Atonement*, p. 136.
3. *Ibid.*, p. 137.
4. *Loc. cit.*
5. Campbell, *The Nature of the Atonement*, p. 137.
6. *Ibid.*, p. 139.
7. A.B. Bruce, *The Humiliation of Christ*, Edinburgh, T. & T. Clark, 1881, p. 318.
8. John MacLeod, *Scottish Theology in Relation to Church History*, Edinburgh, John Knox Press, 1943, p. 258.
9. Campbell, *The Nature of the Atonement*, p. 146.
10. Campbell, *The Nature of the Atonement* (appended notes) p. 397. Cf. T.J. Crawford's claim that Campbell's statements '. . . imply on the part of the Redeemer a self-imputation of the sins of fallen men to an even greater extent than the advocates of His vicarious substitution in the room of sinners would contend for.' *The Doctrine of the Holy Scripture Respecting Atonement*, 4th ed., Edinburgh, William Blackwood and Sons, 1883, p. 332. He is followed by A.B. Bruce, *op. cit.*, pp. 353-4.
11. J.S. Lidgett, *The Spiritual Principle of the Atonement*, 3rd ed., London, Charles H. Kelly, 1901, p. 177. See also R.C. Moberly, *Atonement and Personality*, *op. cit.*, p. 45.
12. Denney, *The Christian Doctrine of Reconciliation*, London, Hodder and Stoughton, 1917, p. 266.
13. H.R. Mackintosh, 'The Vicarious Penitence of Christ, *The Expositor*, Eighth Series, Vol. XI, p. 88. This article is found also as Chapter V in Mackintosh, *Some Aspects of Christian Belief*, London, Hodder and Stoughton Ltd., 1923, p. 79.
14. J.H. Newman, *Discourses Addressed to Mixed Congregations*, Fifth Edition, London, Longmans Green and Co., 1902, pp. 339-40. Cf. the words of the American preacher Newman Smyth in 'The Reality of Faith,' *The Works of the Rev. Newman Smyth*, London, Ward Lock and Co. (Preface dated 1884), p. 83.
15. R.S. Franks, *A History of the Doctrine of the Work of Christ*, Vol. II, pp. 368-9.
16. R.S. Franks, *The Atonement*, p. 184.
17. Emil Brunner, *The Mediator*, trans. by Olive Wyon, London, The Lutterworth Press, 1934, p. 534. Brunner names Campbell as one of three British writers on the atonement whose approach finds special favour with him. He says that from Campbell's book 'we can still learn today.' *The Christian Doctrine of Creation and Redemption*, London, Lutterworth Press, 1952, p. 315.
18. James Martineau, *Mediatorial Religion*, National Review, April, 1856, p. 497.
19. Moberly, *Atonement and Personality*, p. 402.
20. Robert Mackintosh's evangelical loyalties lead him to speak perhaps too strongly of Moberly's notion of 'inclusive humanity.' 'This is a very hard doctrine. We may suffer it as one of those obscure speculations which must be permitted to persons who think they profit by them; but such things ought never to be intruded into our statement of God's central message.' *Historic Theories of Atonement*, p. 220.

21. H. Wheeler Robinson, *Revelation and Redemption*, London, Nisbet, 1942. See especially p. 257ff. Section 3, *The Redeemer as Representative*.

22. John Macquarrie, *John McLeod Campbell*, in *Expository Times*, #83, 9 June 1972, p. 266. The article was republished as a chapter in Macquarrie's *Thinking About God*, London, S.C.M. Press, 1975.

23. Cf. Donald Baillie's insightful pages 11-20 under the heading *The End of Docetism* in *God Was in Christ*, London, Faber & Faber, 1948.

24. At this point Campbell diverges somewhat from Luther whose outlook he had appreciated so much. When Luther contemplated St. Paul's declaration that Christ 'was made sin for us' (II Cor. 5:21) he allowed for the strongest possible language whereby Christ could be named 'the only sinner'; and yet at the same time paradoxically the 'invincible righteous' one who came into conflict with sin, conquered it, and thus set humanity free. Campbell believed himself to be dealing with the same paradoxical person, but he came down on the other side of the paradox with an image of repentance for sin by which every living person may in faith lay hold on pardon. Both men were rooted in revelation. Luther's image carried a double advantage in that first, he had begun by pivoting about a single biblical phrase which was destined to find a firm place in a penal view of atonement, whereas Campbell had been ranging more widely through the New Testament portrayal of the man Christ Jesus and his ministry, including his prayer life. Second, Luther's image was accepted somewhat as a flash of insight having a largely homiletic value while he went on in search of others. Campbell, on the other hand, spent more time on his single image of the repentant Christ more in the style of theologian than preacher, thus leaving himself open to more critical scrutiny.

25. Taylor, *The Atonement in New Testament Teaching*, p. 176.

26. Taylor, 'The Best Books on the Atonement,' *The Expository Times*, XLVIII, No. 6, March 1937, p. 267.

27. J.H. Leckie, *Expository Times*, Vol. XL, No. 5, p. 202; also *The Expositor*, Eighth Series, May 1923, ..373ff.

28. Eugene G. Bewkes, *The Legacy of a Christian Mind*, Philadelphia, Judson Press, 1937, prepared originally as the first doctoral dissertation on Campbell for Edinburgh University. The second was done by a Canadian, Douglas A. Shanks, through the University of Glasgow, 1957 (unpublished).

29. John Macquarrie, *op. cit.*, p. 265.

30. Don S. Browning, *Atonement and Psychotherapy*, Philadelphia, Westminster Press, 1966.

31. *Ibid.*, p. 151.

32. *Ibid.*, p. 211.

33. *Ibid.*, p. 253.

34. See James Torrance's Chapter 6 'The Vicarious Humanity of Christ', in Thomas F. Torrance (Ed.), *The Incarnation*, Edinburgh, The Handsel Press, 1981. See also T.F. Torrance's own earlier consideration of the subject in *Theology in Reconciliation*, London, Geoffrey Chapman, 1975, Chapter Three; also his thoroughgoing emphasis in Chapter Three on the complete humanity of Christ (including the mind of Christ) in whom, as well as through whom, our worship takes place; i.e., a shielding against any Apollinarian tendency in worship, with several notices of Campbell, pp. 139ff, 205, 210.

CHAPTER THIRTEEN

1. See D.W. Simpson, *The Redemption of Man: Discussions Bearing on the Atonement*, Edinburgh, T. & T. Clark, 1889, pp. 9-65; G.B. Stevens, *The Christian Doctrine of Salvation*, pp. 239ff; and Thomas H. Hughes, *The Atonement*, London, George Allen and Unwin Ltd., 1949, p. ix.

2. It is interesting to notice the tendency towards nicety of system in most efforts at classification. According to P.T. Forsyth there are 'three great aspects of the work of Christ which have in turn held the attention of the Church.' These are first, the Triumphant aspect emphasized by the Early Church in which Christ was a victorious champion for man over the Devil; second, the Satisfactionary aspect emphasized by Medievalism and the Reformation in which Christ is the great expiator; and finally the Regenerative aspect characteristic of Moderns who look upon Christ as the sanctifier. (See *The Work of Christ*, p. 199.) John Knox proposes a similar threesome. (See *The Death of Christ*, Chapter Seven, p. 144ff.) J.K. Mozley's series also reveals an interest in tidiness of statement. He arranges theories of the atonement on the basis of the question: Who acts on whom for whom? In one group 'Christ acts on God for man' – the idea of Christ as a substitute. In another, 'Christ acts on God as man' – the idea of Christ as representative. In a third, 'Christ acts on man for God,' – the idea of Christ as example. See *The Doctrine of the Atonement*, p. 173. The temptation to sacrifice individuality and variety in the interest of a balanced system is an obvious hazard.

3. S.T. Coleridge, *Aids to Reflection*, T. Ferby ed., Edinburgh, John Grant, 1905, p. 287.

4. Joseph Butler, *The Analogy of Religion*, Part II, London, The Religious Tract Society, (no date given), Ch. V, p. 223.

5. Leonard Hodgson, *The Doctrine of the Atonement*, London, Nisbet and Co., 1951, p. 147.

6. Vincent Taylor, *The Cross of Christ*, London, Macmillan and Co., 1956, p. 91. Cf. J.K. Moxley, *The Heart of the Gospel*, London, S.P.C.K., 1925, p. 29.

7. R.C. Moberly goes much further by bringing Pentecost to bear upon the subject of the atonement. He thinks Campbell, and presumably almost everyone else, has failed in this regard. R.C. Moberly, *Atonement and Personality*, London, John Murray, 1901, pp. 151-3, 409.

8. N. Micklem, *The Doctrine of Our Redemption*, London, Eyre and Spottiswoode, 1948, p. 60, a chapter with Aulen's title: *Christus Victor*.

9. Sydney Cave, *The Doctrine of the Work of Christ*, London, Hodder and Stoughton, 1937, pp. 255ff; 266ff.

10. Cf. Campbell, *The Nature of the Atonement*, p. 205.

11. John Dickie, *The Organism of Christian Truth*, London, James Clarke, 1930, p. 286.

12. Cf. above, pp. 102-105.

13. See Campbell, *The Nature of the Atonement*, p. 329ff.

14. A.H. Strong, *Systematic Theology*, Rochester N.Y., E.R. Andrews, 1896, p. 200; F.L. Paton, *Fundamental Christianity*, New York, Macmillan, 1928, p. 300.

15. A.B.D. Alexander, *The Thinkers of the Church*, London, James Clarke, 1924, p. 229.

16. Hastings Rashdall, *The Idea of Atonement in Christian Theology*, London, Macmillan and Co., 1920, p. 438.
17. Campbell, *Memorials*, Vol. I, p, 276.
18. C.E. Prichard, 'Modern Views of the Atonement,' *North British Review*, XLVI, June 1867, p. 191.
19. Cf. T.H. Hughes, *The Atonement*, Ch. IV, p. 132; also George Stevens, *The Christian Doctrine of Salvation*, Ch. IV, p. 198.
20. Robert Mackintosh, *Historic Theories of Atonement*, Ch. XII, p. 207. R.C. Moberly used a similar terminology, though he preferred the word 'penitence' in place of 'repentance.'
21. See John McIntyre, *On the Love of God*, London, Collins, 1962, Ch. 7, p. 186.
22. Thomas H. Hughes, *The Atonement*, London, Nisbet and Co., 1951.
23. See F.W. Dillistone, *The Christian Understanding of Atonement*, Herts. England, James Nisbet, 1968. See also Dillistone on Campbell in *Jesus Christ and His Cross*, Philadelphia, Westminster Press, 1944.
24. J.H. Leckie, John McLeod Campbell *The Development of His Thought II*, The Expositor, Eighth Series, XXI, February 1921, p.112.

BIBLIOGRAPHY

Books

Adamson, William. *The Life of the Rev. James Morison.* London, Hodder and Stoughton, 1898.

Alexander, A.B.D. *The Shaping Forces of Religious Thought.* Glasgow, Maclehose, Jackson and Co., 1920.
The Thinkers of the Church. London, James Clarke, 1924.

Allen, W.C. *The Gospel According to S. Matthew* (International Critical Commentaries), New York, Charles Scribner's Sons, 1913.

Athanasius. *Incarnation of the Word,* Nicene and Post Nicene Fathers, Second Series, Vol. IV, p. 36.

Baillie, Donald. *God was in Christ.* London, Faber and Faber Ltd., 1948.

Bewkes, Eugene G. *The Legacy of a Christian Mind.* Philadelphia, Judson Press, 1937.

Brandt, Richard B. *The Philosophy of Schleiermacher.* New York, Harper and Brothers, 1941.

Brooke, Stopford. *Freedom in the Church of England.* London, H.S. King and Co., 2nd ed., 1871.

Bruce, Alexander B. *The Humiliation of Christ.* Edinburgh, T. and T. Clark, 1881.

Brunner, Emil. *The Mediator,* Translated by Olive Wyon. London, The Lutterworth Press, 1934.
The Christian Doctrine of Creation and Redemption, *Dogmatics II.* Translated by Olive Wyon. London, Lutterworth Press, 1952.

Burnaby, John. *Christian Words and Christian Meanings.* New York, Harper and Brothers, 1955.

Burns, Robert. *The Gareloch Heresy Tried in a Letter to the Rev. John Campbell, of Row, and A Sermon Preached at Helensburg.* 2nd ed., Paisley, Alex Gardner, 1830.

Butler, Joseph. *The Analogy of Religion.* London, The Religious Tract Society. No date given.

Caird, John. *The Fundamental Ideas of Christianity.* Glasgow, Maclehose, 1899.

Campbell, A.J. *Two Centuries of the Church of Scotland, 1707-1929.* Paisley, Gardner, 1930.

Campbell, Donald (ed.). *Memorials of John McLeod Campbell D.D.* London, Macmillan and Co., 1877. 2 vols.

Campbell, John McLeod. *Christ the Bread of Life*. London, Macmillan and Co., 1851.

    The Nature of the Atonement And Its Relation To Remission of Sins and Eternal Life. 4th ed. (sic) London, James Clarke and Co. Ltd., 1959. 1st ed. Cambridge, Macmillan and Co., 1856.

    Reminiscences and Reflections. Edited by his son Donald Campbell. London, Macmillan and Co., 1873.

    Responsibility For the Gift of Eternal Life. London, Macmillan and Co., 1873.

    Sermons and Lectures. 3rd ed., Greenock, R.B. Lusk, 1832. 2 vols.

    Thoughts on Revelation. London, Macmillan and Co., 1862.

    Fragments of Truth. 3rd edition, Edinburgh, Edmonston and Douglas, 1861, 4th edition, 1898. Early sermons of Campbell, Erskine, first published anonymously as *Fragments of Exposition*.

Cave, Sydney. *The Doctrine of The Work of Christ*. London, Hodder and Stoughton, 1937

Coleridge, S.T. *Aids to Reflection*. Thomas Ferby (ed.), Edinburgh, John Grant, 1905.

Crawford, Thomas J. *The Doctrine of the Holy Scriptures Respecting Atonement*. 4th ed., Edinburgh, William Blackwood and Sons, 1883.

Culpepper, R.H. *Interpreting the Atonement*., Eerdman's, 1966, pp. 115-117.

Curtis, W.A. *History of Creeds and Confessions of Faith*. Edinburgh, T. and T. Clark, 1911.

Dale, A.W. *The Life of R.W. Dale of Birmingham*. 2nd ed., London, Hodder and Stoughton, 1898.

Dale, R.W. *The Atonement*. London, Hodder and Stoughton, 1875.

Denney, James. *The Christian Doctrine of Reconciliation*. London, Hodder and Stoughton, 1917.

    Studies in Theology. 3rd ed., London, Hodder and Stoughton, 1895.

Dibelius, Martin. *From Tradition to Gospel*. London, Ivor Nicholson and Watson, 1934.

Dickie, John. *The Organism of Christian Truth*. London, James Clarke, 1930.

Dillistone, F.W. *Jesus Christ and His Cross*. Philadelphia, The Westminster Press, 1953.

    The Christian Understanding of the Atonement. Herts, England, James Nisbett, 1968.

Drummond, Andrew L. and Bullock, James. *The Church in Late Victorian Scotland 1874-1900*, Edinburgh, St. Andrew Press, 1978.

Dunlop, William. *The Uses of Creeds and Confessions*, Edinburgh,

James Watson, 2 vols. 1719-22.

Edwards, Jonathan. *The Works of President Edwards*. New York, Leavitt, Trow and Co., 1844.

Erskine, Thomas. *The Brazen Serpent*. Edinburgh, Waugh and Innes, 1831.

An Essay on Faith. 4th ed., Edinburgh, Waugh and Innes, 1825.

The Doctrine of Election And Its Connection with the General Tenor of Christianity. London, James Duncan, 1837.

Remarks on The Internal Evidence for the Truth of Revealed Religion. 4th ed., Edinburgh, Waugh and Innes, 1821.

The Spiritual Order and Other Papers. 3rd ed., Edinburgh, P. Douglas, 1884.

The Unconditional Freeness of the Gospel. 3rd ed., Edinburgh, Waugh and Innes, 1829.

Forsyth, P.T. *The Cruciality of the Cross*. 2nd ed., London, Hodder and Stoughton, 1910.

Positive Preaching and The Modern Mind. (1st ed., 1907). London, Independent Press, 1953.

The Work of Christ. London, Hodder and Stoughton, 1909.

Franks, R.S. *The Atonement*. London, Oxford University Press, 1934. Dale Lectures.

A History of the Doctrine of the Work of Christ. London, Hodder and Stoughton, 1918. 2 vols.

Galbraith, Iain B. *A Village Heritage*: The Parish of Rhu 1648-1980. Published by Rhu and Shagdon Kirk Session (1981).

Garvie, A.E. *The Christian Faith*. London, Duckworth Press, 1936.

Godet, F. *et al. The Atonement in Modern Religious Thought*. 3rd ed., London, James Clarke and Co., 1907.

Gore, Charles (ed.). *Lux Mundi*. From the 5th ed., New York, John W. Lovell Co., 1890.

Gould, William H. (ed.). *The Works of John Owen*. Vol. X, London, Johnstone and Hunter, 1852.

Hanna, William. *Letters of Thomas Erskine of Linlathen*. Edinburgh, David Douglas, 1877. 2 vols.

Memoir of the Life and Writings of Thomas Chalmers. Edinburgh, Sutherland and Knox, 1881. 4 vols.

Henderson, G.D. *The Church of Scotland: A Short History*. Edinburgh, Church of Scotland Youth Committee, 1939.

Henderson, Henry F. *Erskine of Linlathen*. Edinburgh, Oliphant, Anderson and Ferrier, 1899.

The Religious Controversies of Scotland. Edinburgh, T. and T. Clark, 1905.

Heron, Alasdair I.C. (ed.). *The Westminster Confession in the Church Today*. Edinburgh,, St. Andrew Press, 1982.

Hetherington, W.M. *History of the Church of Scotland*. 3rd American from the 3rd Edinburgh ed., New York, Robert Carter, 1844.

History of the Westminster Assembly of Divines. New York, Mark H. Newman, 1843.

Hilary of Poitiers. 'On the Trinity,' Bk. II, 24, *Nicene and Post Nicene Fathers.* Second Series. Vol. IX, p. 59.

Hitchcock, F.R.M. *Atonement in Modern Thought.* London, Wells Gardner, 1911.

Hodges, H.A. *The Pattern of Atonement.* London, S.C.M. Press, 1955.

Hodgson, Leonard. *The Doctrine of the Atonement.* London, Nisbet and Co., 1951.

Hort, A.F. *The Life and Letters of Fenton John Anthony Hort.* London, Macmillan and Co., 1896.

Hughes, Thomas H. *The Atonement.* London, George Allen and Unwin Ltd., 1949.

Irenaeus. 'Against Heresies,' Bk. V, *Ante Nicene Fathers.* A. Roberts and J. Donaldson, eds., New York, Charles Scribner's Sons, 1913. Vol. I, p. 526.

James, M.R. (trans.). *The Apocryphal New Testament.* Oxford, The Clarendon Press, 1924.

Jenkyn, Thomas W. *The Extent of the Atonement, in Its Relation to God, and the Universe.* 2nd American ed., Boston, Gould, Kendall and Lincoln, 1846.

Jowett, Benjamin. *The Epistles of St. Paul to the Thessalonians, Galatians and Romans*, Vol. II. London, John Murray, 2nd ed., 1859.

Kittel, Gerhard. *Theologisches Wörterbuch Zum Neuen Testament.* Trans. J.R. Coates, Stuttgart, 1935. See also Quell and Schrenk.

Knight, William. *Principal Shairp and His Friends.* London, John MacMurray, 1888.

Knox, John. *The Death of Christ.* Collins, 1963.

Lias, J.J. *The Atonement Viewed in the Light of Certain Modern Difficulties.* 2nd ed., London, James Nisbet and Co., 1888.

Lidgett, John Scott. *The Fatherhood of God.* Edinburgh, T. and T. Clark, 1902.

The Spiritual Principle of the Atonement. 3rd ed., London, Charles H. Kelly, 1901.

The Victorian Transformation of Theology. London, Epworth Press, 1934.

Lusk, R.B. (ed.). *The Whole Proceedings in the Case of the Rev. John McLeod Campbell, Late Minister of Row, Before the Presbytery of Dumbarton, The Synod of Glasgow and Ayr, and the General Assembly of the Church of Scotland.* Greenock, R.B. Lusk, 1831, being in three sections as follows:

> *Proceedings of Presbytery* and additional material, called here *Proceedings I.*
> *Proof for the Prosecution and Proceedings in the Synod of Glasgow and Ayr*, called here *Proceedings II.*

A Full Report of the Proceedings in the General Assembly of the Church of Scotland, called here *Proceedings III*.

Luther, Martin. *A Commentary on St. Paul's Epistle to the Galatians*. Trans. by Erasmus Middleton. Edinburgh, Thomas Turnbull, 1822.

Macaulay, A.B. *The Death of Jesus*. London, Hodder and Stoughton, 1938.

McCrie, C.G. *The Confessions of the Church of Scotland*. Edinburgh, MacNiven and Wallace, 1907.

McCrie, Thomas. *The Story of the Scottish Church*. London, Blackie and Son, 1875.

McHugh, J.A. and C.J. Callan. *Catechism of the Council of Trent For Parish Priests*. Joseph Wagner, 9th Printing, 1945.

McIntyre, John. *On the Love of God*. London, Collins, 1962.
    Prophet of Penitence: Our Contemporary Ancestor. A Centenary Lecture Feb. 24, 1072, delivered at the Rhu Church, St. Andrew Press, Edinburgh.

Mackintosh, H.R. *Some Aspects of Christian Belief*. London, Hodder and Stoughton Ltd., 1923.
    With J.S. Stewart, trans. *The Christian Faith* by Friedrich Schleiermacher, 2nd ed., Edinburgh, T. and T. Clark, 1928.

Mackintosh, Robert. *Historic Theories of Atonement*. London, Hodder and Stoughton, 1920.

MacLeod, John. *Scottish Theology – In Relation to Church History*. Edinburgh, The Knox Press, 1943.

Macmillan, Donald. *The Life of Robert Flint*. London, Hodder and Stoughton, 1914.

McNeill, John T. *The History and Character of Calvinism*. New York, Oxford University Press, 1954.

Macpherson, Hector. *Intellectual Development of Scotland*. London, Hodder and Stoughton, 1911.

Macpherson, John. *The Confession of Faith*. Second Edition, Edinburgh, T. and T. Clark, 1882.

Macquarrie, John. *Teaching About God*. London, S.C.M. Press, 1975.

Magee, William. *Discourses and Dissertations on the Scriptural Doctrines of the Atonement and Sacrifice*. (From the fifth London edition) New York, D. Appleton and Co., 1839, 2 vols.

Marshall, Andrew. *The Atonement, Or the Death of Christ the Redemption of His People*. A posthumous treatise edited by John Forbes. Glasgow, Thomas Murray, 1868.

Martineau, James. *Studies of Christianity*. London, Longmans Green and Co., 1879.

Maurice, F. *The Life and Letters of Frederick Denison Maurice*. Edited by his son. New York, Charles Scribner's Sons, 1884.

Maurice, Frederick Denison. *Theological Essays*. London, James Clarke and Co. Ltd., 1957. First published, London, Macmillan and Co., 1853.

The Gospel of St. John. London, Macmillan, 1894 (10th edition).

Micklem, Nathaniel. *The Doctrine of Our Redemption.* London, Eyre and Spottiswoode, 1948.

Mitchell, A.F. and John Struthers, eds. *Minutes of the Sessions of the Westminster Assembly of Divines.* Edinburgh, Blackwood, 1874.

Moberly, R.C. *Atonement and Personality.* London, John Murray, 1901.

Mozley, J.K. *The Doctrine of the Atonement.* London, Duckworth and Co., 1915.

The Heart of the Gospel. London, S.P.C.K., 1925.

Some Tendencies in British Theology. London, S.P.C.K., 1952.

Muirhead, J. and A. Muirhead, eds. *North British Tracts for the Times in Reference to the Controversy in the Scottish Churches on the Atonement.* (Publisher not given), 1846.

Newman, John Henry. *Discourses Addressed to Mixed Congregations.* 5th edition, new impression. London, Longmans Green and Co., 1902.

Orr, James. *The Christian View of God and the World.* 5th ed., Edinburgh, Andrew Elliot, 1902.

God's Image in Man and Its Development. London, Hodder and Stoughton, 1906.

Owen, John. See Gould, William H.

Oxenham, Henry N. *The Catholic Doctrine of the Atonement.* 3rd ed., London, W.H. Allen, 1881.

Paton, F.L. *Fundamental Christianity.* New York, Macmillan, 1928.

Payne, George. *Lectures on Divine Sovereignty, Election, The Atonement, Justification and Regeneration.* London, Hamilton, Adams and co., 1836.

Peake, A.S. *Christianity, Its Nature and Truth.* London, Duckworth, 1935.

Peden, Robert. *The Atonement of Christ.* Toronto, Examiner Office, 1850.

Pfleiderer, Otto. *The Development of Theology in Germany Since Kant, and its Progress in Britain Since 1825.* Translated by J. Frederick Smith. London, Swan Sonnenscheim and Co., 1890.

Quell, Gottfried, and Gottlob Schrenk. *Righteousness.* London, Adam and Charles Black, 1951. (Manual IV, Bible Key Words from Gerhard Kittel's *Theologisches Wörterbuch Zum Neuen Testament,* trans. J.R. Coates, Stuttgart, 1935.)

Ramsay, A.M. *From Gore to Temple.* London, Longmans, 1960.

Randall, Hastings. *The Idea of the Atonement in Christian Theology.* London, Macmillan and Co., 1920.

Rawlinson, A. *St. Mark,* with Introduction, Commentary and Additional Notes (Westminster Commentaries), London, Methuen and Co. Ltd., 2nd ed., 1927.

Reardon, B.M.G. *From Coleridge to Gore: A Century of Religious*

Thought in Britain. London, Longmans, 1971.

Richardson, Alan (ed.). *A Theological Word Book of the Bible.* S.C.M. Press Ltd., 1950.

Robinson, H. Wheeler. *Revelation and Redemption.* London, Nisbet, 1942.

Ross, A.J. *Memoir of Alexander Ewing.* London, Dalby and Isbister, 1877.

Schaff, Philip. *The Creeds of Christendom.* 4th ed., New York, Harper and Brothers, 1905. 3 vols.

Schleiermacher, Friedrich. *The Christian Faith.* Translated by H.R. Mackintosh and J.S. Stewart. 2nd ed., Edinburgh, T. and T. Clark, 1928.

Selwyn, E.G. (ed.). *Essays Catholic and Critical.* London, S.P.C.K., 1926.

Shairp, John C. *Portrait of Friends.* Boston, Haughton, Mifflin and Co., 1889.

Shaw, J.M. *Christian Doctrine.* London, The Lutterworth Press, 1953.

Simon, D.W. *The Redemption of Man: Discussions Bearing on the Atonement.* Edinburgh, T. and T. Clark, 1889.

Smith, John Pye. *Four Discourses on the Sacrifice and Priesthood of Jesus Christ, and the Atonement and Redemption Thence Accruing.* 3rd ed., London, Jackson and Walford, 1847.

Smyth, Newman. *The Works of the Rev. Newman Smyth.* London, Ward Lock and Co. Preface dated 1884.

Stevens, G.B. *The Christian Doctrine of Salvation.* New York, Charles Scribner's Sons, 1911.

Storr, Vernon F. *The Development of English Theology, in the Nineteenth Century, 1800-1860.* London, Longmans Green and Co., 1913.

Story, R.H. *The Apostolic Ministry In the Scottish Church.* London, William Blackwood and Sons, 1897.
The Church of Scotland, Past and Present. London, Wm. McKenzie. 2 vols.
Memoir of the Life of the Reverend Robert Story. London, Macmillan, 1862.

Strong, A.H. *Systematic Theology.* Rochester N.Y., E.R. Andrews, 1896.

Taylor, Vincent. *The Atonement in New Testament Teaching.* London, Epworth Press, 1941.
The Cross of Christ. London, Macmillan and Co., 1956.
Jesus and His Sacrifice. London, Macmillan and Co., 1955.
The Nature of Personality. London, Macmillan and Co., 1911.

Thomson, Andrew. *The Doctrine of Universal Pardon, Considered and Refuted.* Edinburgh, William Whyte and Co., 1830.

Thomson, William. *The Atoning Work of Christ.* London, Longman, Brown, Green and Longmans, 1853.

Torrance, Thomas F. (ed.). *The Incarnation*. Edinburgh, Handsel Press, 1981.

Theology in Reconciliation. London, Geoffrey Chapman, 1975.

Tulloch, John. *Movements of Religious Thought in Britain During the Nineteenth Century*. New York, Charles Scribner's Sons, 1901.

Turner, H.E.W. *The Meaning of the Cross*. London, A.R. Mowbray and Co., 1959.

Tuttle, George M. *The Place of John McLeod Campbell in British Thought Covering the Atonement*. The American Theological Library Association Microtext Project, University of Chicago Library; a doctoral dissertation through Emmanuel College, Victoria University, Toronto, Canada.

Wardlaw, Ralph. *Discourses on the Nature and Extent of the Atonement of Christ*. (Fourth thousand) Glasgow, James Maclehose, 1844.

Warr, C.L. *Scottish Sermons and Addresses*, London, Hodder and Stoughton, 1930.

Westcott, Arthur. *Brooke Foss Westcott Bishop of Durham*. London, Macmillan and Co., 1903. 2 vols.

The Victory of the Cross. London, Macmillan and Co., 1888.

Whitely, Harry C. *Blinded Eagle*. London, S.C.M. Press, 1955.

Wilson, James Maurice. *The Gospel of the Atonement*. London, Macmillan and Co., 1901.

Wilson, William. *The XXXIX Articles of the Church of England*. Oxford, J. Abrams, 1840.

Articles

Brown, William Adams. 'Expiation and Atonement,' *Encyclopaedia of Religion and Ethics*.

Chambers, D. *Doctrinal Attitudes in the Church of Scotland in the Pre-Disruption Era*, Journal of Religious History (Australia) Vol. 8, 1974.

Finlayson, Duncan. *Aspects of the Life and Influence of Thomas Erskine of Linlathen, 1788-1880* in Scottish Church History Society, Vol. XX, 1980.

Gerrish, Brian A. 'Atonement and "Saving Faith",' *Theology Today*, Vol. XVII, July 1960, p. 181.

Graham, J.M. 'John McLeod Campbell and the Atonement', *The Expository Times*, XLVIII, No. 9, June 1937, p. 414.

Johnson, Sherman. 'The Gospel According to St. Matthew, Introduction and Exegesis,' *The Interpreter's Bible*, VII.

Leckie, J.H. 'John McLeod Campbell: The Development of His Thought. I,' *The Expositor*, Eighth Series, XXI, January, 1921, p. 54.

'John Mcleod Campbell: The Development of His Thought. II,' *The Expositor*, Eighth Series, XXI, February, 1921, p. 107.

'The Teaching of John McLeod Campbell,' *The Expositor,* Eighth Series, XXV, May 1923, p. 370.

'Books That Have Influenced Our Epoch – John McLeod Campbell's "The Nature of the Atonement",' *The Expository Times*,XL, No. 5, February 1929, p. 198.

MacGregor, Geddes. 'The Row Heresy,' *The Harvard Theological Review*. XLIII, No. 4, October 1950, p. 281.

MacIntyre, John. *John McLeod Campbell – Heretic and Saint*, Scottish Church History Society Records, Vol. XIV, 1963.

Mackintosh, H.R. 'The Vicarious Penitence of Christ,' *The Expositor*, Eighth Series, XI, February 1916, p. 81.

McLeod, Norman. 'John McLeod Campbell,' *Good Words 1872*, London, Strahan and Co., p. 353.

Macquarrie, John. 'John McLeod Campbell 1800-72,' *The Expository Times*, 83. 9 June 1972. Published also in *Thinking About God*, London, S.C.M. Press, 1975.

Martineau, James. *Mediatorial Religion*, National Review, April 1956, p. 497.

Presbyterian Review, Article by James Barr, Vol. 1, p. 127.

Prichard, C.E. 'Modern Views of the Atonement,' *North British Review*, XLVI, June 1867.

Taylor, Vincent. 'Best Books on the Atonement,' *The Expository Times*, XLVIII, No. 6, March 1937, p. 267.

Torrance, James B. *The Contribution of McLeod Campbell to Scottish Theology*, Paper read to Edinburgh Theological Club, New College, 6 Feb. 1972, Published in the Scottish Journal of Theology, Vol. 26, No. 3, p. 295.

Vaughan, D.J. 'Scottish Influences Upon English Theological Thought,' *Contemporary Review*, XXXII, June 1878, p. 457.

Edinburgh University, Library and Archives at Mound Place holds a variety of relevant pamphlets and letters relating to John McLeod Campbell, published and unpublished, some anonymous. See also Chapter III, footnote #11.

Other Unpublished Material

Anderson, Robert Alexander. *John McLeod Campbell: The Problem of Authority in Religion*. Ph.D. thesis Hertford College, University of Oxford, 1978.

Corbett, Donald J.M. *The Moral Aspect of the Atonement in Scottish Theology From David Dickson to James Denney and H.R. Mackintosh*, doctoral thesis, New College, Edinburgh University, 1965.

Faris, Donald Leonard. *The Nature of Theological Inquiry as Raised by the Conflict of the Teaching of McLeod Campbell And Westminster Theology*, a doctoral thesis, New College, Edinburgh

University, 1967.

Hodges, Louis Igou Jr. *The Doctrine of the Mediator in Classical Scottish Theology (From Knox to Durham)*. Ph.D. thesis, University of Edinburgh, 1975.

Shanks, D.A. *The Life and Thought of John McLeod Campbell,* doctoral thesis, Faculty of Divinity, University of Glasgow, 1957.